AGD - 4745

Looser Ends

Looser Ends
The Practice of Philosophy

Ermanno Bencivenga

University of Minnesota Press *Minneapolis*

Published by the University of Minnesota Press
2037 University Avenue Southeast, Minneapolis MN 55414.
Printed in the United States of America.

Library of Congress Cataloging-in-Publication Data

Bencivenga, Ermanno, 1950-
    Looser ends : the practice of philosophy / Ermanno Bencivenga.
        p. cm.
    Includes bibliographical references.
    ISBN 0-8166-1807-0. — ISBN 0-8166-1808-9 (pbk.)
    1. Philosophy.   I. Title.
    B29.B412   1989
    100—dc20
                                                        89-36828
                                                            CIP

Chapters 1–9 of this book are slightly revised versions of papers that have been published
elsewhere:

"An Epistemic Theory of Reference," *Journal of Philosophy* 80 (1983), 785–805.
"Meinong: A Critique from the Left," *Grazer Philosophische Studien* 25/26 (1985/86),
461–83.
"Philosophy One and Two," *Noûs* 21 (1987), 161–78.
"Theories and Practices," *The Monist* 79 (1987), 212–22.
"A New Paradigm of Meaning,"*Synthèse* 73 (1987), 599–621. Copyright by Kluwer Aca-
demic Publishers.
"Economy of Expression and Aesthetic Pleasure," *Philosophy and Phenomenological Re-
search* 47 (1987), 615–30.
"That Obscure Object of Desire," *Philosophy and Phenomenological Research* 48 (1988),
533–44.
"Metaphors and the Transcendental," *Metaphilosophy*, forthcoming.
"Free from What?", *Erkenntnis*, forthcoming. Copyright by Kluwer Academic Publishers.

The University of Minnesota
is an equal-opportunity
educator and employer.

Contents

Preface

Then the time came when I, too, crossed the Atlantic, and they told me that I had to tie up the loose ends. And I didn't know why, and I didn't much care. I had to make my arguments forceful, they said, knock-down. And I didn't see the point. I knew I wanted my arguments to set people free, to help them realize how much more there was in them than they had imagined, to teach them to imagine more. I certainly didn't want to force them anywhere: they were forced enough already. As for knocking them down, that is an old, obscene story.

But for a long time I had no tale to tell, no explanation of how things could be done differently. Others did; they had a safe and assured tale, and that made me feel weak and embarrassed, and made me wonder at times whether they might be right. The world would be a sad place if they were, but then, perhaps it was.

Finally, a tale came my way. It wasn't my tale, of course, not at first. But I recognized it on sight, and I made it mine, and I made it me. I began to tell it, over and over again, and as I told it, the tale unraveled, it mirrored itself in a thousand other tales, it spread, it loosened. And I knew then that there would be nothing, absolutely nothing, that could tie it up.

E. B.

Introduction

The articles collected here (in chronological order) were written between 1982 and 1987, and emerged as loose ends of my research on Kant, as by-products of the point of view that resulted from that research. Areas of concern that had attracted my interest in the past, even areas that I had been only marginally interested in, suddenly acquired new significance and new implications when seen in the light of my reading of Kant. And I took the time and made a detour to explore these unexpected corners. The moves I thus found myself making were not entirely unfamiliar, for I had been brewing a Kantian perspective of sorts since my first reading of the *Critique of Pure Reason* as a college student. But it is one thing to have some basic (and vague) intuitions and quite another to follow their complicated development (one thing to initiate a practice and quite another to become proficient at it, I would say today).

That such repeated intellectual traumas should occur, and that I should want to use them as an occasion for learning, was consistent with my conclusions about Kant. For I thought that he was responsible for a vast conceptual revolution, one that he had no language to express and that he had been struggling to share with his public through most of his career, while seeing rabbits where they saw ducks — indeed, ugly ducklings. But adopting a new conceptual framework, we know from Kuhn, is like entering a new world, a world populated by new things, things that are new even if the names for them are old. And when you are in a strange new world it may take time to become acquainted with it, time during which things will look odd and will strain your perceptual abilities.

It was thus that I conceived of this project. It was to be an ideal companion to my (1987), which I thought of as a contribution to the history of philosophy, whereas this other book was to be philosophy proper. Of course, there is but a fine line dividing the two fields, and one that is largely conventional: good history is always evidence of a theoretical point, and good theory cannot develop in a vacuum, but only as a dialogue with those who worked before us and from whom we have much to learn. Still, conventional as it is (better: *because* it is conventional), the line each of us draws defines his own (philosophical) stand, determines the options he is willing to be responsible for, and ultimately gives the *incipit* to his personality. So I decided that this enterprise was to be my own, not Kant's, though Kant had been the motivating force, and that it was to be a series of wanderings through the world whose key Kant had given us.

Wanderings, yes, because I thought of turning the conditions in which these essays had originated into a virtue, of making these loose ends into threads that one picks up from the maze and follows through, not quite all the way (if that is even possible) but only enough to make some light, to see some connections. I told myself that this is the only way you can learn a new world, learn *it*, not *about* it: the way you learn a new room. You get in and look from left to right, and then from right to left and from top to bottom and from bottom to top, and you want to do all of this looking back and forth without being committed to any one definite order of seeing things or you would not feel that you really know the room, that you are familiar with it, that you can deal with it effectively. There is something wrong with ordinary books, I told myself, wrong at least for the project I had in mind. A book is linear, one thing after another in a string, and how can a string become the map of a place? Better forget about the usual (linear) consistency and systematicity, and work at a series of loosely connected episodes, of largely independent (though intersecting) paths. The whole thing would have to be published in succession, of course, but the looseness of the structure will itself be a (meta)message, will signal that the order in which the "chapters" come is entirely random, that they could just as well be read in reverse, that perhaps they *should* also be read in reverse, and that only after they are read in reverse and scrambled in various ways will they achieve their goal of picturing a new land. So I told myself, and my words convinced me that a structure like this was the right one. Little did I know then that a much more substantial reason for proceeding in this way would emerge in due time.

1. The Threads

The basic move of Kant's conceptual revolution, in my reading, is the following: whereas in the traditional framework (or, as I would also say, paradigm) the notion of an object was primary, and every other notion was to be characterized with essential reference to it, in the new (Copernican) framework the primary notion is that of an experience—or, in a more Kantian jargon, of a representation. So whereas traditional philosophical accounts began with objects, and everything else was a property of an object, or a relation among objects, or a state of an object, or what have you, from the Kantian point of view objects require a complicated and risky conceptual "construction"; more perspicuously, it takes a lot of work to give philosophical legitimation (in terms of experiences) to our ordinary judgments that this table is an (existent) object[1] but that dinosaur (the one I see out there) is not (which judgments Kant, in view of his empirical realism, would never dream of questioning), and in fact it is not even certain that the work would

pay off. The inconclusiveness of the traditional paradigm in coming up with justifications of this kind is what first suggested to Kant that it might prove useful to
turn things around, but there is no guarantee that the new paradigm would work
any better.[2]

Already at this stage one can pick up a first thread. For think of the debate on
nonexistent objects: some (call them actualists) think it absurd to admit that there
could *be* any, whereas for others (call them nonactualists) it is just as absurd to
deny that when we imagine Pegasus we imagine something, and when we refute
an impossibility there is an object(ive) to our refutation. When accusations of absurdity are thrown around like this, it is likely that the two opposing parties are
seeing different things, possibly because they are *seeing* differently, and, indeed,
this is what we would conclude if we placed the controversy against the background of the Copernican revolution. The actualists live in the traditional framework: for them, the world of objects comes first, it is what it is and you don't mess
around with it. Experiences must be accounted for in terms of this world. If such
accounting can be done without violating their structure, then all is well; otherwise, so much the worse for that structure. The conceptual work is done on the
side of experiences, and it will be as complicated, as revisionary, and as open-
ended as it takes; on the side of objects, there is nothing to learn. For the nonactualists, on the other hand, experiences come (conceptually) first, and their structure is the hard data; the soft data, what can be manipulated, what can be arrived
at (if at all) only after a long conceptual detour, is what it is to be real. It is the
world that needs constructing, and to construct it we will have to refer to those
thoughts or denyings or desirings that undeniably are thoughts and denyings and
desirings of something. Since not all such somethings will turn out to be real (not
everything we think of, or deny, or desire will turn out to exist), there will be
unreal somethings, and from them to (talk of) nonexistent objects it is only a matter of terminology. It is only a matter, that is, of deciding to use the term 'intentional object' to bring out the intentional, directional character of an experience,
and 'real object' or 'object *simpliciter*' for those intentional objects that happen to
be part of the world.

This line of thought (developed in Chapter 2) can be extended to other conflicts
of intuitions in contemporary philosophy. The debate on nondenoting singular
terms, for example, seems a translation of the previous one from the metaphysical
jargon of what objects there are to the linguistic jargon of what names there are.
For the pre-Copernicans, to be a name means to be related in a specific way to
an object, hence something cannot be a name unless it is the name of an (existent)
object; for the post-Copernicans, to be a name means to have a certain role in that
particular kind of experience which is discourse, and it is purely accidental that
some of these linguistic bits should have a correlation with bits of the world. Or
take the debate on what possible worlds are like. Once more, the pre-Copernicans
will start out with what exists and will only admit manipulations and recombina-
tions of it: a possible world is a possible state of *this* world, a possible way in
which these objects — *the* objects — might have evolved. The post-Copernicans, on

the other hand, will start out with discourse and think of a possible world as a structure that discourse can speak of, can describe. On the basis of these two conceptualizations, two quite different research programs will develop, each the natural consequence of one of the paradigms, each unable to even make sense of some of the questions asked within the other program: a good example of this lack of communication is the so-called problem of identifiability through possible worlds. (These issues are discussed in Chapter 9.)

The story of nonexistent objects can also be developed in depth, instead of horizontally. One can, that is, inquire specifically about some interesting classes of unactualized entities, maybe those that have proved most resistant to analysis by traditional means: objects of desire. The problem with these objects is best expressed with an example: if I look for a siren, there seems to be no object that I am looking for, existent *or* nonexistent, for there are no existent sirens and a nonexistent one is not what I am looking for. And the solution (better: dissolution) of the problem is easy within the Kantian framework: one need not decide whether the (intentional) object of an experience of looking for exists to conceptually account for the structure of that experience. It is only when the experience is compared with other (for example, visual) ones that the issue of existence may be posed and (possibly) resolved. But even if the relevant question were never answered or never asked, looking for a siren would continue to be the experience it is, and continue to share its intentional character with seeing a table but not with being hurt. Whence also follows a natural diagnosis of the problem: it is the conceptual primacy of objects in the traditional framework that forces us to the vicious dilemma of the existent vs. nonexistent siren. For in that framework nothing is accounted for unless it is brought to the object level, where we will be forced to face excluded middle, no-win situations such as this one. In the Kantian framework, on the other hand, all sorts of things can and must be decided before the issue of the existential status of intentional objects is even raised, and hence failure of resolving that issue — or even the impossibility of resolving it — will prove nothing against the adequacy of the conceptual analyses we have carried out. In conclusion, objects of desire and search are an anomaly in the Kuhnian sense for the traditional paradigm: a set of data that find no natural position of rest in the logical space defined by the paradigm, but happen to fall in place perfectly as soon as there is a paradigm shift. (See details in Chapter 7.)

Stop and pick up another thread. Are our references mediated by our conceptual abilities, as Frege and Russell (allegedly) thought, or are they determined by factual chains of events, as is intimated by the more recent "causal theory"? Both alternatives have their intractable problems, for on the one hand we seem able to refer to things even when we are "in fact" wrong about any characterization we might give of them, and on the other causal chains turn reference into an obscure, quasi-mystical phenomenon, entirely disconnected from understanding. The Kantian point of view seems to offer a way out of this impasse: blame it all on transcendental realism, on the claim that reference is to transcendentally real, conceptually primary "things in themselves," and make it instead into a relation with intentional objects of discourse, or of thought, or of whatever. Then, even if I am wrong about Romulus being Rome's first king, even if there had never "really" been a Romulus or a king of Rome, I would still be referring to Romulus when I say 'Romulus' and when I say 'Rome's first king' – to Romulus as a member of my cognitive, intentional space, which is to say the only kind of space there *is*: a phenomenal one, the space of an experience. The noumenal space that is the theater of the struggle between the Fregeans and the Kripkeans is a delusion, hence that mythical battle can be disregarded as an irrelevancy.

But this account went too quickly and lost something crucial on the way: the conceptual room for mistakes. If what I refer to when I say 'Romulus' is my Romulus, how can I ever be wrong about him? Answering this question means unpacking the difference between (merely) intentional and real objects, spelling out the details of how the world gets "constructed" out of experiences. Which in turn means realizing that the relation between the two paradigms cannot be one of mutual exclusion: the transcendental idealist who does not want to lose all grip on ordinary reality (that is, who wants to remain an empirical realist) must continue to refer to the *idea* of a transcendental reality as providing him with a set of criteria to be used in assessing his experience. If such a transcendental reality would have to be consistent, for example, and if different points of view on it would have to agree, then he must require consistency of his judgments and agreement between them and what he construes as the judgments of others. For the transcendental idealist, the world in itself is no less essential for being a delusion, and no less a focus for being an imaginary one. (See Chapter 1.)

And again, one might ask, why should transcendental reality be a delusion? Could we not reconstruct it *once and for all*, and thereby legitimize it, within the new framework? Could not the dissent between the two paradigms thus resolve itself into a temporary state – one that is terminated as soon as conceptual priorities and relations of conceptual dependence are set straight, without loss to anybody? That the answers to these questions should be in the negative is argued in detail in my (1987), on the basis of an analysis of the antinomies. Here (in Chapter 10) I examine a consequence of that analysis (and of those negative answers): the inextricable link that comes to be established between the reconstruction of the world and an element of activity (Kant would say: synthesis), of arbitrariness, of freedom. Which also means, in the end: an element of responsibility and guilt. Not only is somebody's decision involved in making the world what it is: that decision is also a burden that somebody must carry.

"Somebody who?," you will ask, and with this question our path is ready for a new twist. For the answer will be, in the first place, "the subject," but insofar as that subject is to become itself an *object* of discourse, a character in a story, it must be possible that there are other objects like it: centers of decision and action, initiators of causal chains, free interpreters and "constructors" of a world. So a task is set for *this* subject, the subject of *this* experience: to find within the experience itself the traces of those *other* subjects of similar experiences that he needs to establish his own objectivity. An unfulfillable task, since an*other* experience is by definition without the bounds of this one, but still a necessary task, one that keeps imposing itself, in spite of all the temporary, revisable "solutions" found for it.

So we must construe ourselves as living in a world *together with* other agents if we want to account for the possibility of that agent which is ourselves; we must learn to impute intentions to others if we want to make sense of our own. With a curious reversal, notions such as that of an intention, a motive, a plan, which were central for those who first spoke of "intentionality" and "intentional objects," now become dislocated to a secondary position, conceptually dependent on an operation of interpretation which is just as necessary for oneself as it is for others. Which is just as well, for talk of a meaning "intentionally" expressed and carried around from speaker to hearer under the "perceptual garb of a sentence"[3] proves to be of little help in understanding most of what ordinarily counts as interpretation and communication (see Chapter 5).

Yet another thread. If our intellectual reconstruction cannot be completed, if the world can never be reached and finally accounted for, if all that our revolution promises is a bunch of inescapable but unfulfillable tasks, is not this evidence that there is something wrong with the revolution after all? Maybe, but then again, maybe not. Nobody will ever be able to establish the *necessity* of this (or any other) conceptual turnaround, but still *we* can find a role, *within* the revolutionary framework, for an activity as inconclusive as explaining has (for us) turned out to be. Such an operation will take two major steps.

First, we must reverse the traditional hierarchy of values that puts theories and theorizers on top and practices and practitioners on the bottom, judges the former wiser, and makes them responsible for guiding the latter. Wisdom consists more in doing and not doing than in knowing, Kant says[4]: knowing, or, better, pretending to know, is often only a way of confusing those automatic, unreflective concatenations of moves in which true wisdom (that is, true efficacy) resides. The main argument in favor of the traditional view, and one that is considered decisive by most, is based on the *development* (some say: progress) of practices, and on the fact that theorizing seems to have something to do with it. To give intellectual dignity to the opposite view, this argument must be undermined, which task is taken up in Chapter 4: mutation and selection apply to practices as much as to biological traits, and theorizing is possibly the safest means to maximize mutation. Thus theories are indeed a precious component of our form of life, but not for the (noble) reasons ordinarily alleged.

Which brings us to the next step. Within my framework, it is best to concentrate not so much on theories themselves, that is, on their content, which would make us insist on properties of that content (such as truth, consistency, and the like), but rather on the practice of building theories. It is this practice that we need to assess, it is for it that we must find a function, and as soon as we realize this we are well on our way to resolving the issue. Even from under the ideological cover-up of promoting integration and resolution of conflicts, it is easy to unveil the transgressive, game-like, liberating nature of the intellectual activity of "construction" and interpretation, it is easy to see that the stories and the characters we supposedly "build" in order to "make sense of things" are just so many occasions for drifting away from existing (linguistic) practices. The point of this drifting is an important one: the environment will change, and when it does, it will already be too late for those whose automatisms are well adapted to the *present* state of affairs. At that point, it may prove useful to have bred a gang of professional children who made play into a living, cooked up the wildest hypotheses and tried to follow them through, at least "in thought": it just may, if in fact some of those hypotheses turn out to be verified by the world gone crazy.

That this task is useful is confirmed by the pleasure that comes with it, a pleasure that for many is confined to the "odd moments" of "aesthetic appreciation" (see Chapter 6). Those who do it for a living, on the other hand, are best advised to turn their attention away from establishing idle "necessities" and concentrate instead on extending the range of what is possible (see Chapter 3), to try and forget their current "gut reactions" and think of what *other* gut reactions they might want to instill in people, if only they could (see Chapter 11). All this with a great deal of care, using the fortunate accident that made available to us a *medium* for cheap revolutions, using the airy substance of words, that is, not the flesh and blood of human lives, where the most fantastic dreams easily turn into nightmares (see Chapter 8).

2. Philosophy

Possibly the most debated philosophical "subject," at least in this century, has been philosophy itself, and most of the debate has centered around criticisms of devastating scope. We have been told that there was something deeply wrong with this activity since the time of Plato, that philosophical explanation should come to an end and (scientific?) description take its place, and more recently that the classical "problems of philosophy" should not be answered in a new way but quite simply forgotten, since there is nothing "interesting" at stake there.[5] In the Anglo-Saxon world, talk of "postanalytic philosophy" has matched the European emphasis on postmodernism and poststructuralism in expressing the embarrassment of professionals to come up with any definite proposal for a role that they can play. "What we do," these people seem to say with their purely "chronological" labels, "is whatever it is that comes after what was done under those other labels, in the old days when philosophers suffered from the delusion that there was something specific for them to do." And while the boundaries between philosophy and science, philosophy and literature, philosophy and art become shaky, on both sides of the Atlantic philosophers put pressure on society to tell them what they are (think of when they believed they could say what a society was to be!): philosophers are professors of philosophy, the members of philosophical associations, the people who aggregate around Congresses of Philosophy, those who receive grant money for projects in philosophy, those who publish in philosophy journals. Since I have now crossed paths with the themes of this debate, it seems that I should have a position on them, and in fact I do—and an introduction is as good a place as any to throw it at the public, sketchy and programmatic as it is bound to be (see also the next section).

In the best spirit of the good old days, I think that everything everybody has said on this subject is right, *when properly understood, and* that from the standpoint of this proper understanding virtually everything everybody has said (including the many "precursors" of my proposal, insofar as they were "limited" by lack of an "adequate language") falls short of stating the matter clearly. Of course, all of these convictions may later turn out to be delusive, but—and here is a qualifying point—*only* later. *Now* it is time to spell out the convictions.

If philosophy is the transgressive, game-like activity I depicted, the luxury of an insurance policy that some societies seem able to afford while hoping that the time for payment will never come, can we still think of philosophers as professional explorers of a "conceptual realm" neatly separated from the empirical concerns that infest "ordinary life" and still somehow able to reveal the "essence" of those concerns? In a way, no. What philosophers "in fact" do is decontextualize things, separate them, that is, from their ordinary contexts, or even better, since language is their major arena, separate words from other words ordinarily associated with them and put them together in strange ways, to ask strange questions and elaborate strange stories as answers. The conceptual realm is not a place: it is the imaginary prize that they pursue as they thus leave words hanging in the air, deprived of their usual, automatic, reassuring connections. And the wisdom that an excursion through the forms would give them is wishful thinking: when they re-enter the cave, they are just dizzy, lost to those conditioned reflexes which are our best hope for survival. Nor, for that matter, is there any difference in principle between frolicking in the godly sun of truth like this and selecting some other form of deliverance from customary moves: that of the painter who violates our visual expectations about walls and ceilings, say, or that of the musician who teaches us what we can do with our breath.

But then, should we want to phase out philosophy, absorb it into a general "intellectual" practice of deviation and amazement, or perhaps just remind philosophers that whatever they want to call themselves, there is nothing specific that they do? Not quite: there is room for cats and dogs in this world, if both can find their ecological niche. Philosophers and poets and clowns and who knows who else all contribute to challenge our habits, yes, but they do it differently, and that is because they have different images of themselves and their ends. Poets want to achieve formal perfection or aesthetic value or something of the sort, clowns have laughter as a goal, and philosophers, well, they go for a general understanding of how the whole comes together, nothing less.[6] Of course, as they try to understand any one thing, they end up going further and further from it; as they answer the question "Why X?" they are led to a Y which is *not* X, and from that to a Z which is not Y, and pretty soon they have forgotten X altogether and succeeded in changing the subject. But why should we want them to have something else in mind and some other idea of themselves while they thus proceed to always change the subject, if that one works for them, and ultimately for us the policy owners? Why should we want them (and us) to stop deriving a modest psychological advantage, a tenuous boost, a slight pat in the back, from the consistency of moves and ends that our lives show, within themselves and within the grand picture, when told *in retrospect* by a successful professional Candide, if that *placebo* may be just the thing that will encourage the unwilling *agent provocateur* to continue to plant his seeds of rebellion? Why should we want to prevent the scientist or the writer who has made a revolutionary move in some limited area of concern from thinking of the "general significance" of his move, *that is*, of its *philosophical* significance, *and* from thinking that he is then doing something different from his ordinary activities? After all, even if a tyrant is a gangster blown large, and a capitalist a lucky gambler, few of us would want to deprive *them* of their denominations.

But perhaps it is the history of philosophy that we want to dispense with. Who cares about the questions philosophers have *already* asked and the stories they have *already* been able to invent? If cross-fertilization and breeding is their line of work, tell them we need *new* puns, *new* voices to be added to the general pandemonium, and forget about the steps that belong to the past. But no: only the most irresponsible optimists may think that it is enough for our species if something was said once and is written somewhere, probably the same optimists who think that they know something if their computer does. Those who have more realistic expectations know that the work must be done again at every generation, even the work of deviation and catharsis, and that it requires repetition and discipline—indeed, more and more repetition and discipline with every generation, unless, of course, the thread is cut and a whole civilization is wiped out. They know that there is a temporal dimension to this work, that some steps can be taken only after some others, *because* those others were taken. They are not ready to dispense with the old vocabulary of concepts and abstraction and reflection, even as they claim that that vocabulary is ready to explode, since they know that it can explode only for those who have lived and felt at home with it. Only for them will the event have the proper impact, and only this impact—not the simple, unnoticed slip into oblivion—is a relevant "philosophical" goal.[7]

Besides, history is a great reservoir of tricks. Certainly more exist there than any one of us, or even all of us together, could come up with, and it is the tricks that matter, it is the articulations, the twists that make stories worthwhile. No philosophical depth resists being summarized in a paragraph: the best it can hope for then is the status of a solemn banality. But to give flesh and blood to our empty stands, to turn our prephilosophical intuitions (and what else could something as unquestioned as an intuition be?) into chapters and books, and books with interesting, complicated plots, what better training can be imagined than the patient inspection of the meanders created by previous artisans? After some apprenticeship of this kind, you will appropriate (some of) those artisans, you will be able to answer counterfactual questions like "What would X say if I said Y?," you will internalize part of that dialogue of conflicting points of view, of that dialectic of arguments and priorities, of that babelic confusion of tongues, from which telling tales come.

Am I saying then that philosophy *must* be a profession? Am I providing a legitimation for philosophy as an academic discipline? Yes and no: perhaps I am only explaining why philosophy *had to* become a profession and an academic discipline, when the meanders got to be too tortuous. Clearly, the neutral ground of a philosophy department, the (little) money granted there to graduate students, and the close contact they thus are able to establish with older professionals and virtually nobody else constitute an ideal setup for philosophical apprenticeship: few distractions are offered (or can be afforded) as they explore the conceptual ways. The problem with such an institution is that it tends to go beyond schooling the young, to transform the "older professionals" into older schoolboys, good at regurgitating what has already happened and was notarized in the professional journals. Instead of promoting a subtler creativity, the fifteeen years that ordinarily elapse between entering a Ph.D. program and achieving tenure, *that is*, realizing the mythical state that optimally combines freedom and expertise, end up promoting conformism and acquiescence, and a daily reality of routine and boredom.

So, shall we throw philosophers out of the institutions, and make them practice their transgressions within society at large? Possibly, but beware. Transgression is a risky business, and isolating its practitioners is a convenient device for avoiding that the violence done to conceptual frameworks and verbal constructions turn too easily into violence done to humans. This is, ultimately, the major social role of the academic discipline of philosophy and of the technical jargon that comes with it[8]: to bracket the philosophers' "silly," extreme proposals, to make immediate application of those proposals impossible, to leave them as the last resources they are, the desperate answers needed by a despairing world.

Does this mean, again, that philosophers will have to give up all hope of understanding, all expectation of ever becoming able to guide society toward a better, juster, more rational future? Do we want them, humbled by the discovery of their foolishness, buried under the weight of all their predecessors' moves and countermoves, terrorized by the potentially destructive consequences of their "mental experiments," to quietly withdraw into a think-tank and continue to play the game they have been taught, just because they know no better and it sure can't hurt? Do we want their records to be consigned to the irrelevance of dusty shelves, to be hidden by the hieroglyphics of a formal language or the contortions of a convoluted prose? Do we want them, in other words, to (be forced to) help us defend ourselves from them, while keeping them ready for the time they might become useful?

Affirmative answers to these questions would be the premise of one more invocation of doom on the future of philosophy: after the relativity of all claims has been shown (not *said*, for that would involve us in a paradox!), after we have appreciated that only what works survives and that there is no reason why it *should* work, after we have seen the light and espoused "pragmatism," the most we can do is continue our conversation until somebody shuts us up, or wait for others to make a move and then tear them apart. In the same vein, those who discovered that their values are not the only values, or their God a member of a large set, may conclude that there is nothing interesting to discover about values or Gods (not even that there aren't any) and learn not to worry. But the (false) prophets suggesting these escapes are the last systematizers, and the worst kind: the disillusioned ones, the ones turned cynical. They are the last, tedious act of an absolutist era, the spoilers of future games because theirs was spoiled, the Cronoses who would eat their own conclusions so that they won't leave them and prove them wrong. What they say must be said and understood, that is, it must become part of us, *and then* we must go a step further and learn to live in a world in which those words are true, which ultimately means: learn to live *as if* they were false. It may be that if God is dead then all is possible, but only something will be real and to some small extent it will depend on me, too. So I better stop the nonsense of not speaking because I cannot say the whole truth and begin to say what I believe; I better stop doing someone else's work of bringing my position down and do my own of shoring it up. Even if my practice is the destabilizing, doubt-ridden, confused and confusing one of the philosopher.

Of course, philosophers who come after the Age of the System and who have shaken off the hangover of "negative thought" will be convinced that the world would be much better if more people believed their stories and operated on the basis of them; they would be irresponsible if they thought otherwise. And of course, there will be many who are just as convinced that they are entirely off track, and will do their best to prove it: this is what the children's world looks like, once dad has been sent to bed with a big stone in his belly. Neither party must be deterred by competition or scare itself into a closet: it is for the others to try to lock them there if that is their interest. As one more social force, philosophers will try to blossom out of academia and bring their message to the world, and of course there will be resistance; or better, we hope there is, to keep the game honest.

All stories have a moral — and philosophical ones are no exception. So even if my story about philosophy attempts to give a proper reading to everything everyone said on the matter, it is certainly not indifferent to all possible courses of action. It suggests that after proper "stylistic" training philosophers try to state and defend provocative, ambitious claims, and express them in ways that make them resonate for many, not just their fellow professional players. It calls for a showdown with the obscurities under which philosophers like to conceal themselves and their gratuitousness,[9] for a limpid cry that reveals those secret codes for what they are: an uneasy compromise between a childlike exploration of the resources of language, on the one hand, and, on the other, the magical evocation of a specious competence that will protect the faint at heart from recognition of the nothingness of their concerns, of the unreality of their possible worlds. It invites to a public discussion of philosophical theses, so that wide familiarity with most of the moves will make society less of an easy prey to the charisma of that one who every once in a while, no matter what we do, will happen to hit upon an idea, or a slogan, or a creed that strikes the imagination, and threaten to send us all down the stony road of single-mindedness.[10] And clearly, it favors keeping open the academic sanctuaries, where philosophers can retrieve their steps when they are beaten up, and recover forces for the next round, and study some formidable moves with their seconds; it wouldn't be an academic philosopher's story if it didn't.

3. Why Not a Treatise?

The most perplexing consequences of a philosophical theory are always those concerning self-applicability, and the present case is no exception. My theory says that philosophical theories are ideological constructs, that they hide under a pretense of superior insight repeated attempts at rocking the boat of the only workable insight we have, the practical wisdom that makes us move right when circumstances and expectations are familiar enough, and it *also* says that philosophical theorizers are best advised to proceed under the assumption that they *have* superior insight and indeed will make it possible for all to move better in the future. Briefly stated, my theory says that my practice should disregard, indeed should antagonize, my theory.

Now this conclusion is strange, I admit, but only because none of us can forget that primacy of theories which is inscribed in our culture and our nerves: not even I can, not even if I deny it in words. *What* I say, *the content* of what I say, makes no difference: what can make a difference is a patient work of severance and renovation, of initiating *and perseverating in* new practices, and this work will have to use whatever *practical* resources are available, *including, as one of the most powerful*, the confidence that I stolidly keep on having in what I say, even when what I say is that there is no confidence to be had. There is nothing strange in the conclusion following from my theory if one thinks that practices are *in general* unaffected by any theory, not just by this one, that their development follows its own blind laws, and that the explanations we hang on them, reassuring or disconcerting as they may sound, have little power to found them or shake them, or indeed no power at all unless for reasons that are certainly not theoretical the practice of telling them happens to interfere with what else we do. But then, nobody really thinks that way (yet?).

So self-application will not crucify me on some logic or pragmatic trap, it seems. Can it have more positive consequences? Consider the following: if I am convinced of the truth (usefulness, desirability; I am not too fussy about which word(s) you use here[11]) of my theory, as all philosophers on the good side of the Copernican Acheron are supposed to be (according to my theory), I will try to maximize its impact on people. And since I am also convinced that people are not moved by rational motives, theoretical convictions, valid arguments, or anything of the sort, but rather by example, by seeing something concretely at work and then trying it themselves, and best if they can do it in various contexts, so that not only will the essential reactions be imprinted in them but there will also be enough flexibility built in the system to allow it not to collapse against the first hurdle, because I am convinced of all that, I will not dream of writing a theoretically unassailable treatise to expound and defend my point of view. Instead, I will want to write a series of sketches, detailed enough to give a clue to the procedure, and yet open enough to have readers continue on their own. I will want to put together a series of beginnings of works that would in any case be interminable, but beginnings that, to be effective, will not even *give the idea* of terminating somewhere, will not even have the format of something that terminates. A bunch of loose ends, in sum.

So we have gone full circle, are back where we started, at the format of this book, and it seems that we have learned something crucially relevant to it. Whereas earlier the looseness of the structure was a natural choice in an unnatural, unique situation, that of one who wakes up in a new world and wants to tell the others what it looks like, now that character has become an essential component of the destabilizing enterprise of philosophy. And, quite appropriately, the new account is not independent of (much less in conflict with) the old one: it results instead from "deepening" our analysis. Doing philosophy is always, to some extent, changing the world, hence it requires provocative ways of generating the active cooperation of readers, of involving them in the process, of stirring their attention and interest, or nothing will be done. You may try the dialogue to personify the multifariousness of "conceptual issues,"[12] the libel to rouse general aggressiveness and enthusiasm and have others join the fight, and even the treatise if you would rather become a well-defined target. But in all cases you will be doing philosophy insofar as you leave stones unturned, nerves exposed, tensions unresolved, ambiguous messages, bits and pieces that one might want to pick up and fit together in a puzzle, beginnings. So a book like this one is philosophy in its purest form. I could have sown my threads into a fabric of sorts, I could have done more bringing together of my various themes, more ironing out of their oddities and inconsistencies, I could have waited longer and written the many books of which these are the beginnings. But then I would only have clouded the issue. Philosophers are permanently in the temporary state of entering a new land and are most effective when they are clear about it.

Do I believe all of this? Of course I do, or I would not say it. I believe it and I am ready to defend it and go down with it, but still I can't help observing that the loose ends were there before this demonstration of their necessity was thought out. The curiosity, the desire to experiment with various styles and subjects came first, then the urge to have others share the game, and finally the rationalization proving that they should, and that these should be the game's rules. This rationalization tells me that I was right not to pen a unified treatise in the philosophy of language, or aesthetics, or perhaps metaphilosophy and philosophical methodology; but then, if I ever feel like writing a treatise, and if I do, there will be another story telling me that I had to.

Also, as *this* story pacifies me for a moment, as the theorizing activity thus comes to a temporary halt in the unsettling progression it itself has initiated, I cannot help noting where all of this leaves me. I was happy pursuing my loose ends when they were not yet that, when I had not yet asked what they were and whether and why I should pursue them: happy and unconscious. Now all those questions have been asked, and even if I have answers I am no longer innocent. I know that I could have done something else, I know that then I would have had different answers, and I begin to wonder whether I should.

Notes

1. It will become clear later that the conceptual construction of objects proceeds in this paradigm through the imposing of conditions on some more elementary notion for which the word 'object' can still be used, qualified in some way. But this does not mean that the attribute of existence is to become less redundant for objects once constructed. Real, existent objects are *the only* objects; "intentional" objects and the like are only a manner of speaking, a conceptual stance on the way to objects—or, as I say when I want to be most explicit about this point, to objects *simpliciter*.

2. And indeed, it won't (see p. xiii below). Thus, in the end, the whole notion of philosophical *legitimation* will come under attack, and I will find the essence of philosophy in the very operation of turning things around, not in any *outcome* of this operation.

3. The expression is Frege's (1918), p. 354.

4. See below, p. 48.

5. In the next section, reasons will be offered for the frequency of such apocalyptic statements in philosophical circles, and for my own statements falling in the same category.

6. Sellars put it suggestively when he called philosophy "an attempt to see how things, in the broadest possible sense of the term, hang together, in the broadest possible sense of the term." (Quoted by Rorty, 1982, p. xiv.)

7. These remarks apply to my own use of expressions like 'conceptual level of discourse' or 'conceptual framework,' for example in Chapters 2, 7, and 10, and to the "deconstruction" of such expressions in Chapter 8. What is a contradiction from the synchronic, delusive point of view of "pure theory" is often a necessary dialectic within the practice of theorizing, where attention shifts from what is true (which is all true at once) to what is said (which *cannot* all be said at once).

8. As opposed to the role they play for philosophy itself: that of the garden where it can tend its roses without too much anxiety. Note also that by the end of this section the suggestion will surface of an alternative social "safety device": making the game of philosophy more familiar to "ordinary people" may be an effective strategy to build up their "immune system."

9. Their *act*-gratuitousness, to coin an expression (and work on my own hide); for *as a rule*, there is a point to having philosophers around and letting them play with what is not (yet) the case.

10. See note 8 above and the attending text.

11. I am not because each of these convictions can be used to rationalize the same practical attitude, which is what matters here.

12. This is what I have tried, in my native Italian, in my (1988).

Looser Ends

1

An Epistemic Theory of Reference

The theory I will present here was first sketched in a series of papers published in Italian between 1974 and 1979.[1] I go back to it now for basically two reasons. First, I am dissatisfied with those sketches. None of them provides anything close to a systematic presentation of the theory. Second, I think that the theory may give an interesting perspective on some puzzles that seem to be of great concern for contemporary analytic philosophy of language. Indeed, I will begin by mentioning one such puzzle and showing how the theory would handle it. However, this is only an expository device. It is clear to me that what the theory provides is not so much a solution as a *dis*solution of the puzzle in question (and similar ones): the puzzle simply does not arise anymore, because the whole context has changed. I think it is far more interesting to see where the theory must pay its dues, that is, to consider the puzzles *it* must face. Thus, after presenting the essence of the theory and its most basic motivations, I will devote quite a substantial part of the chapter to some such puzzles. Finally, let me note that—as will become apparent later—the expression 'epistemic theory of reference' is in an important sense a misnomer for the theory.[2] However, I think it is the expression that might best of all at this stage give some idea of what the theory is about without at the same time connoting it negatively.

I thank Terence Parsons, David Smith, Bas van Fraassen, and Peter Woodruff for their comments on an earlier draft of this chapter.

1. The Puzzle[3]

Pierre is a native of France. He does not speak English. He does not know that the expression 'London' names anything. But he saw pictures of a city that was referred to as 'Londres,' and from those pictures he concluded that

(1) Londres est jolie.

Some time later, Pierre moves to England, and takes up residence in London. He learns English, learns that 'London' is the name of the city where he lives, but does not realize that London is the same as Londres. He concludes from examining his surroundings that

(2) London is not pretty,

but he has no reason for changing his mind about Londres. Indeed, he can now express his beliefs about Londres in English, by saying

(3) Londres is pretty,

and would certainly feel committed to assenting to

(4) Londres is pretty and London is not pretty.

Since he knows about Leibniz's law, Pierre can conclude from (4) that

(5) Londres $\neq$ London.

But, *in fact*, what is the case is

(6) Londres = London

and according to a popular view, an identity like (6) is, if true, then necessarily true. Does this mean that Pierre believes an impossibility? Does it mean that— appearances to the contrary—he is an irrational agent?

2. A Diagnosis

To the extent that we find the above case puzzling, we might try to attack one or the other of the principles involved in its description. A very natural candidate, for example, would be the last principle mentioned: that (6) is either false or necessarily true. We might want to argue that proper names are disguised definite descriptions, and thus that (5) is only contingently false. Pierre is wrong, but he is not irrational.[4]

However, this is not my line. The principle I would attack instead is

(7) *In fact*, 'Londres' and 'London' refer to the same thing,

from which, of course, it follows that—contrary to what Pierre believes (or assents to)—(6) is true. To indicate what form my attack will take, I find it useful to give a brief sketch of a theory which is an alternative to my own and from which (7) would follow. Before proceeding, however, two remarks are in order. First, I am not at all suggesting that (7) in any sense "implies" the theory in question (or, since the theory is to a large extent metaphysical in nature, that (7) carries so much metaphysical baggage). If anything, the implication goes the other way around: the relation between (7) and the theory is more like the relation between a set of (linguistic) data and a system of philosophical assumptions that entail, and thus far explain, the data. Second, though I think that the theory is a relatively popular one in contemporary analytic philosophy of language (and one that would fit well, for example, with Russell's "robust sense of reality"[5]), I am not attributing it here to anybody in particular. The reason I introduce it is theoretical, not historical. As I point out later, there are two basic construes of (or metaphors about) 'referring,' and this theory is as natural a fit to one as mine (I think) is to the other. It is, of course, possible (and interesting) to compromise between the two construes, and later I will mention some such compromise. At the present introductory stage, however, it may be illuminating – as part of my expository device – to contrast my theory with its most natural antagonist, to make it clearer.

Here, then, are the "principles" of the alternative theory (from now on, *the realist's* theory), in order of decreasing generality:

(8) There is some such thing as *the real world*. What exactly it is like is a matter of (metaphysical) debate, but a number of things about it seem to be relatively uncontroversial. For example, there is exactly one real world, which contains objects, and these objects have properties and bear relations to one another. (To put it briefly, the real world is a *structure*, not just a *set*.)

(9) Some of the objects contained in the real world are human beings. You and I are some of them. One of the most important relations human beings can have to anything in the real world (including themselves) is the relation of *knowing* it, that is, becoming aware of its structure.[6] To the extent that they know anything in the world, they can be said to know the world itself.

(10) Knowledge is expressed in language; so language must somehow hook up with the real world. The way it does this is by using words or expressions (singular terms) that are somehow associated with objects in the world, and words or expressions (general terms) that are associated with properties of those objects or relations among them.

(11) The association is largely conventional to start with, but, once it is made, it conditions further uses of those words and expressions, so that it makes sense to say that a given singular term *refers to* a given object in the world, and that anyone using it with the intention of referring to anything else is using it incorrectly.

(12) One of the objects contained in the real world is a city in England, with several million inhabitants. 'Londres' and 'London' are two singular terms referring to this object.

I have various relations to (8)-(12). I can't say I accept any of them. Some I reject; with respect to others I am simply agnostic. But I do not think that this is the appropriate context to discuss all of them. What I most want to challenge here is (10), and, more precisely, the idea that singular terms in a language are associated with (or refer to) objects in the real world. Rejecting this thesis will make it possible for me to deny (7), and if we deny (7) we have no more puzzle. In what follows, I will try to make all of this precise.

3. The Basic Proposal

If singular terms (and in particular proper names) do not refer to objects, real objects, objects out there, what do they refer to? Well, my first intuition is that this is the wrong question, that names do not refer *simpliciter*; rather, it is speakers that refer *by using them*. But this is not a new idea. Strawson (1950), for example, claimed that it is not linguistic expressions that refer, but uses of them. Thus, it is not the expression 'the present King of France' that refers (or does not refer): it is its use in 1790, or 1880, or 1970 that does. And Donnellan (1966) claimed that different utterances of the expression 'the man over there drinking champagne,' in different circumstances and by different speakers, may refer to very disparate entities, including men who never drank champagne, and possibly trees and lamp-posts. So far, then, we are on well-trodden ground, but things change when we reformulate the question in a way that would make it acceptable to me — as well as, I take it, to Strawson and Donnellan. The question I have in mind, of course, is: "What do speakers refer to by using singular terms?"

My feeling is that not only Strawson and Donnellan but also most other authors in the analytic tradition would still answer: "Objects in the real world." They might qualify their answer, they might add that the object referred to in a given situation is a function of context, or of the intentions of the speaker, or of what he expects from his hearers, but with all these qualifications they would still stick to basically the same answer.[7] And here is where our roads part. For in my opinion, whether or not there is a real world (and in this regard I want to remain agnostic, at least here), such a world is largely irrelevant to the phenomenon of reference.

My second intuition is that a structure is associated with each speaker, which I call his *cognitive space*. The best way to approach my conception of different cognitive spaces is to think of different possible worlds, and to take an anti-haecceitist view with respect to them: it does not even make sense to say that an object in one world is the same as (or different from) an object in another world.[8] However, the image suggested by possible worlds is a static one: possible worlds simply *are* in a certain way. In this sense, the image must be corrected. Cognitive spaces are evolving, dynamic structures. They change as a function of time and of their bearers' experience, in at least three ways. First, objects get added to cognitive spaces, or dropped from them. The moment I found out there was a mountain called 'Aconcagua,' my cognitive space got richer; the moment I found out there was no Santa Claus, it (as well as my hopes) got poorer.[9] Second, distinct members of a cognitive space may get to be identified, or one and the same object split into two or more. My cognitive space contracted when I realized that New York and the Big Apple were the same, but expanded when I realized that what I thought was a single person was in fact identical twins. Third, entities in a cognitive space may themselves become richer, by acquiring new properties or entering into new relations with one another, or poorer, by losing properties or relations. In my cognitive space Niels Bohr has the properties of being a man, being a physicist, and having lived in the twentieth century. With respect to most of the properties it would be reasonable to predicate of him, he fails to have either those properties or their negations. But I may learn more about him tomorrow, or realize that he was an engineer instead, in which cases my cognitive space would be modified accordingly.

My third intuition is that when a speaker uses a singular term he uses it to refer to an entity in his cognitive space, and nothing else. Now Pierre's cognitive space contains (at least) two objects: the city he once saw pictures of and the city he lives in. Such objects are definitely distinct; indeed, one is pretty and the other is not. Typically, Pierre uses 'Londres' to refer to the first and 'London' to refer to the second. So 'Londres' and 'London' — in Pierre's usage — do *not* refer to the same thing. Not only is Pierre not irrational. In a sense, he is not even wrong.

4. Qualifications

I am sure the reader has a number of objections to my last few statements. I know that my account must face a number of difficulties, and I intend to address those which I consider most serious in a moment. But before I do that, I think it is appropriate (a) to make a number of qualifications, so that my position be better defined, and (b) to present my basic motivations. First, the qualifications.

The members of a cognitive space are not (all) *ideas*. Some of them, of course, are — if the bearer of the space admits such mental entities. But such things as the referents of 'Londres' or 'London' are not. They are objects, exactly as in the alternative account I sketched earlier. Only, these objects belong to a different (kind of) world. The introduction of ideas into the picture — I think — is a move toward capturing some of the intuitions I am trying to express without giving up realism. For my idea of London may be distinct from your idea of it,[10] and Pierre's idea of London distinct from his idea of Londres, but still we may think of such ideas as real objects.

For analogous reasons, members of a cognitive space are not (all) Fregean *Sinne*. Again, cognitive spaces may well contain *Sinne*, and *Sinne* would probably be the referents of expressions such as 'the *Sinn* of "London" '. But the referent of 'London' is not a *Sinn*: it is a city.

Also, members of a cognitive space are not (all) Meinongian nonexistent objects. There may be some such, depending on what position we take on fictional entities (more precisely, entities that are taken by the speaker to be fictional), but in general objects of reference *do* exist, *in* the cognitive spaces to which they belong. The winged horse existed in the cognitive spaces of Greek mythologists, and the round square may have existed in the cognitive space of some medieval alchemist. Still, there are two important analogies with Meinongian intuitions here. On the one hand, if by 'existence' we mean 'existence in the real world' then members of a cognitive space are not so much nonexistent as "beyond existence and nonexistence": the question whether they "really" exist is totally irrelevant to *what* they are. On the other hand, we have already seen that members of a cognitive space are often "incomplete objects": they are not determined with respect to properties that it would be reasonable to predicate of them.[11]

And finally, I think it might be clear by now why I think that the expression 'epistemic theory of reference' is partly a misnomer for the position I advocate. Such an expression might suggest that the essential claim of this position is something like the following: what we know (or believe) in a given situation is important to determine what we refer to (by using some expression or other) in that situation. Certainly, I accept this claim, but so probably would Donnellan and others. What I take to be essential to my position is the kind of things that are objects of reference. It would be clearer to characterize my theory as anti-realist or idealist (in the sense of transcendental, not of empirical, idealism[12]), but, as van Fraassen noted in a different context, "realists have appropriated a most persuasive name for themselves,"[13] and it is bad politics to imply right from the start that you are going against the good guys.

5. Motivations

Suppose you ask me what I am thinking of. I answer, "I am thinking of the winged horse," and you say, "You can't possibly be thinking of the winged horse, because there is no such thing." Chances are I would find your objection inadequate, and I would point out to you (following a tradition that goes back at least as far as Brentano) that the "real" existence of an object is totally irrelevant to my ability to think of it.

On the other hand, suppose I am attacked by a bunch of different animals on a very dark night. I am carrying a big stick with me, and I succeed in hitting one of the animals with it. The animals escape, I get home safe, and you ask me: "Which animal did you hit?" I answer, "I am pretty sure I hit the winged horse," and you say, "You can't possibly have hit the winged horse, because there is no such thing." In this case, I think your objection (if accepted) would be destructive for my belief.

The point of these examples should be clear. There are transitive verbs φ such that the "real" existence of b seems to be a necessary condition for the truth of

(13) a φ's b

and transitive verbs ψ such that the existence of b seems to be no necessary condition for the truth of

(14) *a* ψ's *b*.

I will call the latter verbs *intentional*, and the former *nonintentional*.[14]

Ultimately, the reason I came up with a theory of reference like the one I sketched above is that I think of 'referring' as being more like 'thinking of' than like 'hitting,' that is, as being an intentional verb. But I do not want to put up here an obdurate defense of my own intuitions on the matter. I don't see why we could not think of the verb 'referring' as an ambiguous one, and have a theory of 'referring' as an intentional verb *as well as* a theory of 'referring' as a nonintentional verb. Only, I think that the first theory should come first, if for no other reason than that of conceptual economy. The second theory depends on the acceptance of real existence and the real world, whereas the first one does not.

In any event, the moment you think of 'referring' as an intentional verb, that is, in analogy with 'thinking of' rather than 'hitting,' a number of things become natural which are not at all natural in the realist theory I sketched above. It becomes natural to think that I can refer to winged horses even if there "really" aren't any, and it becomes natural to think that when I say

(15) The brown table over there is rectangular

I am referring to a brown table even if "in fact" there is only a blue table there (or maybe no table at all). But where shall we find a "brown table over there" or a winged horse when there are "really" no existing ones? Talking about ideas or *Sinne* will not do, because ideas and *Sinne* are not *tables* or *horses*. And talking about nonexistent objects will not do either, because it may well be that when I say (15) *I* am referring to an *existent* brown table over there—as I certainly would be, it seems to me, were I to say (under the same circumstances)

(16) The existent brown table over there is rectangular.

The only viable alternatives in the vicinity are the following: either you say that I am not *really* referring to what I think I am referring to, or I find my reference in a different world from the actual one. However, the first way out is not practicable if 'referring' is taken to be intentional, for it then seems that what I "really" refer to should not be relevant, or at least not be allowed to overrule what I *think* I refer to.[15] The second solution, on the other hand, may have vast consequences and may ultimately open the way to a theory such as mine. For once we decide that *in some cases* the reference of a term (for a given speaker) is to be found in a non-"actual" world (and a world—I should add—that is definitely shaped and determined by the speaker's belief-system) it may seem natural that it should be so *in all cases*. After all,

(17) There really is a brown table over there

is at best a contingent truth, and though we may expect contingent truths to determine what object our reference is in a given circumstance, it may seem less desirable that contingent truths should determine what *kind* of object our reference should be, in particular, in what world this reference should be found. We would expect our philosophy of language to make such decisions, and we would like our philosophy of language to be as independent as possible from the metaphysical structure of the "actual" world.

It seems to me that the most important breakthroughs in recent analytic reference theory had to do with the recognition of the pragmatic and intentional factors I am emphasizing here. Only, these breakthroughs did not go very far because the various authors did not definitely choose an intentional reading of 'referring,' or at least distinguish clearly between the two readings. What they did primarily was to introduce intentional elements into a nonintentional construe, often creating awkward mixtures. This is not the place for an extensive discussion of the matter, but a few remarks may be in order.

One of the arguments given by Kripke (1972) for the rigidity of proper names is based on the following mental experiment. Suppose Gödel was not in fact the person who proved the incompleteness of arithmetic. Suppose a man named 'Schmidt' actually proved it, but Gödel got hold of the manuscript and the proof was thereafter attributed to Gödel. Now it may be that the only description the ordinary man can associate with the proper name 'Gödel' is 'the man who proved the incompleteness of arithmetic.' Since this description "really" refers to Schmidt, the view according to which proper names get their reference through the association to some description[16] would have it that when the ordinary man says

(18) Gödel was born in Vienna

he is actually referring to Schmidt. "But," says Kripke, "it seems to me that we are not [referring to Schmidt]. We simply are not." (p. 84) Therefore, proper names do not get their reference through association with some description.

The basic point of the mental experiment is well taken. To refer to an object by a proper name, we need not know of any property the object "really" has. But one should go further. For suppose that, under the circumstances of the experiment, the ordinary man says:

(19) The man who proved the incompleteness of arithmetic was born in Vienna.

Whom do you think the ordinary man is then referring to, Schmidt or Gödel? If you find the second answer more plausible (as I do), then you may begin to think that the knowledge of "real" properties of the object of reference is just as unimportant with descriptions as it is with proper names.

A natural answer to my last suggestion would run as follows. Of course, the ordinary man typically refers to Gödel when uttering (19), but that is only because he is making a referential use of the description 'the man who proved the incompleteness of arithmetic.' In its attributive use, the description refers to Schmidt. However, this answer is ultimately unsatisfactory. Just as calling a class of contexts 'referentially opaque' does not even begin to address the problems that class of contexts presents, calling a use of a description 'referential' does not make that use more perspicuous. Finding a name for a problem may be useful to identify the problem, but it certainly does not solve it. And here is a serious problem: how is it that descriptions, apparently the referring expressions whose use depends most strictly on the correct identification of some property or properties of the object of reference, may succeed in referring to objects that blatantly contradict the description used?

I have an answer for this question. Reference is primarily an intentional operation, which is performed in an intentional, cognitive domain. The properties "real" objects "really" have do not matter for reference because reference is not to such objects. But, of course, the properties objects in cognitive spaces have do matter. It is only because the ordinary man's cognitive space contains a Gödel who proved the incompleteness of arithmetic that he can succeed in referring to Gödel (whatever the case "really" is) by the description 'the man who proved the incompleteness of arithmetic.' He could not, and would not, refer to Gödel (referentially or otherwise) as 'the man who discovered America' (unless his cognitive space were quite peculiar).

The so-called Frege-Russell view of proper names[17] embodied a simple idea of how reference works. A description picks out the (unique) entity described; a name picks out its reference through association with some description or other. Unfortunately, however, this view also conceived of reference as a nonintentional act, as an act that picks out objects in the "real" world. So when people tried to apply that simple idea to current phenomena of reference, they found that virtually everything was an exception to it. This outcome, however, did not bring them to a clear recognition of the intentional character of reference; instead, they preferred to complicate matters on the side of how reference works. Names are used "rigidly" and descriptions are used "referentially," and never mind if this generates an impression of general arbitrariness, the impression that perhaps one can use any expression to refer to anything.

On the other hand, when the intentional character of referring is rightly emphasized, things fall back into place. It then becomes possible to say again that descriptions refer to the entities described, and names like 'Gödel' get their reference (in a cognitive space) through association with some description. And this is reasonable, since for most of us Gödel is neither more nor less than the man who proved the incompleteness of arithmetic.

So much for my motivations. As I suggested in the introductory paragraph, I think that, though it is interesting to see what the theory can do, it is more interesting to see how it reacts to objections and criticisms. The rest of this chapter deals with such reactions.

6. Communication

Suppose I tell you

(20) He is tall,

and assume for the sake of argument that the realist's construe of reference is correct. 'He,' of course, is an ambiguous singular term, so we may also suppose that what you understand as the referent of 'he' is a different (real) entity from what I intended that referent to be. This, the realist might claim, is a case in which we would normally say that there was a failure of communication. But, he would continue, does not *every* case of (alleged) communication end up in a similar failure, according to my theory? Isn't *every* singular term systematically ambiguous there, and isn't it *always* the case that the referent of a singular term *for you* is a different entity from the referent of that singular term *for me*? Apparently, the realist is in a much better position: he certainly must admit that there are cases of ambiguity and misunderstanding, but he can also claim that in most cases we *succeed* in communicating with each other *because we are talking about the same things, real* things, things that belong to the single *real* world.

In addressing this objection, let me note first of all that the realist's explanation of successful communication may be explaining too much. There seems to be a lot more systematic misunderstanding among human beings than that explanation would allow, and whether or not we successfully communicate with each other seems to depend very little on what our reference supposedly is in the real world and a lot instead on whether we share a culture, had similar experiences, adopt the same system of values, and so on. Thus no sooner has the realist "explained" successful communication than he has to account for the numerous cases in which we *seem* to communicate (just because our referent "out there" is the same) but in fact we don't.

But I do not want to answer an objection by a counterobjection. Nor do I want to underestimate the objection. Clearly, I must conceive of (verbal) communication in terms of how a hearer's cognitive space is modified as a result of some utterance(s) by a speaker. But now the problem is: can I formulate within my theory plausible criteria of *successful* communication? Can I specify when a modification of a hearer's cognitive space (resulting from the utterance(s) of a speaker) counts as *appropriate*? The discussion above makes an affirmative answer to such questions doubtful because it makes clear that I cannot use here the numerical identity of referents, which is likely to play a major role in the realist's account of the matter. I cannot say that a necessary condition for two (or more) people to communicate successfully with each other is that they talk about (numerically) the same things, because in my account they are never going to. But then is there in this account some substitute for the realist's numerical identity, and if there is, what is it?

To begin with, note that I cannot replace the numerical identity of referents with their *qualitative* identity. For suppose that I require the following: in order that A successfully communicate something to B about, say, Aristotle, the referents of 'Aristotle' in A's and B's cognitive spaces must have the same properties and be involved in the same network of relations. More precisely, suppose that the minimal subspaces including those referents and all the entities to which they are related must be isomorphic. Then some communication would indeed be possible, but it would be impossible to communicate something *new*.

So it must be something weaker than qualitative identity. What I propose is the conjunction of two conditions. The first condition seems relatively unproblematical.[18] For something to count as a case of successful communication across cognitive spaces, the hearer must be able to map the information received *unambiguously* into his cognitive space. For example, suppose that A says

(21) Aristotle was a student of Plato

to four hearers B, C, D, E. B has no idea who Aristotle and Plato are. C's cognitive space contains only one Aristotle, a Greek philosopher. D's cognitive space contains two Aristotles, a Greek philosopher and a Greek shipowner, but no Plato. E's cognitive space contains two Aristotles, a Greek philosopher of the fourth century B.C. and a Greek shipowner of the twentieth century A.D., and it also contains exactly one Plato, a Greek philosopher of the fifth/fourth centuries B.C. I think we could agree that A is successfully communicating something to $B, C,$ and E but not to D, and that the *reason* D is receiving no communication is that he has no way of knowing to which Aristotle in his cognitive space he should relate the statement (21).

To understand the need for the second condition, suppose now that A says

(22) Aristotle was born in Greece

to F, whose cognitive space contains exactly one Aristotle, a Labrador dog. Surely F can map (22) unambiguously into his cognitive space, but probably we would not consider the result a paradigm of successful communication.

My second condition is supposed to take care of such problems. I require that for A to successfully communicate something to B about x (by using the singular term 'x'), the information B already has about x not contradict the information that A has. In more technical terms, I require that the minimal subspaces including the referents of 'x' in the two spaces with their networks of relations be such that they can "merge" into a single (sub)space.

This second condition is open to the following objection. Suppose that A believes that Aristotle died in 322 B.C. and G believes that Aristotle died in 323 B.C. Would this alone be enough to block any communication between A and G on the subject of Aristotle? According to the condition in question, the answer is yes, but this answer seems counterintuitive.

My approach to this objection has two components. First, I think that the question "Is there successful communication between A and B at time t?" is not one to be answered straightforwardly with a yes or a no. My intuition is that to have *perfect* communication between A and B (the Platonic idea of perfect communication, if you wish[19]), both my conditions must be satisfied; that is, it must be the case *both* that B can unambiguously map the information received into his cognitive space *and* that the information A and B have about the relevant entities is not in conflict. But—I would also claim—this notion of perfect communication works only as a *standard* of successful communication: communication among human beings is successful *to the extent to which* it approaches the ideal case. Thus we cannot simply say that there is or there isn't successful communication between *A* and *B* (at *t*): we can only say that there is (or there isn't) a certain *degree* of successful communication between the two.

Second, I want to emphasize that communication is not an end in itself. Communication has pragmatic value: it allows us to direct our actions, modify our goals, and so on. Therefore, whether or not some communication is successful depends also on whether or not we are successful in doing those things. Possibly most of our communication is imperfect to a point, but still it may be imperfect for *practically irrelevant* reasons, in which case I would tend to consider it successful to a very high degree. Thus if the only conflict between *A*'s and *G*'s cognitive spaces — as regards Aristotle — were about Aristotle's date of death, I think that whatever information one gave to the other about Aristotle would be used in an efficient way. Of course, if one ever referred to Aristotle as "the philosopher who died in 322 B.C." (say in the course of a parlor game), they might realize that they were having a communication problem, but in most other cases their communication about Aristotle would work practically very well.[20]

7. Truth

At this point, readers may feel they've been patient enough. Understanding how communication would work in a theory like mine may be of some marginal interest, but they may also think that the theory will never get off the ground unless I have an answer for a much more decisive objection. The objection is: if what we refer to is members of cognitive spaces, and more precisely *our* cognitive spaces, how can we help concluding that everything anyone ever says is *true*?

Return to the puzzle we discussed at the beginning. When Pierre says that Londres is not London, he is referring to *his* Londres and *his* London, and, of course, his Londres is distinct from his London. This is why I said that "not only is Pierre not irrational. In a sense, he is not even wrong." But now those words come back to haunt me. Unless I specify what "In a sense" means, and I also find a sense in which Pierre may be said to *be* wrong, I will have no place in my theory for error, and consequently no significant place for truth either.

To begin with, consider how simply this problem is solved within the realist account. There is exactly one real world. This world is a structure, in that it contains objects and these objects have properties and bear relations to one another. Singular terms refer to real objects, and general terms to real properties and relations. The singular sentence

(23) Londres is a city

is true if the real object referred to by 'Londres' has the real property referred to by 'is a city.' Since in the real world Londres is a city and is the same city as London, Pierre is right in believing (23) and wrong in believing (5).

Now note that, even if we accept the claim that objects of reference are not in the real world but in cognitive spaces, we are not necessarily forced to give up the essence of the above realist characterization of truth. We can retain that characterization if we are ready to admit (a) that there is a real world (over and above all cognitive spaces), and (b) that a cognitive space represents an attempt at mimicking the structure of the real world. For if we hold these views, we can claim that Pierre is *really* right in asserting (23) (as opposed to being right "within his cognitive space") if the relevant area of his cognitive space constitutes a "largely adequate representation" of (part of) the real world. More precisely, we can claim that Pierre is really right in asserting (23) if (i) there is an area in the real world which is structurally analogous to the area around Londres in his cognitive space, (ii) there is an object in this area which is structurally analogous to the Londres in his cognitive space, and (iii) this (real) object is a city. The claim that Pierre is *really* wrong in asserting (5) could be explicated along similar lines.

I said on p. 6 that in the present context I want to remain agnostic on whether or not there is a real world. So surely I cannot accept here anything like belief (a). (And by the way, if I may for a moment interject my own metaphysical biases into the matter, I would not accept any such belief anyhow, since I am convinced (with Kant) that the real world is not an object of experience,[21] hence that we have no way of establishing its existence.) However, this does not mean that I cannot accept and use belief (b). The reason is simple. To strive to mimic (the structure of) something, there is no need that that something exist. All one needs is to have *an idea of* that something, and this idea in the case of the real world we most certainly have.

My move here is a Platonic and Kantian one. Our common everyday experience makes the sense it makes for us only when seen in the light of things that may not themselves be objects of experience, but work in an essential way as *standards* by which to assess, judge, and ultimately (try to) act on that experience.[22] The idea of a real world, whether or not we have experience of such a world, is one of these standards. We do conceive of ourselves as trying to mimic the structure of this world by our cognitive structures, and our cognitive spaces are (among other things) the result of such a striving. So the fact that the real world may be (or is, in my metaphysical view) beyond our horizon does not mean that thinking of it and striving toward it (as a Kantian "imaginary focus") does not have important effects. For example, since we think of there being a *single* real world and we think of truth as correspondence with it, we think of there being a single truth, and as a consequence we see agreement among people as a positive factor. This is what is wrong with Pierre's beliefs about Londres and London: they are (to a certain extent) too peculiar, they conflict with most other people's beliefs on the same subject. Of course, Pierre does not realize *that*; if he did, he would start having doubts himself. And, of course, the judgment that such beliefs are mistaken can be made only inside another cognitive space, whose perspective may turn out in the end to be just as deviant as Pierre's is supposed to be. There is no rock bottom in this process.

So to put it simply, my answer to the present objection is as follows. Somebody who has *the idea of* a real world may have *the idea of* (absolute) truth as correspondence with this world. This idea will allow him to understand what it is (or what it would be) for Pierre's (or anybody's) beliefs to be true, and will determine in important ways the structure and development of his cognitive space. This in spite of the fact that the idea might never (and I think will never) find an experiential realization.

8. Theory and Metatheory

But now my answer to the last objection may generate a new objection. If all acts of reference and judgment are made inside a cognitive space, what is the status *of my theory*? Apparently, I am in a paradoxical situation, for though continuously denying or questioning the realist's *beliefs*, through all of this discussion I have been speaking the realist's *language*. I said that human beings have cognitive spaces, that they refer to entities in them, and I have even tried to describe communication *across* cognitive spaces. How can I do such things? Do I have a point of view outside all cognitive spaces from which to look at them? But according to my theory no such point of view exists!

This problem is not peculiar to my position. Kant's philosophical theory runs into a similar paradox by claiming that things in themselves are unknowable and at the same time making all sorts of statements about them.[23] And I might point out that not even the realist is completely immune to this difficulty, not when he starts recognizing that what people believe has an effect on what they refer to. For then, of course, his own description of how things *really* work is seen as determined by his beliefs about the matter. He may try to address the problem by distinguishing metaphysics from epistemology and claiming that what he believes has nothing to do with whether or not what he believes *is true*, but the fact is that the very distinction between metaphysics and epistemology is a belief of his. At any rate, I am not concerned here with the realist's problems, save to the extent that I share them. Thus I will address this problem as a problem *of mine*.

The analogy with Kant may help, so let me pursue it for a moment. Kant claims that no metaphysical theory can ever be known to be true, and then proceeds to give his own metaphysical theory. This sounds paradoxical, but is it really? Only if we add an extra assumption, which probably most of us are ready to attribute to Kant. The assumption is that Kant's own metaphysical theory be known (by Kant) to be true.

A principle of charity should always be at work in our interpretation of the history of philosophy. In particular, we should not rush to conclude from the above that Kant's position is contradictory, but rather explore the possibility that the assumption generating the contradiction be denied.[24] What would happen in that case?

Kant himself has the answer. When the claim to ultimate and absolute truth is given up, metaphysical (and—I would like to say more generally—philosophical) theories may be seen as a product of the human reason's inevitable tendency to construct complete and systematic answers to its most basic questions.[25] No such answer will ever be found satisfactory, (at least) because no such answer will ever be known to be true. But the questions will always be there and will always create a gap that human reason will perpetually try to fill by philosophical theorizing. So this is what my theory is, too: one more product of transcendental illusion. There is no point of view from which the theory may be seen to be true: all that there is is the striving toward such a point of view.

But then why not say so from the beginning, and then keep saying it all the time? Why present the theory in realist terms? Why continuously slip into a realist jargon? The answer, very simply, is that there is no choice. It is just a fact that the language we speak—the only language we have—is a realist language. This language contains names, and names at least purport to refer to *things*. This language allows for the construction of sentences, and sentences at least purport to describe *facts*. If we use this language to formulate theories, these theories will inevitably have a realist look: they will at least purport to tell us *the way things are*.

It may seem then that the realist has an unsurmountable philosophical advantage over his opponent and that whoever, like myself, has different views should follow Wittgenstein's advice (in the *Tractatus*) and just shut up.[26] But there is an alternative solution, whose essence is to be found in the very "paradox" we are discussing here. The very fact that the realist finds so objectionable—that is, the fact that theories like Kant's in a way deny themselves—is in the position I am advocating an absolutely indispensable critical reminder. It tells us that, though it is important to take the theory and its realist presumption seriously in order to understand it, the theory itself *is only a theory*. What we do in this way is try to escape from the realist constrictions on language by having language fight against itself.

9. The Ultimate Objection

It seems that I can answer objections to my theory only by getting myself into deeper trouble. This is what seems to happen, in particular, after my last answer. For after that answer one more objection comes very naturally, possibly the most basic objection I will consider here. (For this reason I call it "the ultimate objection.") It goes like this. What right do I have to propose a theory like mine, and to expect anybody to take it seriously? It is a highly sophisticated theory, and one that is sometimes in conflict with ordinary people's intuitions. After all, ordinary people do not think or say that they refer to tables or chairs in their cognitive spaces: they think and say that they refer to *real* tables and chairs. If I were a realist, I could at least claim that—no matter what ordinary people think or say—what *I* say *is true*, and is what they *should* think and say. But as it is, I certainly do not have any such absolutist conception of my position, so why should anybody else find all this complicated machinery worthy of attention?

My answer to this objection has two components. First, I think that the discovery of philosophical truth is not the only purpose of a philosophical theory. A philosophical theory is also (and perhaps primarily) an attempt to face a certain area of our experience and make consistent sense out of it. In this process (which is ultimately a process of *understanding*) some of our intuitions are reshaped and modified, whereas others are followed to their last consequences. The choice of which ones will go and which will stay, of course, is motivated by our hierarchy of values, hence the resulting theory will also be *expressive* of that hierarchy. So, even if I am not convinced of the absolute truth of my position, even if in fact I would find such a claim absurd, it is not out of the question that somebody who shares with me the belief that reference is primarily an intentional operation, and who attributes to such a belief the importance I do, will want to follow me in all the consequences that intuition forces me to (if, in fact, it forces me to them), giving up in the process other intuitions ordinary people might have.

The second component of my answer is that in the end it is irrelevant whether anybody will be convinced by my theory, or even whether I am. I think that a position like this must be elaborated, at the very least as a significant polemical objective. I think that it is instructive to see how the position can answer some natural (and apparently fatal) criticisms, and in the process reveal more vitality than one might have expected. I think that all of this is crucial if we want to avoid having analytic philosophy of language develop in a vacuum, where its most basic principles are unreflectively accepted as truisms.

Notes

1. See for example my (1974, 1978, 1979). In the same years, some analytic philosophers have been developing positions that partially overlap with mine: most notably, Hilary Putnam (see, for example, his 1978). But this is not the place to discuss such connections in any detail.

2. On this matter, see the end of Section 4.

3. This puzzle was first presented by Saul Kripke (1979). Authors dealing with it include Putnam (1979), David Lewis (1981), and Ruth Barcan Marcus (1983).

4. Kripke examines this option in his paper, and finds it equally unsatisfactory. Indeed, he has "no firm belief as to how to solve" the puzzle (p. 259), and says that "the primary moral" to be drawn from it "is that the puzzle *is* a puzzle" (p. 267).

5. See his (1919a), p. 170.

6. Of course, the object of knowledge is often taken to be *propositions*. Since I am working in a Kantian framework, I find it more natural to talk about knowledge of *objects*, but what I say could easily be reformulated in the propositional jargon.

7. An example of an author who makes such qualifications but in the end remains committed to a form of metaphysical realism is David Smith (1982). See also Horwich (1982), which follows Smith's paper in the same issue of *Noûs*.

8. This does not imply that I am an anti-haecceitist in connection with modal semantics; here I am using possible worlds only as an analogy. For the notions of haecceitism and anti-haecceitism, see Kaplan (1975), pp. 722–23.

9. Of course, all this talk about "finding out" is part of realist jargon. In Section 8, I will face the problems posed by my use of such jargon.

10. To be more precise, I should be speaking of the ideas you and I associate with 'London.'

11. For an excellent discussion of Meinongian incomplete objects and *Aussersein* see Findlay (1963).

12. The sense in which this idealism is transcendental will become clear later, especially after my discussion of ideas in Section 7.

13. See his (1980), p. 5.

14. Of course, by using these terms I intend to suggest that there are important analogies between my position and current intentionality theories. However, such analogies (as well as the differences that also exist) will not be discussed here.

15. The situation would be different if 'referring' were conceived as more like 'hitting' than like 'thinking of.' So in a theory of 'referring' as a *non*intentional verb (which, as I said, I don't want to rule out) the first alternative would be a perfectly viable one.

16. By using the vague expression 'association' I am deliberately not distinguishing between the description giving the *meaning* of the name, and only helping to *fix* its *reference*. The reason is that this distinction—though interesting—is irrelevant to the present discussion. For on the one hand, Kripke thinks that people before him were usually unclear about the distinction, and on the other, even after making the distinction, he is going to reject *both* construes of the "association" in question by "counterexamples" like the one discussed in the text.

17. Of course, this "Frege-Russell view" is largely a fiction—especially with regard to Russell. Kripke, who discusses the view at great length, acknowledges its fictional character in footnote 4 (p. 27). But I would agree that the fiction is a useful one.

18. But see note 20 below.

19. What I mean by ideas here will become clearer in the next section.

20. This approach can be extended to the first condition, too. For even a hearer who does not know exactly to what in his cognitive space he should attribute a certain property or relation may be receiving *some degree* of information (the property or relation should be attributed to *one of many* entities, without it being clear to *which* one), and may make some practical use of that information.

21. As far as Kant is concerned, of course, 'real' means 'noumenal.'

22. The whole section on Transcendental Dialectic in the *Critique of Pure Reason* is relevant here, and in particular the appendix to it on the regulative employment of the ideas of pure reason.

23. This apparent paradox is what brought about the transcendental excision of Kant's theory (the term is John Findlay's) operated by Strawson and others.

24. Of course, Kant did not help by often claiming apodeictic certainty for his system. But we have his own authorization for discounting such metatheoretical remarks, since he said (of Plato): "it is by no means unusual, upon comparing the thoughts which an author has expressed in regard to his subject, whether in ordinary conversation or in writing, to find that we understand him better than he has understood himself." (*Critique of Pure Reason*, p. 310)

25. See, for example, the following passage from the *Prolegomena*: "Although an absolute whole of experience is impossible, the Idea of a whole of knowledge according to principles must impart to our knowledge a peculiar kind of unity, that of a system, without which it is nothing but piecework. . . . The transcendental Ideas therefore express the peculiar vocation of reason as a principle of systematic unity." (pp. 97–98)

26. See *Tractatus* 7. Note, however, that Wittgenstein himself does not remain silent. In *Tractatus* 6.54 he says we should throw away the ladder, but only *after* climbing up it. So even what ultimately turns out (in the *Tractatus* view) to be nonsense is judged crucial to "see the world aright."

2

Meinong: A Critique from the Left

But if *it* ain't
then *it* must be.
Else what is the it that ain't? (Meinong)
But what are the it's that ain't?
Take any it you like
and it ain't *it*.
Trouble is
there just ain't no it's that ain't. (Russell)
Whatever "it" is, it is truly comical. (Nietzsche)
Those who ask such questions need (and deserve)
a sharp blow to the head. (Smullyan)

[Graffiti in a philosophy department bathroom]

1. A Delusive Generalization?

Early in his (1904),[1] Alexius Meinong says:

The intent of the problem raised here is to call attention to just such an area of knowledge, which is sometimes overlooked, sometimes not sufficiently appreciated in its distinctive character. (p. 77)

The new *Gegenstandstheorie* he proceeds to articulate in the rest of the essay is supposed to remedy this oversight, and do justice to a category (or perhaps, several categories) of objects that had not received proper attention by either scientists or philosophers. Specifically, not even the most general of disciplines, metaphysics, that discipline for which (an excess of) generality had been the

20

source of recurring trouble, could advance a reasonable claim to covering this unexplored territory.

If we remember how metaphysics has always been conceived as including in its subject matter the farthest and the nearest, the greatest and the smallest alike, we may be surprised to be told that metaphysics cannot take on such a task. It may sound strange to hear that metaphysics is not universal enough for a science of Objects, and hence cannot take on the task just formulated. For the intentions of metaphysics have been universal (a fact which has so often been disastrous to its success). (p. 79)

There are two (closely related) aspects of Meinong's rhetoric strategy here that make it look very promising. First, the drive to generalization may be the most fundamental not only in philosophy but in all theoretical disciplines. As Aristotle put it in *Metaphysics* A,

We suppose first, then, that the wise man knows all things, as far as possible, although he has not knowledge of each of them individually. (*Works*, p. 1554)

So if a discipline (or a theory) can be successfully represented as a generalization of existing disciplines (or theories), this fact alone will be an advantage for it, in that it will allow one to see it as a step in the right direction: in the direction of that most comprehensive account of "the world" theoreticians depict as their ultimate goal. Think of the sense of intellectual satisfaction usually associated (at least within "historical," student-directed or opinion-making reconstructions[2]) to the discovery that some earlier theories could be considered "special cases" of later ones, say classical thermodynamics of statistical mechanics or optics of the theory of electromagnetic radiation.

Second, the move toward generalization, especially if, as was allegedly the case with Meinong's theory, it consists of extending scientific study to areas never considered before, is one that minimizes the importance of conflict and promotes an ideology of integration. The "mistake" of earlier ages reduces to their not having paid (enough) attention to a class (or classes) of phenomena; what was done then can very well be unquestionable and unquestioned, and it is just a matter of adding to it. This reading of the relation between past and present is reassuring, for it allows one to see the cognitive development of a culture as linear and cumulative, as rarely if ever going "off track," and therefore once again as proceeding in the right direction—if convergence and agreement are considered evidence of truth.

The work by Kuhn and Feyerabend has done much to undermine this peaceful representation of cultural progress, and to emphasize that conflicts and tensions play a crucial role in the making of that progress, though not usually in the most popular rationalizations of it. But be it as it may in the general case, part of my purpose here is to point out that Meinong's reference to generalization is disingenuous. What he is proposing, in fact, is a revolutionary move of enormous scope that *contradicts* some of the most basic features of the opposing (that is, the traditional) conceptual framework, so his characterization of this move as a conservative extension of traditional concerns results in a dramatic misrepresentation of the significance of the *Gegenstandstheorie*, which in turn may be responsible for the most typical misunderstandings and criticisms of this theory. *In spite of* Meinong's misrepresentation, the true import of his position is finally beginning to emerge,[3] but it is high time to pass from scattered, almost casual remarks to a full appreciation of the revolution he (did not initiate but certainly) contributed to in an important way. I hope to reach such an appreciation here; to do so, I will have to criticize Meinong not (as is usually the case) for being *too radical* (that is, from the conservative right) but, rather, for not being (at least in his exposition) radical enough (that is, from the left).[4]

To begin with, what is the new "area of knowledge" the *Gegenstandstheorie* studies? The answer appears simple[5] if we compare this theory with what Meinong understands as metaphysics:

> Without doubt, metaphysics has to do with everything that exists. (p. 79)

> metaphysics . . . is the science of reality in general. (p. 106)

If metaphysics covers all objects that exist (are real), the only extension the *more general* theory of objects can be sensibly credited with is to objects *that do not exist*. And this conclusion is confirmed by Meinong:

> the totality of what exists, including what has existed and will exist, is infinitely small in comparison with the totality of the Objects of knowledge. (p. 79)

> No matter how generally the problems of metaphysics are construed, there are questions which are even more general; these questions, unlike those of metaphysics, are not oriented exclusively toward reality. The questions of theory of Objects are of this kind. (p. 107)

Meinong anticipates the criticism that the extension of science to nonexistent objects may be regarded as unimportant:

> the lively interest in reality which is part of our nature tends to favor that exaggeration which finds the non-real a mere nothing — or, more precisely, which finds the non-real to be something for which science has no application at all or at least no application of any worth. (p. 79)

His basic response to this criticism consists of two parts: on the one hand, he admits that "[t]he theory of Objects . . . is, in the main, a science that for the time being hardly exists at all" (p. 100), and on the other, he qualifies this very statement by pointing out "that, although the theory of Objects may not have been pursued 'explicitly' heretofore, it has all the more frequently been pursued 'implicitly' " (ibid.), that is, that subjects and problems traditionally regarded as of great importance can be seen — after the theory of objects and its relations to the other sciences have been properly characterized — to fall within the scope of the new discipline. It is by developing the second part of this response that Meinong will be led eventually to show some sensitivity to the revolutionary import of his proposals, but *prima facie* his moves here are once more conciliatory. The claim that nonexistents are unimportant ('don't cares,' Quine would say) is provisionally accepted: the only way to defend them against this claim is by reorganizing the field of what is recognized as important, but nobody will agree to such a reorganization unless the theory of objects is shown to have some additional, independent fruitfulness. So the burden is on the object-theorist to show that he is a Prometheus and not an Epimetheus, and Meinong thinks that the decades spent working on the theory will be evidence that he has been (and is) ready to carry this burden and substantively develop, not simply talk and make plans about, this "young . . . very young science" (p. 115).[6]

However, there is another, much more damaging criticism Meinong does not consider: that the extension promised by the theory of objects is not simply unimportant, but is *no extension at all*. A witty expression of this criticism can be found in the following remark by Bertrand Russell (1905):

if we enumerated the things that are bald, and then the things that are not bald, we should not find the present King of France in either list. Hegelians, who love a synthesis, will probably conclude that he wears a wig. (p. 485)

The present King of France, of course, is precisely one of those (nonexistent) objects to which Meinong is trying to make us address our scientific attention. So a superficial reading of Russell's statement might suggest that Russell is being unsympathetic (and perhaps unfair) to Meinong's position, whose "refutation" he takes up in the same essay. A more sympathetic, and less question-begging, formulation—according to this superficial reading—would begin by saying that

if we enumerated the *existent* things that are bald, and then the *existent* things that are not bald, we should not find the present King of France in either list.

From which—if we accept Meinong's theory—no problem about the law of excluded middle (Russell's immediate concern here) and no conclusion of a Hegelian nature follow.

But I suggest that this formulation would be *too* sympathetic to Meinong, since Russell has very good reasons for not adding the qualification 'existent' here. Meinong himself points out that, for "[t]hose who like paradoxical modes of expression," one of the major tenets of his theory could be expressed as "There are objects of which it is true that there are no such objects" (p. 83). He does not elaborate on the paradoxical character of this statement; if he had, he might have come close to a clearer appreciation (and expression) of just how revolutionary that tenet was.

The word 'object' has a long history in philosophy, and one that shows some continuity with the (previous) history of the Latin '*substantia*' and the Greek '*ousia*.' At least, many of the problems philosophers formulate today in terms of (a reference to) objects, the Schoolmen would have formulated in terms of *substantiae* and the Greeks in terms of *ousiai*. Consider now the following statement by Aristotle, in *Metaphysics* Z:

> And indeed the question which, both now and of old, has always been raised, and always been the subject of doubt, viz. what being is, is just the question, what is substance [*ousia*]? For it is this that some assert to be one, others more than one, and that some assert to be limited in number, others unlimited. (*Works*, p. 1624)

To ask what there is is primarily to ask what substances there are. Substances are what is in the most basic, fundamental sense, and for everything else to be is to be a determination of substances:

> obviously that which is primarily is the 'what,' which indicates the substance of the thing. . . . And all other things are said to be because they are, some of them, quantities of that which *is* in this primary sense, others qualities of it, others affections of it, and others some other determination of it. (p. 1623)

Substances themselves, on the other hand, are ontologically undifferentiated: as we read in the *Categories*, no (primary) substance[7] is more substance than another (p. 5).

I argued elsewhere[8] that the traditional conceptual framework typified by these Aristotelian statements was alive and well at least until Kant's time, and that it constituted the target of Kant's Copernican revolution. Later I will explore the relevance of that revolution to the matter at hand, but for the moment it will be instructive to point out that Kant's attack did not result in the demise of the old paradigm. That paradigm is still the most popular one today, at least in analytic circles, and it was certainly active and influential in Meinong's time. Consider for example the following statement by Gottlob Frege (1892):

> A logically perfect language (*Begriffsschrift*) should satisfy the conditions, that every expression grammatically well constructed as a proper name out of signs already introduced shall in fact designate an object, and that no new sign shall be introduced as a proper name without being secured a meaning. (p. 169)

What Frege is worried about here is the problem of what were later called improper definite descriptions, but note that he does not express this problem (and the relevant requirement on a language) as that of names that designate no *existent* objects. He talks of these *Eigennamen* as designating *no objects at all*, in fact as having no meaning (*Bedeutung*) at all. Which suggests that objects for him are what *ousiai* are for Aristotle: the most primary, most fundamental beings, for which it is unnecessary to add the qualification 'existent' (and would be absurd to add the opposite qualification).[9]

Returning to Meinong, one may begin to see now the delusiveness of his claim to generalization. The claim that, say, a general cosmology is a generalization of a theory of the solar system is understood as follows: a general cosmology treats of all heavenly bodies, and *there are* heavenly bodies outside the solar system. But Meinong's claim that the theory of objects is a generalization of metaphysics (in his sense) cannot be understood in the same way, for *there are no* objects that are not (real). Or at least there are no such objects if we go along with Aristotle and Frege and believe that objects are precisely what is in the most primary sense, that in terms of which the being (or not being) of everything else is to be characterized. Thus Meinong's superficial rhetoric seems to fall flat, and his conciliatory statements fail to substantiate the peaceful impression of a science that slowly but surely approximates possession of "the whole truth."

2. The Revolutionary Standpoint

A sympathetic Meinong interpreter might still be unimpressed by the points made so far. Apparently, Aristotle thought that no (primary) substance is more substance than any other, and Frege thought that a non-denoting description has no *Bedeutung* at all, but are these opinions a *necessary component* of what I have been calling the traditional paradigm? Why could we not think that Meinong's was, in fact, a generalization of the paradigm in question, in that he was to attribute to an object the most basic kind of being *if that object had any being at all*?

To answer these questions, I must bring out more of the nature and function of paradigms. A paradigm is first and foremost an intellectual tool,[10] something that we use to (begin to) understand some area of our experience,[11] or perhaps all of it. And a tool is a *better* tool if it carries no extra baggage, if it is not encumbered by elements that add nothing to its performance *relative to the tasks for which it is used*. If a knife is something I use to cut, then my knife will be a better knife if I do not hang my keys on it, since the keys are of no help in cutting and make the whole thing heavier to carry and more awkward to handle. When this simple economical consideration is applied to tools of a conceptual kind, it may justify the acceptance of a variant of Ockham's razor, not as a grand (and suspicious) metaphysical principle about the simplicity of nature but, rather, as a pragmatic offspring of plain good sense.

Think, for example, of a geocentric model of the universe as a tool for understanding our astronomical observations, and suppose that at first the earth sits still at the center of the model. Then somebody comes along and says: "This business of the earth necessarily being still is a *limitation* of the model. Let us proceed therefore to modify the model in the following way: the earth rotates around its axis with some angular velocity or other, anywhere from 0 on, but all the rest of the universe rotates with it at the same velocity (in addition to whatever other kinds of motions it has), so that this rotation cannot be detected and makes no difference to our observations. The modified model is a *generalization* of the old one because in the particular case in which the velocity of the earth's rotation is 0 it reduces to the old one, but of course it allows for infinitely many other cases."

Our reaction to this proposal would probably be a negative one, and *the reason why* it would be negative, I claim, is of a pragmatic nature: the proposal would add nothing to our explanatory powers, and the only effect of adopting it would be to complicate the mathematics of the explanations.

Consider now the Aristotelian framework discussed earlier. The point of this framework is that of allowing us to conceptualize the totality of our experience. Given the central role objects have in the framework, experience is to be explained as depending on them, and the most natural articulation of this general recipe will come in something like the following form: experience is a property that one of these objects (i.e., the subject) has, and a property that results from the interactions of this object with itself and other ones, that is, ultimately, from the causal efficacy that all objects (including the subject) have on the subject. Now suppose that someone proposes to add nonexistent objects to the paradigm. Nonexistent objects have no causal efficacy on the subject, and not because they are somehow objects "of a different level," to be correlated in various ways to those that do have causal efficacy (as one might say numbers or sets are): they are just ordinary objects, "low-level" objects, objects like tables and chairs and humans, but *nonexistent* tables and chairs and humans. They cannot explain any more of our experience than existent objects alone do, so they are at best a useless appendage of this intellectual tool, and we are authorized to feel about them as we did earlier about the proposed "generalization" of the geocentric model.[12]

But the Meinongian might still have a response to this argument, indeed one that uses the very metaphor of a tool I have been using. For he might say: if a tool is used for some purpose A, making it more proficient at executing A is not the only way to make it a better tool. One can also *extend its use*, that is, make it a tool that can be used for A and for (some distinct purpose) B. For example, hanging the keys on my pocket knife might lower the probability that I forget one or the other, and this is as good a pragmatic consideration as any. Of course, in contexts in which a *concrete* tool such as a knife is in question, one must take into account all sorts of limitations of a physical nature: for example, hanging the keys on the pocket knife might make the resulting tool *too* heavy or awkward. But when it comes to a paradigm, that is, an *intellectual* tool, we may be more liberal, and if something can be added *consistently* to such a tool and extend its use, this is enough of a justification for making the addition. Now (a large part of) Meinong's *Gegenstandstheorie* can be added consistently to the traditional paradigm,[13] and when this is done the result is an instrument of wider applicability. Therefore, there is nothing wrong in seeing Meinong's move as a generalization of Aristotle's conception of objects.

In the abstract, this strategy of defense is reasonable. But successful implementation of it depends on specifying what the *other* uses are that the generalized framework could serve. And here the strategy runs into trouble. For such specifications amount usually to pointing out that reference to nonexistent objects may allow me (in addition to simply accounting for experience *in some way or other*) to explain *what* it is that I think of when I think of a winged horse, or *what* it is that I talk about when I talk about the round square,[14] and for concerns such as these to even make sense it is already necessary to think of objects in ways that are in sharp contrast with the Aristotelian paradigm.

To phrase the issue in the form of a question, why *should* there be something I think of when I think of a winged horse, or something I talk about when I talk about the round square? Unless we recognize the *necessity* of postulating such a "something," it will be enough to go along with the sober assessment that in cases like these I simply think of (or talk about) *nothing at all*. And the only way I see to justify this necessity is by making objects *conceptually dependent* on the having of thoughts or the occurrence of talk,[15] that is, by claiming that (in some cases at least) there are objects *because* there is some kind of consciousness of them, not the other way around. But this move is essentially the same as (what I take to be) Kant's in my interpretation of the Copernican revolution mentioned earlier; so it will be useful to give a brief account of that interpretation.

In the traditional conceptual framework objects are not only ontologically *but also conceptually* primary,[16] that is, *the thought of* objects, *the notion* of an object is the starting point of philosophical explanations, and in particular consciousness is conceptualized as consciousness *of objects*. In the new Kantian framework, on the other hand, it is the thought of consciousness that is primary, and objects are conceptualized as objects *of consciousness*. Given how destabilizing Kant's move is, it is not surprising that he should have serious difficulty giving a clear expression of it. For he has no language with which to give such an expression: the traditional one is still permeated by the conceptual primacy of objects, and the new language required by the revolutionary standpoint is in the process of being articulated. Many of Kant's obscure and contradictory statements may be understood as the results of his attempts at providing this articulation; for example, his insistence that empirical objects (appearances) are *representations* may be seen as an attempt to attribute to objects of experience the kind of (conceptual) dependence on consciousness representations had in the traditional framework.

Thus Kant's is work in progress, and a substantial part of post-Kantian philosophy results in further actualizing his project; in particular, in providing the new language that (he lacked and that) is necessary for formulating the Copernican standpoint. Of central historical importance in the elaboration of such a language is the notion of an *intentional object*—a notion that was originated and developed within the cultural climate to which Meinong belonged, in part by Meinong himself. For an intentional object is an *object*, not (for example) a representation; a clear statement is made in this context of the difference between objects *and contents* of consciousness, and in terms of this distinction representations and objects would in general fall on opposite sides.[17] And clearly, an intentional object is conceptually posterior to (and dependent on) consciousness: it is characterized as the target of a mental attitude, as an object *of* cognition, *of* fear, *of* desire.

On the other hand, the new language must not be taken too seriously and be allowed to force us to the conclusion that all objects *in the new sense*, all intentional objects, are real; indeed, such a conclusion would be foreign to Kant's declared empirical realism (and conservatism).[18] As a consequence, a new conceptualization of what it is to be real must be developed; for Kant, this conceptualization will bring to the fore the characters of spatio-temporality and rule-directedness. But aside from details, the thing to emphasize here is that, whereas in the traditional framework reality is virtually *defined* in terms of objects, so that *green* and *square* are real *because* there are green and square objects, in the new framework reality is defined otherwise, and in fact it becomes imperative, in the interest of elementary credibility, to so define it that some objects *in the new sense* turn out *not to be real*.

It is within a conceptual framework of this Kantian variety that Meinong's *Gegenstandstheorie* becomes a useful (indeed, probably necessary) project. For if objects are objects of consciousness, and if not all objects of consciousness exist, it becomes important not only to admit that not all objects exist, but also to study what is true in general of objects, whether they exist or not.

If this reading is accepted, one can see that the Meinong-Russell debate is a debate across conflicting paradigms, and in particular across conflicting ways of thinking of objects (not simply of what objects there are). Take a statement asserting the nonexistence of something, say of the difference between *A* and *B*. Russell finds such statements puzzling; for he, following a clearly Aristotelian line (see Aristotle's *Works*, pp. 4–5), thinks of the subject of a proposition as an object, *and thinks of an object as something that is*, thus ending in a conceptual bind:

> 'I think, therefore I am' is no more evident than 'I am the subject of a proposition, therefore I am.' . . . Hence, it should appear, it must always be self-contradictory to deny the being of anything. (1905, p. 485)

Consistent with this conclusion is Russell's making it impossible to even formulate singular nonexistence statements. Meinong, on the other hand, who not only wants to allow for the meaningfulness of these statements (and the truth of some of them) but is inclined to regard them (or, more precisely, to regard the corresponding judgments) as evidence in favor of his theory,[19] can do so because he is changing the notion of what it is to be an object and admitting that objects enter the picture whenever there is (say) *thought* of objects.

3. Metaphysics

I suggested in the first section that there is in Meinong some (imperfect) recognition of the revolutionary character of his pronouncements. Such recognition comes out primarily in the context of his peculiar proposal for an understanding of the word 'metaphysics':

> What can be known about an Object in virtue of its nature, hence *a priori*, belongs to the theory of Objects. . . . On the other hand, that which is to be determined about Objects only *a posteriori* belongs to metaphysics, provided that the knowledge is of a sufficiently general character. (p. 109)

For once, in giving this definition, Meinong recognizes that it will probably issue (not just in a generalization of traditional concerns but) in a conflict with both ordinary intuitions[20] and historical data. And he also claims that he is ready to live with this conflict and to regard the view expressed here as regimentary and normative rather than descriptive (perhaps of a larger universe of things):

> But even if our present view of the character of metaphysics up to this time should not convince everyone, indeed even if it should be shown to be historically incorrect, the error concerns only the definition "*de lege lata*," as it were, and the definition "*de lege ferenda*" would remain open for consideration. (p. 107)

Given the recurrent emphasis on the *necessary* status of metaphysical statements, hardly anything could be more devastating for the traditional point of view than this proposal to make metaphysics empirical. Meinong tries to defend the proposal by suggesting that it renders "a just account of the claims of empiricism" (p. 110), but once again his defense is disingenuous. For on the one hand, empiricism in general does not deny that there are legitimate nonempirical statements asserting nonempirical truths,[21] and on the other (and more important), nonempirical statements are not excluded by Meinong's framework: they are assigned a solid, perfectly respectable location in the theory of objects. So the problem reduces to which science should be competent to deal with nonempirical, conceptual matters: the old metaphysics or the new *Gegenstandstheorie*. And given how differently objects were thought of by traditional metaphysicians (say, Aristotle) and by Meinong, this conflict of conceptual competence can be seen as expressing a conflict of conceptual framework. Meinong does not try to drive the old framework out of business directly, by giving a clear statement of its opposition to his new point of view, but tries instead to cut the ground out from under it by definitionally depriving it of the area in which it normally operated.

Interestingly enough, Kant, too, fought a battle on the word 'metaphysics.' It was largely an underground battle, whose immediate results were once again textual obscurities. Thus metaphysics was sometimes said, in substantial agreement with the tradition, to have "as the proper object of its enquiries three ideas only: *God, freedom*, and *immortality*," and at other times it was made to be, in a more modern vein, "nothing but the *inventory* of all our possessions through pure reason, systematically arranged."[22] Given that Kant's "inventory" will show the delusiveness of the three ideas above, an attempt at putting these two characterizations together would result in making metaphysics a totally empty pursuit. But, of course, part of what Kant takes himself to be doing in the first *Critique* is establishing the possibility of metaphysics "as a science." Also, in Kant's case as in Meinong's a new discipline comes into the picture, transcendental philosophy, and the relations between this discipline and metaphysics are far from unambiguous: sometimes metaphysics seems to be supplanted by it, and sometimes it seems to be a part of it. Ultimately, the best way to make sense of this textual morass[23] is by thinking that there are two *senses* of the word 'metaphysics': a traditional one and a new one *defined by Kant*. And if this reading is accepted, one can see that Kant is doing essentially the same thing as Meinong, that is, redefining the area in which one is supposed to address conceptual concerns instead of (or perhaps, in his case, in addition to) making it clear that those concerns are to be addressed in a novel way.

4. An Objection

The interpretation of Meinong's (implicit) strategy I have been proposing here must face an important textual difficulty. For the following statement is to be found in his (1904):

> However, I cannot conceal from myself at present that it is no more necessary to an Object that it be presented in order not to exist than it is in order to exist. (p. 83)

Prima facie, this statement is in direct contradiction to my claims in the previous two sections, since it ostensibly asserts the independence of objects — existent *and* nonexistent — from our consciousness. In fact, the statement seems to suggest that Meinong is still thinking of objects à la Aristotle, as primary and independent — even when they do not exist.

I do not want to deny that some such confusion may in fact have occurred. Mine is, after all, not a defense but a criticism of Meinong, a way of *forcing* his position in directions he might not have approved of with the intent of making it more defensible and perhaps (in view of the problems that haunt the old conceptual framework[24]) even more palatable. But the statement above is not where I would like to draw the line between what I accept and what I reject in Meinong, for that statement makes perfectly good sense to me, indeed brings out an important (and often misunderstood) aspect of the operation involved here.

Once again, the dependence of objects on consciousness in the Copernican paradigm is *conceptual* dependence: it is dependence of *the thought* of objects on *the thought* of consciousness. Admitting this dependence amounts to the following: thinking of objects is something one arrives at (or, given the normative nature of a paradigm, *should* arrive at) by first thinking of consciousness and then putting conditions on this consciousness. Once one has arrived at the notion of an object, on the other hand, one can well admit objects no one has ever been aware of.[25] Similarly, I can conceptualize colors as dependent upon experiences people have (and not as features of an independent reality) and then admit the possibility of colors nobody has ever experienced. The dependence of colors on experiences here, or of objects on consciousness above, is not (empirical) *psychological* dependence.

It is precisely of this psychologism — Kant would have said *empirical idealism* — that Meinong is afraid here, because confusing his theory of objects with psychology would deprive the former of its conceptual, *a priori* character:

Psychology can take interest only in those Objects toward which some psychological event is *actually* directed. Perhaps we could put this more briefly: psychology can take interest only in those Objects which are *actually* presented, *whose presentations thus exist*. (p. 89; italics mine)

The conceptual rearrangements we are discussing are not without consequences, but these consequences surface only when we move from the empirical level of *actuality* to the conceptual level of *possibility*. Consider again the conceptualization of colors in terms of experiences: if I accept it I can certainly admit the possibility of colors no one has ever experienced (or will ever experience), but I cannot admit the possibility of colors no one *could* ever experience, for that a color *can* be experienced is built into the very notion of what it is to be a color. Similarly, if I conceptualize objects in terms of awareness, I can admit the possibility of objects no one has ever been (or will be) aware of, but I cannot admit the possibility of objects no one *could* be aware of, for that objects *can* be objects of awareness is built into the very notion of what it is to be an object. On the other hand, I could admit the possibility of such inaccessible objects if I stuck to the traditional paradigm, since there thought of objects is totally independent of thought of consciousness. So the two paradigms are really opposed on this issue, and it is interesting (as well as in agreement with my reading) to note where Meinong falls in terms of the opposition:

there is no Object which could not at least in possibility be an Object of cognition. All that is knowable is given—namely, given to cognition. To this extent, all objects are knowable. Given-ness as a most general property can be ascribed to Objects without exception, whether they are or are not. (p. 92)

Many Kant commentators have serious problems with (at least some of) the statements of transcendental idealism, in that these statements seem to express an unacceptable empirical dependence of objects on the mind.[26] In my reading, they do not: the dependence in question is of a conceptual nature. The reason why they *appear* to have such an empirical significance, on the other hand, is to be found in the linguistic limitations Kant was facing, and the resulting difficulties of expression he experienced. I have pointed out here that Meinong's language is better equipped than Kant's; as a consequence, the conceptual character of his concerns may (and does) emerge more clearly—*precisely* through passages like the one quoted at the beginning of this section. So such passages, far from representing a problem for my reading, allow for a welcome articulation of one of its major themes.

5. Concluding Remarks

I have criticized Meinong for not doing full justice to the novelty of his position, and for presenting it (misleadingly) as a generalization of, not an alternative to, the tradition. But I must point out that Meinong's attitude in this regard is (probably for the reasons mentioned on p. 21) a relatively common one, common in particular to various positions in the vicinity of the *Gegenstandstheorie*. It may be instructive to give a few examples.

As Karel Lambert (1983) pointed out, there are clear similarities between Meinong's theory of existent *and nonexistent* objects and the attempts on the part of free logicians to systematize our use of denoting *and nondenoting* singular terms. The difference between the two projects is to a large extent one of philosophical jargon: though not insensitive to the importance of language,[27] Meinong is still (as Kant before him) deeply under the influence of psychological metaphors. The free logicians, on the other hand, are well within "the heyday of sentences,"[28] and so what could be expressed in terms of objects *of consciousness* (or *of cognition*) they express in terms of objects *of discourse*. But when their proposals (or Meinong's) are suitably reformulated, the two parties can be seen as making essentially the same moves, and as having essentially the same relation of conceptual conflict with the tradition.[29] In the case of free logic, the tradition is represented by classical quantification theory, which is based on the primacy of objects and conceptualizes names in terms of the objects they name — whence it follows that *as a logical (conceptual) truth* all names refer. Free logic, on the other hand, is best seen as having discourse itself as the conceptual starting point: thus for it the notion of a name is prior to the notion of the object that constitutes the reference of that name, and it is in fact perfectly possible that some names refer to no object at all.

The official act of birth of free logic was a seminal paper by Henry Leonard (1956). At the very beginning of this paper, Leonard says:

> Every abstract, formal system — hence every system of logic — is developed against a background of presuppositions and assumptions. . . . The presuppositions are of tremendous importance when one undertakes to apply the abstract system to a concrete subject matter. Unless the field of application satisfies the presuppositions, both the explicit and the tacit ones, the application is invalid and the result of the application can be serious errors of belief about the subject matter in question. (pp. 49–50)

Classical quantification theory, according to Leonard, contains tacit assumptions concerning existence, and the *revised* logic he proposes (which Lambert later called *free*) has the effect (among other things) of eliminating those assumptions and thereby making it possible for logic to have wider applicability. Thus Leonard's justification for the enterprise of free logic is in the same vein as Meinong's for his *Gegenstandstheorie*, that is, it is conducted in terms of a reference to generalization. And this justification is just as delusive as Meinong's, for when it comes to specifying some "concrete subject matter" to which the new tool would be applicable but the old one would not, Leonard brings in Santa Claus. And that is no generalization of traditional concerns, because there is no Santa Claus, and so we are not giving our logical tools wider applicability if we make them applicable to him. Of course, there is *talk* of Santa Claus, but for such talk to be taken seriously, and not simply dismissed as talk *of nothing*, indeed for it to become important to study its structure, our attention must be focused on talk — not on objects — from the very beginning. Otherwise, one might simply conclude that if people talk of Santa Claus that is too bad: they should not, at least in respectable scientific contexts.[30]

Not even Kant eludes the attractiveness of the generalization ploy. At the very end of the Transcendental Analytic (in the first *Critique*), he finds it useful to "add some remarks which, although in themselves not of special importance, might nevertheless be regarded as requisite for the completeness of the system." (p. 294) Such remarks begin as follows:

> The supreme concept with which it is customary to begin a transcendental philosophy is the division into the possible and the impossible. But since all division presupposes a concept to be divided, a still higher one is required, and this is the concept of an object in general, taken problematically, without its having been decided whether it is something or nothing.

It is part of what I have been claiming in this chapter that that of an object which is nothing is a notion that makes sense in the Copernican paradigm *but not* in the traditional one. So it is not surprising that Kant should express interest in this notion here and proceed to give a conceptualization of nothing. But it is surprising (or perhaps no longer surprising, given the other examples discussed above, but still disingenuous) that he should describe his conceptualization of nothing as (in effect) a generalization of what was "customary." For in terms of what was customary this is no generalization and there is no need of a higher concept here: objects *cannot* be nothing.

Finally, a comment may be in order on this chapter's motto, which I see as a brilliant and economical synthesis of the major theme of my discussion, as well as of other (related) ones that I had to leave aside. The quotes attributed in that motto to Meinong and Russell bring out the fact that theirs is a conflict of paradigms: specifically, of paradigms concerning what it is to be an "it" — or an object. But it has been a frequent occurrence in the scientific literature at least since the time of Ptolemy[31] that the view of an opposing paradigm be described as ridiculous, and this makes sense, for if we try to look at the world from that foreign standpoint, we do in fact see it topsy-turvy, and the experience is likely to relieve the tensions that maintain our assurance of where is up and where is down, and excite laughter as a result. Hence the quote attributed to Nietzsche. Finally, the one attributed to Smullyan emphasizes that when it comes to paradigms, noncognitive factors are crucial. Part of what it is to be committed to a paradigm is to be convinced that the paradigm will ultimately make sense of what we do not yet understand and smooth out what now appears absurd or contradictory; so no amount of negative data will ever be enough to logically necessitate abandonment of such a commitment. The step from one paradigm to another is to be made on (at least partly) noncognitive grounds: as a result of a blow to the head perhaps, or of some other instrument of "enlightenment," that will suddenly make us see the world, or part of it, with new eyes.[32]

Notes

1. All Meinong quotes below are from this source.

2. Kuhn and Feyerabend (to be mentioned again shortly) have illustrated with a number of examples the unreliability of later reconstructions of scientific achievements, especially when these reconstructions fulfill purposes of indoctrination.

3. Thus consider the following statement by William Rapaport (1985):

Part of the problem is that 'object' is ambiguous. Meinong used '*Gegenstand*' (= object) in the sense of "object-of- thought"; that to which our acts of thinking are directed. In ordinary use, 'object' tends to mean something like "thing out there in the (real) world." . . . On the second reading, modifiers such as 'existing' or 'actual' seem redundant. (p. 257)

Though I argue below that much more than an "ambiguity" is at stake here, and that the modifiers do not just *seem* to be redundant in the traditional reading of 'object,' this statement goes at least in the same general direction as my present discussion.

4. In a statement quoted by Findlay (1963), p. xiii, Gilbert Ryle has already criticized Meinong for being "the sort of reformer who makes revolutions inevitable, yet himself stops short of seeing that they are even possible," that is from what seems to be a radical standpoint. But the revolution Ryle is talking about here consists of adopting the general strategy of Russell's theory of descriptions—in Ryle's words, "wherever possible logical constructions are to be substituted for inferred entities"—and though the issue of what modifications of a given position qualify as conceptual revolutions is one that probably cannot be resolved in an unpartisan way, there is evidence that Meinong's position as reconstructed here goes further than Russell's (though probably not far enough) in breaking with the tradition. For the primacy of objects discussed below is more central to the traditional paradigm than the claim (denied by Russell) that the grammatical form of natural language does justice to its logical form; in fact, the latter claim seems already denied by Aristotle. So Russell's strategy can be seen as an instrument of restoration, which by giving up nonessential features of the tradition tries to effectively safeguard (what is essential to) it from some irritating puzzles. Similarly, if one thinks that civil liberties are less essential to bourgeois society than the capitalistic mode of production, one can conclude that a fascist *coup* is a conservative move and not a revolutionary one.

5. That things are not so simple will be shown later, when I discuss Meinong's notion of metaphysics in more detail.

6. I will argue in the next section that the issue of fruitfulness cannot be decided here without some commitment to one or the other of the parties in conflict. Then it will become apparent that even in the present case Meinong's exposition is *misleadingly* conciliatory.

7. We may disregard here secondary substances, since they clearly do not fit the more mature discussion in *Metaphysics* Z.

8. In my (1985, 1987). The conclusions of those arguments will be summarized in the next section.

9. Of course, this is not to say that there are the same objects for Frege as for Aristotle, but that the two have (roughly) the same notion of what it is to be an object. Note also that the admission of this necessary (that is, conceptual) equivalence between 'object' and 'existent object' may be the basis of Frege's attitude toward singular existence statements. See my (1980).

10. This practical significance of paradigms is evident from their first characterization (in Kuhn, 1962) as "universally recognized scientific achievements that for a time provide model problems and solutions to a community of practitioners" (p. x). Later, for example in his (1974), Kuhn acknowledged that his original use of the word 'paradigm' was somewhat ambiguous, and distinguished paradigms as *disciplinary matrices* from paradigms as *exemplars* (even suggesting that perhaps the word 'paradigm' should be dropped altogether). But both of the senses thus identified have the prag-

matic dimension I emphasize here, hence for present purposes I may disregard such distinctions. (I focus on them in Chapter 8 below, where I also question the conventional identification accepted here between *paradigm* and *conceptual framework*).

11. Or, if you find this formulation slanted toward idealism, some area of the world. The substitution would not affect my arguments below.

12. Though I know of no one who holds this view, it might be possible to claim that nonexistent objects do have causal efficacy on existent ones, and hence can contribute to explaining experience – for example, that Hamlet is causally involved in (hence can account for) my thought of Hamlet. But it would be hard to deny that one who made this claim was involved in a major overhaul of basic features of the traditional conceptual landscape, though possibly features different from existence and objectivity (in this case, causality would rather be under attack). So this hypothetical defender of the significance of nonexistent objects for traditional concerns would in fact just be proposing a different (kind of) conceptual revolution.

13. Proving this is the aim of efforts such as Parsons (1980), which, however, must stop short of admitting contradictory objects – unless they give up classical logic.

14. Thus Meinong (1904) begins with the following statement:

> That knowing is impossible without something being known, and more generally, that judgments and ideas or presentations are impossible without being judgments about and presentations of something, is revealed to be self-evident by a quite elementary examination of these experiences. (p. 76)

Probably, a supporter of the traditional paradigm would claim the self-evidence of the contradictory claim that some presentations (say, my current presentation of a pink elephant in the corner) simply *fail* to have an object.

15. There may be other uses for the addition of nonexistent objects to the traditional paradigm, but to my knowledge none has yet been pointed out. The following lucid statement by Parsons (1980) – to be found in the concluding paragraph of the (short) section on evidence for the theory – is a good summary of the attempts of recent Meinongians: "Of course I have not proved that there are nonexistent objects; I don't believe that anyone could do that in a non-question-begging way." (p. 37)

16. In the Aristotelian passages quoted earlier the reader will find suggestions of both kinds of primacy, but no clear statement of the distinction; indeed, part of my concern (here and elsewhere) is to bring out this distinction explicitly. Note also that, as I show in my (1987), the ontological primacy of objects will not be questioned by Kant: after the revolution, it will still be possible to say that the being of properties, relations, states, and the like depends on the being of objects – of those, that is, which *are*.

17. Of course, I could make a representation the object of an act of awareness, but even then the content of my experience would be different from its object.

18. In third chapter of my (1987) I argue that Kant intended his new conceptualization of experience to change nothing of *ordinary* (cognitive) practices. The changes it involves concern the way in which philosophy is to *think of* those practices.

19. Consider, for example, the following passage: "Any particular thing that isn't real (*Nichtseiendes*) must at least be capable of serving as the Object for those judgments which grasp its *Nichtsein*." (p. 82)

20. Another passage where this awareness surfaces is the following: "But such things may be alien to our natural way of thinking." (p. 82)

21. The only significant philosophical alternative to admitting nonempirical knowledge is not empiricism but, rather, epistemological holism. And Meinong clearly rejects any such position:

> Nowadays, we occasionally meet with failure to recognize this distinction [between empirical and *a priori* knowledge], but such failure no more affects the validity of the distinction than does the fact of color blindness affect the distinction between the various colors.

22. Both quotes are from the *Critique of Pure Reason*, p. 325 and p. 14, respectively.

23. What makes things even more complicated is that transcendental philosophy, too, will turn

out to be in some sense an empty pursuit (see the next chapter) — a conclusion that Kant never quite accepted "officially." Even if he had, however, he would have claimed that this empty pursuit is a valuable one, whereas traditional attempts at dealing with God and the like in conceptual terms are not (in fact, they are counterproductive).

24. I discuss the problems the old framework has with knowledge in the second chapter of my (1987).

25. And Meinong wants to admit such objects and is concerned about the (Berkeleian) argument that I cannot think of an object nobody thinks of without thinking of it — an argument that would apply if the dependence in question were of an empirical nature (see his pp. 89–90).

26. See for example Strawson (1966), pp. 21ff.

27. Consider for example the following passages:

In dealing with the meaning of words and sentences, linguistic science is necessarily also concerned with Objects, and grammar has done the spadework for a theoretical grasp of Objects in a very basic way. (p. 88)

one is tempted to say that the general theory of Objects must learn from grammar just as the specialized theory of Objects must learn from mathematics. (p. 103)

On the other hand, it is still true that Meinong's jargon is largely psychological, probably because, as he admits, "much of the essential nature of the way in which the theory of Objects frames its questions originally occurred to [him] while [he] was engaged in supposedly exclusively psychological labors" (p. 102).

28. The expression is Ian Hacking's: see his (1975).

29. The points made in the rest of this paragraph are articulated in Chapter 9 below.

30. The proposal that free logics be regarded as extensions of (rather than alternatives to) classical logic has surfaced again within Bas van Fraassen's semantical analysis of the former. I discuss this issue in my (1986), pp. 414–15.

31. See *The Almagest*, p. 11.

32. I discuss the noncognitive aspects of a paradigm shift in the fourth chapter of my (1987).

3

Philosophy One and Two

> *I have experienced it myself, with all the horror of seeing an-*
> other woman *in me* — that other woman — *besides this one that I*
> *am here for you and for myself:* two women, *within a single*
> *person!*
>
> Luigi Pirandello, *Mrs. Morli One and Two*, Act III;
> my translation

The end of systematic philosophy has been promulgated.[1] But the modalities of this demise leave open a major question. For while the millenarists seem convinced that "there will be something called 'philosophy' on the other side of the transition" they are advocating, they have little to offer as to what this something will or should be except admittedly "idle" speculations or uninformative remarks such as "that philosophers' moral concern should be with continuing the conversation of the West." Later in this chapter I will suggest an explanation for such inconclusiveness, but my main concern here is with going beyond it, with indicating an important social task that a group of intellectuals, probably best called (largely for reasons of tradition) philosophers, should find the time to attend to. I hope it will become apparent to the reader that my proposal is not motivated by a desire to find something significant for some otherwise useless academics to do, but, rather, by a desire to see a certain *job* done, a job that those academics — if they overcome some basic mis(self-)conceptions — may be best equipped to do. To put it briefly, the job in question is a *critical* one, not, however, one that will set definitive, unsurpassable limits to human thought and action, but, rather, one that will patiently oppose myth to myth, story to story, possibility to possibility, trying all along to avoid unilaterality and single-mindedness.

In justifying my proposal, I will be making constant references to the most provocative and misunderstood of edifying philosophers, that is (of all people) Immanuel Kant. But I will not be defending my interpretation of Kant here.[2] The present discussion is not intended as a contribution to the history of philosophy: my references will only have the purpose of discharging a duty of intellectual honesty and attributing the main ideas mobilized below where they belong.

1. Transcendental Arguments

One of the (few) classical topics of Kantian scholarship within the analytic tradition is the issue of transcendental arguments. Here are the fundamental features of such arguments according to a recent (and relatively standard) exposition:[3]

(a) transcendental arguments are supposed to answer the skeptic;
(b) they (attempt to) do that by undercutting the skeptic's position, that is, by showing that the truth of some proposition p that the skeptic wants to deny is required for the very formulation of intelligible thought, so that if the skeptic denies p he ends up making no sense at all;
(c) it is unlikely that any transcendental argument purporting to prove some interesting proposition can be made to work (though examples can be found of sound transcendental arguments proving relatively trivial conclusions).

Stock examples of such arguments are—within this interpretive tradition—the transcendental deduction and the analogies of experience; for example, the "transcendental argument" of the second analogy is taken (as trying) to establish in some sense or other the "objective validity" of the Principle of Causality against Hume's attack.

I am not concerned here with challenging this reading of the deduction or the analogies.[4] But I am concerned with pointing out that Kant himself used the expression 'transcendental argument' (and analogous ones) in a different way, *and* that the different uses of this key expression by Kant and his analytic commentators suggest two different pictures of transcendental philosophy—which ultimately means, from a Kantian point of view, of philosophy in general. Since it is these two different pictures that I want to articulate and discuss here, the issue of transcendental arguments is probably as useful and stimulating a starting point as any.

In the only two occurrences of the phrase 'transcendental argument' ('*transzendentales Argument*') in the *Critique of Pure Reason*, 'transcendental' is to be understood as 'purely conceptual,' and Kant is clearly not endorsing any such arguments, even less indicating that they are central to his enterprise. On the contrary, he says:

> To prove the contingency of matter itself, we should have to resort to a transcendental argument, and this is precisely what we have here set out to avoid. (p. 522)

Similar remarks apply to the expressions 'transcendental proof' ('*transzendentaler Beweis*') and 'transcendental mode of proof' ('*transzendentale Beweisart*'). Thus, for example, Kant says:

Both the above proofs were transcendental, *that is, were attempted independently of empirical principles.* (p. 514; italics mine)

And in the section of the Transcendental Doctrine of Method entitled *The Discipline of Pure Reason in Regard to Its Proofs*, where he covers both legitimate proofs (as, say, that of the Principle of Causality) and illegitimate ones (as, say, the classical arguments for the existence of God), he makes it clear that what unifies these "transcendental" proofs is not any specific structure they have, or any specific aim of answering the skeptic, but, rather, the fact that they are conducted at a purely conceptual level.

The apparent simplicity of this characterization is ultimately delusive, since it is not at all clear what it means to conduct an activity (say an activity of inquiry or reflection) "at a purely conceptual level." I will return later to this puzzle, but for the moment I point out that, *whatever it means to do something at a conceptual level*, Kant faces a serious problem here. For he claims that "[i]ntuition and concepts constitute . . . the elements of all our knowledge, so that neither concepts without an intuition in some way corresponding to them, nor intuition without concepts, can yield knowledge." (p. 92) So how is a proof conducted at a purely conceptual level going to extend our knowledge?

An answer to this question is suggested by the only occurrence of "transcendental proof" in the Analytic, which is contained in the following passage:

Almost all natural philosophers, observing . . . a great difference in the quantity of various kinds of matter in bodies that have the same volume, unanimously conclude that this volume, which constitutes the extensive magnitude of the appearance, must in all material bodies be empty in varying degrees. Who would ever have dreamt of believing that these students of nature . . . would base such an inference solely on a metaphysical presupposition—the sort of assumption they so stoutly profess to avoid? They assume that the real in space . . . is everywhere uniform and varies only in extensive magnitude, that is, in amount. Now to this presupposition, for which they could find no support in experience, and which is therefore purely metaphysical, I oppose a *transcendental proof*, which does not indeed explain the differences in the filling of spaces, but completely destroys the supposed necessity of the above presupposition. . . . My proof has the merit at least of freeing the understanding, so that it is at liberty to think this difference in some other manner. (p. 206; italics mine)

Kant's "transcendental proof" here consists of pointing out that the phenomena of different density could be explained by introducing a notion of *degree of reality*, and saying that all space is completely filled, but in different degrees. Note, however, that he does not

intend to assert that this is what actually occurs when material bodies differ in specific gravity, but only to establish from a principle of pure understanding that the nature of our perceptions allows of such a mode of explanation, that we are not justified in assuming the real in appearances to be uniform in degree, . . . and that we are especially in error when we claim that such interpretation can be based on an *a priori* principle of the understanding. (p. 207)

"Proofs" of this kind belong to what Kant calls the "polemical employment of pure reason," which consists in "the defence of its propositions as against the counterpropositions through which they are denied" (pp. 593–94). There are several examples of such an employment in the *Critique*. At p. 342 Kant shows that the (formal) unity of self-consciousness at different times does not entail the numerical identity of the subject (that is, the entity that *has* the consciousness), since one could imagine self-consciousness to be transmitted from one substance to another the way motion is transmitted from one elastic ball to another. At pp. 373–75 he counteracts Mendelssohn's proof of the permanence of the soul after death by imagining that the soul's powers are lost in a gradual and continuous way. And at p. 618 he "weakens the force" of the argument against the immateriality of the soul based on the influence of the state of physical organs on mental powers by "postulating that our body may be nothing more than a fundamental appearance which in this our present state (in this life) serves as a condition of our whole faculty of sensibility."

Peter Strawson (1966) claims that the transcendental deduction "is not only an argument. It is also an explanation, a description, a story" (p. 86). That it is an explanation, incidentally, agrees with *Kant's own* account of what the deduction is (at p. 121), but according to Strawson the two aspects of the deduction must be separated out, "disentangled" in his terminology, to identify Kant's real contribution. The "austere" transcendental argument must be purified of its connections with the "transcendental drama." On the other hand, the above remarks on Kant's use of what *he* calls transcendental proofs suggest quite naturally a way in which the two aspects of the deduction are best seen *together*, a sense in which the deduction (and possibly other sections of the *Critique*) may be presenting an argument *that takes the form of a story*.

To begin to see what I mean, suppose that your polemical objective is a philosopher who has argued that a class of statements that we ordinarily, in our everyday life, take as true are really *impossible*. For example, we ordinarily assume (the truth of the statement) that we *know* of the existence of certain causal connections, but Hume comes along and argues that such knowledge is impossible, that we can never legitimately claim that we have a successful epistemic relation with a causal statement. Or, alternatively, we ordinarily assume that we are free, in at least some limited area of our activity, but d'Holbach or some other mechanist philosopher comes along and argues that such freedom is impossible, that insofar as we are part of a deterministic world (which, for the sake of argument, we might assume we are), the determinants of any (alleged) action of ours are always to be found in a causal network which ultimately extends far beyond the spatiotemporal scope of our life. Then you might conceive of the following philosophical project. Let us accept the challenge that Hume and d'Holbach implicitly make and argue *not for the reality* of knowledge or freedom, but, rather, *for their possibility*. The success of this project would not in any way *found* or *ground* our ordinary judgments of knowledge or freedom, but would at least allow us to *defend* those ordinary judgments against the "scandal" of a philosophy that proclaims their illegitimacy.[5] And how can you argue for the possibility, not the reality or the truth, of a statement or a class of statements? A natural strategy would seem to be that of telling a coherent *story* that includes such a statement or class of statements, or, less provocatively put, that of characterizing a model of the statement or class of statements in question, a way in which the world *could be* to make that statement or class of statements true. On the face of it, you should be able to successfully pursue this strategy without abandoning a purely conceptual level of reflection, since what you need to know in order to tell your story is not, say, what objects or causal connections *there really are* (which you could only know from experience), but at most *what it is* to be an object or a causal connection.

With an important qualification to be made later, I think that this is essentially Kant's project. But, as I said, I do not want to make historical points here; rather, I want to use the suggestions provided by (my understanding of) Kant to make some theoretical points. The first of these points is as follows. Systematic philosophy is usually identified with an attempt at founding or grounding some belief(s) or practice(s), in the sense of showing their logical or metaphysical "necessity." And usually, the skeptic is seen as the opponent of the systematic philosopher, the spoiler of systematic projects. But, in fact, (many) skeptics have something in common with (virtually all) systematic philosophers, insofar as they want to establish the *impossibility* of some belief(s) or practice(s).[6] To begin with a trivial logical point, an impossibility is after all a necessity (of the negation). And to show the significance of the logical point, what this means is that the success of many skeptical, as well as of virtually all systematic, philosophical projects would claim to have a vast impact on ordinary, everyday life, though, of course, a very different impact in the two cases: in the latter, usually, the effect would be that of providing ordinary life with a solid rational assurance, whereas in the former the effect would be a challenging, revisionary one. Once this similarity is appreciated, the suggestion may surface of conceiving yet another philosophical activity, one that has absolutely no interest in necessities of any sort. It is this suggestion that Kant is offering when he characterizes the main aim of the *Critique* as that of establishing how synthetic *a priori* judgments are *possible*. Here is how I would flesh it out.

There are two ways of doing philosophy.[7] For the sake of labels, we might call them the *philosophy of necessity* and the *philosophy of possibility*. The philosophy of necessity tends to *reduce* the number of alternatives to be considered in a rational approach to the world by showing the impossibility (that is, the *ir*rationality) of certain alternatives and thereby establishing the necessity of (the disjunction of) the alternatives left. If the (possibly degenerate) disjunction a given philosopher of necessity argues for includes (the statement of) some ordinary belief or some ordinary practice, the philosopher may be construed as attempting to give a rational foundation to that belief or practice; otherwise, he may be construed as adopting a revisionary attitude with respect to them. *The philosophy of possibility, on the other hand, tends to extend the number of alternatives to be considered.* It does not either question or try to legitimize ordinary beliefs or practices; at most, it can be construed as trying to protect them from the attacks of some philosophers of necessity.

The philosophy of necessity is also a philosophy of coercion, which tries to set *limits* to our conceptual framework.[8] The philosophy of possibility is also a liberating philosophy, which tries to break open any limits our conceptual framework might be construed as having. The main instrument of the philosophy of necessity is an argument or proof from a set of (assertoric) premises to a(n assertoric) conclusion[9]; if such an argument is accepted, then a necessary link is established between premises and conclusion, and one avenue of thought is sealed off, the one including the premises and *the negation of* the conclusion. The main instrument of the philosophy of possibility is a story, or, described more respectfully, a theory or a model, which tries to show that a certain avenue of thought is coherent by articulating it in a plausible way. If we want, we can see such a story as an argument, not, however, one with an assertoric conclusion, but one with a *problematic* conclusion of the form 'It is possible that *p*.'

Traditionally, the methodology (though not necessarily the aim) of the philosophy of possibility was appropriated by the skeptics, who reacted to alleged natural or logical necessities by cooking up the wildest hypotheses on how the world could be.[10] To my knowledge, Kant was the first to realize that the method of the skeptics could be put to a nonskeptical use,[11] so long as one gave up on the attempt to legitimize ordinary practice and rested content with resisting (philosophical) threats to its coherence. The obsession of analytic philosophers with arguments is a good indication that most of their professional activities fall within the scope of the philosophy of necessity, and hence that (if I am right in my interpretation) they are probably going to be at a loss in understanding Kant *and in pursuing the suggestions of a different philosophical practice that are implicit in his work.* The conflicting uses of the phrases 'transcendental argument' and 'transcendental proof' signaled above are a tip of this iceberg of misunderstanding: whereas Kant's non-negative uses of such phrases seem to refer to solutions of a possibility problem, and hence to stories, his analytic critics use them to refer to (attempted) refutations of the skeptic. No wonder that they find so few such refutations successful!

2. Real Possibility

The Kantian program as I characterized it so far looks very similar to (a limited form of) Hilbert's. Ordinary beliefs and practices are best left alone: the philosopher is not to delude himself into thinking that he can provide a "solid ground" for them (or, for that matter, refute them). But he can investigate their possibility, and so long as he can establish it, provide a guarantee that no incoherence will ever surface from assuming such beliefs and practices. We know that Hilbert's program (even in the limited form considered here[12]) failed, on account of Gödel's theorem; interestingly enough, the (provisional) Kantian program sketched above failed, too, for different (but related) reasons. I will now turn to this failure and to what we can learn from it.

One of the most obscure Kantian doctrines is the thesis, proposed in the Postulates of Empirical Thought, that the field of the possible extends no further than the field of the actual.[13] At first, one might hope to make sense of this doctrine by mobilizing Kant's distinction between *logical* and *real* possibility, where the former is simple absence of contradiction and the latter is the possibility *of being experienced*. But a reference to this distinction by itself will not do, since even if real possibility is stronger than the logical variety, it still does not follow that it should collapse into actuality. In Gordon Brittan's recent reconstruction, for example,[14] logical possibility is characterized in terms of what is true in some logically possible world, and real possibility in terms of what is true in some really possible world, where really possible worlds are a (proper) subclass of logically possible ones, but a subclass that, though it contains the real world, does not— according to Brittan—reduce to it. So something more is involved here: an insight about possibility that proves Kant to have seen further and deeper than most contemporary philosophers of logic, though perhaps what he saw he did not like. Understanding this insight will require a digression.

Suppose that in propositional modal logic we follow Leibnizian intuitions and characterize necessity and possibility as truth in all possible worlds and in some possible worlds, respectively. Given the level of logical analysis at which we are, it will be natural for us to identify possible worlds with assignments of truth-values to atomic propositions. Now consider a proposition of the form

(1) It is possible that p.

Since p is an atomic proposition, there certainly is a world (that is, an assignment) in which p is true, and hence (1) is *logically* true. But if we substitute q-and-not-q for p, the result is something that not only is not logically true, but is in fact logically *false*. And the reason why this creates a serious problem is that p and q-and-not-q might represent two distinct stages in the logical analysis of one and the same English proposition, so that depending on how far we analyze that proposition we end up judging it coherent and incoherent!

Contemporary modal logic carefully avoids any such problem by concentrating on *schemes* rather than propositions. Its subject matter, that is, is construed as being constituted not by those propositions that are true in all possible worlds but by those schemes of propositions *whose instances* are all true in all possible worlds. But avoiding the problem does not solve it. What we believe, argue for, or (claim to) base our activity on, are propositions, not schemes, hence we must still face the problem that a proposition considered possible at one stage of logical (that is, conceptual) analysis could be found to be impossible at a subsequent stage of the same analysis.[15]

This problem could be deflated if we were dealing with an artificial language, a language defined once and for all. For then we could conceivably make sense of a *last* stage of logical analysis, and count a proposition as *really* possible if it were recognized as possible at that stage. But natural language does not work this way. Conceptual analysis in natural language may not be an infinite process as Leibniz suggested, but it certainly is an indefinite, open-ended one, and this is enough to rule out any chance of successfully applying the strategy above. However long we have taken examining the network of concepts mobilized by a proposition of ours (especially if the "proposition" is complicated enough, as the conjunction of all that a story says is likely to be), we may never be conclusively certain that a contradiction that has not surfaced yet will not surface later.[16]

The digression is thus at an end, and we can return to the obscure claim that possibility extends no further than actuality. A natural way to make sense of this claim might now be the following. Conceptual analysis by itself will never allow us to prove the possibility of any*thing*. We can attribute logical possibility to our concepts, meaning by that that we have not discovered any contradiction in them (yet), but there is no way that consideration of concepts alone can convince us that they even *can* have an object. The only way we can convince ourselves of that is by having an object presented to us, and, of course, if this happens then not only the possibility of the object is proved, but its actuality is as well. So the only things whose possibility we can establish are the actual ones. "Real" possibility, that is, *true* (as opposed to apparent) possibility ultimately coincides for us with reality.

This devastating analysis of possibility is the missile that sinks the "Kantian" program sketched in the previous section. In line with most of the tradition, Kant thinks[17] that the characteristic mark of philosophical activity, what distinguishes it from empirical activities, is its being performed at a purely conceptual, rational level—with all the vagueness and obscurity that this characterization still retains. But at that level no object is ever presented to us, hence no account can ever be proved to be *really* possible. So there is no way of arguing transcendentally for the (real) possibility of a belief or a practice: transcendental proofs of problematic statements are just as delusive as those of assertoric (or apodeictic) ones.

Incidentally, note the connection between this negative result and the dire consequences that Gödel's theorem had for Hilbert's program. If we were *presented* with the totality of mathematical entities, or at least by the totality that constitutes the subject matter of some mathematical theory, this actual presentation could provide us with the best evidence one might wish of the truth, hence the consistency, of that theory. But since no such presentation is possible, for any interesting mathematical theory, in view (at least) of its infinite scope, we are left with the project of trying to argue for consistency at a conceptual level, where the thing turns out to be impossible. The point has often been made in this century that Kant's invocation of the notion of intuition in mathematics is based on the limits of the logic he used: now we know better—it is said or implied—hence we need no such invocation.[18] The fact that without intuition we may not be able to prove the consistency of what we are talking about, hence ultimately the great significance that Kant's proposal could have for contemporary reflection, is carefully kept out of sight in this perspective by sticking to the notion mentioned above of a *logic of schemes* in which results are established once and for all (but their relevance is never certain).

Now where does all of this leave us? Have we entirely deconstructed philosophy, in both its aspects of philosophy of necessity and philosophy of possibility? What, if anything, is left for a professional philosopher to do? To answer these questions, we must turn to Kant once more.

3. Weapons of War

In the *Groundwork of the Metaphysic of Morals*, we find the following passage:

> Freedom . . . is a mere idea: its objective validity can in no way be exhibited by reference to laws of nature and consequently cannot be exhibited in any possible experience. . . . But where determination by laws of nature comes to an end, all *explanation* comes to an end as well. Nothing is left but *defence*—that is, to repel the objections of those who profess to have seen more deeply into the essence of things and on this ground audaciously declare freedom to be impossible. (p. 127)

I have already mentioned above the defensive function that the philosophy of possibility can have—as opposed to the founding or revisionary functions the philosophy of necessity usually depicts itself as having. But the strategy of defense suggested then was a *definitive* one, based on a definitive proof that some ordinary practice or belief is coherent, hence possible to maintain. To say that there is no hope of such a final solution is not to say that no defensive strategy is at hand; only, it will have to be a more modest one. It will not be one that establishes *once and for all* the inconclusiveness of all attacks, but one that concentrates on specific forms attacks have in fact taken, on concrete "philosophical arguments" for the necessity or impossibility of a practice or a belief, and that shows the inconclusiveness of *those* attacks and arguments. The everlasting harmony promised by the local "peacekeeper" is a delusion: one's "empirical" territory must be protected by a continuous fight, with the conventional weapons of creativity and imagination.

In the section of the *Critique* entitled Architectonic of Pure Reason, Kant says:

> philosophy is a mere idea of a possible science which nowhere exists *in concreto*, but to which, by many different paths, we endeavour to approximate, until the one true path . . . has at last been discovered, and the image, hitherto so abortive, has achieved likeness to the archetype, so far as this is granted to man. Till then we cannot learn philosophy; for where is it, who

is in possession of it, and how shall we recognise it? We can only learn to philosophise, that is, to exercise the talent of reason, in accordance with its universal principles, on certain actually existing attempts at philosophy, always, however, reserving the right of reason to investigate, to confirm, or to reject these principles in their very sources. (p. 657)

This passage is surprising, coming as it does near the end of the *Critique*, which is supposed to contain "all that is essential in transcendental philosophy" (p. 61). After having laid down all the essential groundwork for his new philosophy, Kant still claims that philosophy "nowhere exists *in concreto*," and that all we can do is "learn to philosophise." But, in fact, there is nothing to be surprised about: what Kant is doing is reminding us that transcendental philosophy is first and foremost *critical* philosophy, and that the role of a critic is the primary one (maybe even the only one) a philosopher is to have in society.

The general picture is as follows. *Pace* Wittgenstein and Rorty, a purely empirical conduct, in which words are used only when they make (empirical) sense, is not part of our form of life[19]: ordinary practice is constantly guided by myths that strain words beyond their ordinary conditions of application and end up with no guarantee of meaningfulness. We take the notion of a father, that we know perfectly well how to use in everyday contexts, and tell a story about a universal Father, who is supposed to make the same general impression on us as our fathers did when we were small children, only on a much larger scale, on such a scale indeed that we do not know whether the whole thing makes sense. We take the notion of a particle, unproblematically exploited when we talk of particles of dust, and blow it into something very small and perfectly elastic, thus making it not at all clear that we should be allowed to talk of particles any longer. And so on and so forth.

If pressed, we might try to defend this analogical, metaphorical use of language by claiming that what we do is mobilize our *concept* of a father or a particle, as opposed to concrete *images* or *experiences* of fathers or particles. And there is nothing necessarily wrong with this terminology, so long as we understand the limits of such a "purely conceptual" activity, in particular the limits we have in establishing the coherence of its results. Because of such limits, *we* can assign our myths no empirical significance, though we can toy with the idea that the analogies might "hold" and the theories actually "get things right": *for all we know*, such theories may represent little more than playing with words.[20] But if this is true of the theories and analogies themselves, *the having of them* is a phenomenon of vast empirical implications, in that it implicitly sets projects for action, indicates a direction for inquiry, makes us look for things we cannot find and in the process run into more of those we can find.[21]

This is the first, mythopoetic function of philosophy: "metaphysics in general" or "metaphysics as natural disposition," as Kant called it. For this function, however, we do not need a *professional* philosopher: all of us are natural metaphysicians to a degree and have some (more or less sophisticated) story to tell to rationalize our activities. In fact, the professional philosopher is probably the least likely person to come up with interesting and exciting myths: insofar as his *activity* is professional philosophy, the myths he may need are Hegelian or Platonic irrelevancies concerning Absolute Spirit or the philosopher-king.[22] How much more productive is, say, the myth of a physicist who (like Galileo) thinks of God writing the book of the world with mathematical characters, or that of a biologist who (like Konrad Lorenz) thinks of human cultures as obeying the evolutionary laws of living organisms![23]

The problem with myths is that people might take them too seriously. And I do not mean individual people; as far as individual people are concerned, it is probably most effective if they believe "blindly" in what they are doing. It becomes dangerous when too many people happen to share the same myth, and the same "blind" belief in it: then the system of checks and balances usefully provided by *opposing* myths is going to fail, and generalized single-mindedness is going to reveal not just its intolerance, but its *unproductivity* as well, in a way that is instantiated most instructively by the wings of the argus pheasant.[24]

If human societies displayed more of what literary critics call *irony*, if people were able, individually and collectively, to occasionally distance themselves with a laugh from the "business" to which they devote the "serious" part of their lives, the risk mentioned above might not be a real one. But given that humor is not very popular, there is a point for that philosophical activity whose problems, Wittgenstein says, "arise when language goes on holiday,"[25] and a significant role for the professional philosopher. For he can (indeed, must) constantly remind us of the mythical character of the myths, both of those that would vindicate ordinary practices or beliefs and of those that would challenge them, in the attempt at either substituting different practices or beliefs for them or just leaving us in a vacuum. To convince one of the mythical character of his myths is to convince him of what Rorty calls their "optional" character, that is, of the fact that they are some of the many *possible* stories one could tell on the matter. However, one cannot perform this operation once and for all, by proving the optional character of all stories, for one does not have the theoretical room to do it: such a "proof" would simply be one more story and would *prove* nothing at all. What is left then is a case-by-case approach, the one Kant suggests in the last quote above. Give me an "actually existing attempt at philosophy" and I will try to take it apart, using my ingenuity to construct an alternative story with the same ending, an alternative explanation of the same data. I will not be able to prove the coherence of my story, but the opposition may not be able to prove its *in*coherence, either: after all, they do not "see more deeply into the essence of things" than I do, and this may give me enough ammunition to successfully fight *this* battle. Another day there will be *another* battle; whether I will be successful then cannot be decided now, on the basis of some "universal therapy." It will depend on what I can come up with, on what "transcendental story" (or "transcendental proof") I can generate, if any.

The image of man promoted by the philosophy of necessity, in both its skeptic and its anti-skeptic variants, is one of integration and resolution of conflicts. The

claims men make, and the myths they build to justify such claims, are either
necessary or impossible, and hence men are ultimately to acquiesce in either their
wisdom or their ignorance. Besides, the philosopher has a crucial role in this resolution: he gets back into the cave with a clearer picture of things, and can tell the
prisoners the true story.

The image of man we get from Kant, on the other hand (and the one I have
been promoting here), is one of disintegration and dissolution. The penultimate
work Kant published was called *The Conflict of Faculties*. The faculties mentioned in the title are the university faculties, though there is for Kant a close connection between them and the faculties of the mind. In this work we find the following passage, where Kant comments on the conflict between the philosophy
faculty and the "higher" faculties of theology, law and medicine:

> This conflict cannot and should not be settled by an amicable accommoda-
> tion. . . . For the dispute could be settled only through dishonesty, by
> [the lower faculty's] concealing the cause of the dissension and letting itself
> be persuaded. . . . This conflict can never end, and it is the philosophy
> faculty that must always be prepared to keep it going. (p. 55)

This is by no means the only reference to the inevitability and usefulness of
conflict in the Kantian corpus, but it is one of the clearest and the most relevant
to our present concerns. Philosophers have a definite role to play in society: a critical one. Coming to an agreement with the targets of their criticism would amount
to abdicating this role, hence to displaying intellectual and moral dishonesty. This
may be taken as a defense of the philosopher's independence, and to some extent
it was, but note that if "this conflict can never end" then philosophers can never
win it, either. In fact, nobody can or should win it. The best thing is to keep the
conflict going, to have theology and law and medicine and physics construct their
myths, and philosophy (try to) take them apart, one by one, without any pretense
of superior insight or wisdom, simply by illustrating with appropriate "counter-
myths" that those other disciplines have no superior insight either. Ultimately,
this may (and, according to Kant, will) be for the better; for wisdom after all "consists more in doing and not doing than in knowing,"[26] hence is compatible with
(declared) ignorance.

There is a tendency for those who share the intuitions expressed here and
recognize philosophy as an essentially deconstructive activity to try to protect
themselves from that very deconstruction. The net result of this timid policy is
to call oneself out, to refuse to search for interesting, exciting stories, and to end
up with banalities such as that everything is connected with everything else, or
that things will go the way they will go, or that they should go the way we think
they should go.[27] I do not think that this policy is right, and my moral judgment
here is justified by a myth, the one I sketched in this chapter. Of course, the myth
could be debunked, and maybe even I could debunk it. But I do not want to do
so by refusing to tell any story and thereby refusing to make any move in this
game. I would rather tell a story, *this* story, and maybe later tell *another story*,

where the first one is characterized as *only a story*. To discover the laws of myth-making is not to exempt oneself from them, any more than discovering the laws of gravitation is. Even after discovering them (or deluding themselves that they have discovered them), philosophers remain members of the same world, and if they want to do something in it they must involve themselves in the same delusions they just found out about.

> *One can only become a philosopher, not be one. As soon as one believes one is a philosopher, one stops becoming one.*

Friedrich Schlegel, Fragment 54 from the *Athenaeum*;
my translation

Notes

1. The reference here is to Rorty (1979). All quotes in this paragraph come from p. 394 of Rorty's book. Of course, the end of systematic philosophy was promulgated many times before, but Rorty's statement has recently contributed to a serious reconsideration of the issue, hence it is a natural starting point for those who (like, for example, Peter Strawson, 1959) think that a substantial part of philosophy consists of rethinking permanent thoughts in an impermanent idiom (and even more for those who deny the existence of any such permanent thoughts). Also, insofar as the present chapter is concerned with addressing what seems to me a central difficulty of Rorty's position (and of a number of analogous ones), I take no direct issue here with Rorty's opponents (that is, the systematic philosophers themselves), who in general have not been convinced by Rorty's or other similar statements that their discipline is at an end. However, I surmise that some of their resistances may be overcome by resolving the difficulty I am concerned with, and thereby giving a clearer and more articulate picture of edifying philosophy.

2. I carry out this defense in my (1987).

3. See Walker (1978), pp. 14–27.

4. The reader will find enough *material* below (but no sustained argument) for an alternative interpretation.

5. My running together the Kantian defenses of causality and freedom might raise some eyebrows, since according to many current interpretations (a) Kant proves the *necessity* of the Principle of Causality but only the *possibility* of freedom, and (b) the latter has to do with the noumenal world and the former with the phenomenal world. Though a better articulation of my alternatives to (a) and (b) must be left to my (1987), at least the following remarks are in order here. As for (a), I think that it is false: at most, Kant is concerned with the *possibility* that the Principle of Causality is necessary (as in general with the possibility of synthetic *a priori* judgments). As for (b), to say that freedom is noumenal is simply to say that nothing spatio-temporal can count as a presentation of it. But then neither can we have a presentation of the necessity mobilized by the Principle of Causality: in both cases, all we can do is correlate them with empirical notions that are unsatisfactory in an absolute sense but work well enough for the purposes relevant to a specific (and limited) context.

6. However, not all skeptics fall in this category. The distinction between academic and pyrrhonian skeptics, insisted on by Sextus Empiricus and Montaigne and recently utilized by Curley (1978), is relevant here. In fact, there is a close similarity between the role of the philosopher that I will be advocating in this chapter and the attitude of a pyrrhonian skeptic.

7. Something like this distinction is advocated by Robert Nozick (1981). From my point of view, he simply does not go far enough, insofar as he is "tempted to say that explanation locates something in actuality," and that "a hypothesis known to be false will not explain how something *is* possible" (p. 12). Part of what the philosophy that I call here *of possibility* is supposed to do is precisely chal-

lenge the (alleged) fact that some things be "known to be false (or true)." So I think of this philosophy as more concerned with the enterprise that Nozick calls "understanding" (and that does not figure centrally in his book).

8. Of course, philosophers of necessity will often claim that the limits in question are not limits *they* set, but limits the concepts themselves have. It would take me too far afield to argue here against such "conceptual realism." For a statement of its impracticability, at least in the specific area of the *meanings* of words and phrases, see Chapter 5 below.

9. Given the Kantian flavor of this discussion, I find it natural to retain the terminology of problematic, assertoric, and apodeictic statements (or judgments). But essentially the same points could be made by utilizing the more contemporary terminology of modal operators.

10. The distinction between the methodology and the aim of a philosophical project is crucial in the present context, hence it may be worth insisting on it a little further. Though pyrrhonian skeptics are likely to use stories in much the way I recommend, academic skeptics will probably use them to establish necessities (or impossibilities) of sorts. For example, they may use the story that I am always dreaming to prove that it is impossible for me to rely on sensory experience. So, once more, the distinction I am making has nothing to do with that between skeptics and nonskeptics, though it is, in fact, among the skeptics that one is more likely to find instances of the mode of operation I favor.

11. For the distinction between skepticism and skeptical method see for example the *Critique*, p. 395.

12. The other aims of Hilbert's program (such as proving the completeness and decidability of mathematical theories) are not relevant here.

13. See the *Critique*, pp. 249–51.

14. See his (1978), pp. 13–28.

15. For more on this problem, see Nino Cocchiarella's (1975) and my (1981).

16. Compare this remark with the following passage from Wittgenstein's *Philosophical Investigations*:

"But the fairy tale only invents what is not the case: it does not talk *nonsense*."—It is not as simple as that. Is it false or nonsensical to say that a pot talks? Have we a clear picture of the circumstances in which we should say of a pot that it talked? (p. 97)

17. See, for example, the *Critique*, pp. 656–57.

18. A good recent example of this position is Michael Friedman (1985). Note that I do not question here the accuracy of Friedman's reconstruction, but his judgment concerning the contemporary (ir)relevance of Kant's thought, best expressed when he says that Russell was "exactly right" when he "blamed all the traditional obscurities surrounding space and geometry—including Kant's views of course—on ignorance of the modern theory of relations and uncritical reliance on Aristotelian subject-predicate logic" (p. 457).

19. See, for example, the following passages from the *Philosophical Investigations* and Rorty (1979), respectively:

When philosophers use a word—'knowledge,' 'being,' 'object,' 'I,' 'proposition,' 'name'—and try to grasp the *essence* of the thing, one must always ask oneself: is the word ever actually used in this way in the language-game which is its original home? What *we* do is to bring words back from their metaphysical to their everyday use. (p. 48)

In its homely and shopworn sense, the reason why 'good' is indefinable is not that we might be altogether wrong about what good men or good apples are, but simply that *no* interesting descriptive term has any interesting necessary and sufficient conditions. In the first, philosophical sense of 'good,' the term is indefinable because anything we say about what is good may "logically" be quite irrelevant to what goodness is. The only way to get a homely and shopworn mind to grasp this first sense is to start it off with Plato or Moore and hope that it gets the idea. (pp. 307–8).

The point I am making here is that the invidious contrast suggested in such passages between a "metaphysical" and an "everyday" use (or a "homely and shopworn" and a "philosophical" sense) of words is reductive and simplistic.

20. For more details on this play, see Chapter 8 below.

21. Such, at least, is the way (frustrated) theoreticians might like to put it, as a last-ditch effort to reserve to themselves the role of a guide. But since there is no end to frustration, it is possible that not even as blind oracles will they be able to gain leadership: maybe all we need them for is to try little tricks in the nursery (see Chapters 4, 8, and 11 below). Still, they must play the game right, *as if it were for real*, or they will forfeit whatever (little) use they have.

22. Thus it might be profitable, now and then, to violate philosophers' confidence in their professionalism, and force them out of the conventional games they enjoy so much. See the introduction and Chapter 11.

23. Interestingly enough, the scientists themselves are often aware of the creative value of this "free" talk. Thus Lorenz devoted his Nobel lecture to "Analogy as a Source of Knowledge," and in Galileo we find passages like the following:

> I will not consent that our Poem should be so confined to that unity as not to leave us fields open for Epsody's. Every small connection should be worth introducing with almost as much liberty as if we were telling stories; it shall be lawful for me to speak whatever your discourse brings to my mind. (*Dialogue on the Great World Systems*, p. 176)

24. See Lorenz (1963), p. 40.

25. *Philosophical Investigations*, p. 19.

26. *Groundwork of the Metaphysic of Morals*, p. 73. See also the following chapter.

27. One obvious polemical objective in this sentence is Rorty. But note that Rorty's position is a complex one. He does have a positive suggestion to offer in his (1979) as to what philosophers should do, and one that goes in the same general direction as mine. "Edifying" philosophers, qualified as "the heroes" of the book, are primarily "reactive" (p. 369) and "want to keep space open for the sense of wonder which poets can sometimes cause" (p. 370). Also, his underlying (and related) values surface in his use of such key words as 'interesting' and 'important' (see, for example, p. 359). But because he wants to escape the very "Sisiphean task" or "self-defeating obsession" he has identified (p. 374), because he wants to remain on firm ground, he ends up with not enough consciousness of his myth to come out in the open with anything more than the banalities mentioned above. Ultimately, this pragmatic inconsistency is based on an analogous inconsistency in his treatment of Kantian Ideas of reason. Whereas "officially" he has disparaging things to say about them (see, for example, p. 309), when it comes to making positive proposals he is inevitably led to reintroducing them into the picture, but attributing them *to Lessing* and not to Kant to save at least superficial coherence (p. 377).

4

Theories and Practices

At the beginning of the *Metaphysics*, Aristotle says:

> But as more arts were invented, and some were directed to the necessities of life, others to its recreation, the inventors of the latter were always regarded as wiser than the inventors of the former, because their branches of knowledge did not aim at utility. Hence when all such inventions were already established, the sciences which do not aim at giving pleasure or at the necessities of life were discovered, and first in the places where men first began to have leisure. . . . The point of our present discussion is this, that all men suppose what is called wisdom to deal with the first causes and the principles of things. This is why . . . the man of experience is thought to be wiser than the possessors of any perception whatever, the artist wiser than the men of experience, the master-worker than the mechanic, and the theoretical kinds of knowledge to be more of the nature of wisdom than the productive. (*Works*, p. 1553)[1]

The picture suggested by passages such as this has been criticized by various radical thinkers as elitist and nonhumanitarian, for at least two (related) reasons. First, this picture makes (disinterested) theorizing independent of productive practice, and embodies a "contrast between contemplation and action, between representing the world and coping with it."[2] Second (and more important), the terms being contrasted here are not assigned equal dignity: the word 'wisdom' is thrown onto the side of contemplation and representation, thus ultimately legitimizing a social hierarchy that puts intellectuals on top and makes them responsible for decisions involving many of those "manual workers" who, among other things, provide for the intellectuals' survival and well-being.[3]

For those who share the feeling that this traditional picture does no justice to human practices and human values, the necessity arises of coming up with alternatives to it. A natural move in such a process, most recently exploited by Paul Feyerabend (1978), consists of describing theories as fairy tales that people need to bring order into their tortuous minds, and of inciting to an anarchistic multiplication of such tales. Then—one hopes—once philosophy (and science, and perhaps law as well) has dissolved into literature and myth, one will be able to turn the castle upside down and put *practices* on top, *especially* those that prove useful.

The strange thing about this strategy is how unpopular it has always been, and how often radicals have been co-opted by the traditional picture. Thus Feyerabend observes that "[i]t is surprising to see how rarely the stultifying effect of 'the Laws of Reason' or of scientific practice is examined by professional anarchists" (p. 20). And, I might add, even those who have tried to turn Hegel on his head, and in the process assert the primacy of practice, have ended up ironically enough calling their enterprise 'scientific socialism.' But there is a good reason for the "surprising" persistent attractiveness of the scientistic model, and one of which Feyerabend is well aware:

> The image of 20th-century science in the minds of scientists and laymen is determined by technological miracles such as colour television, the moon shots, the infra-red oven, as well as by a somewhat vague but still quite influential rumour, or fairy-tale, concerning the manner in which these miracles are produced.
>
> According to the fairy-tale the success of science is the result of a subtle, but carefully balanced combination of inventiveness and control. Scientists have *ideas*. And they have special *methods* for improving ideas. The theories of science have passed the test of method. They give a better account of the world than ideas which have not passed the test. (p. 300)

It is not enough to want to put practice first: one has to explain what makes practice progress, what makes us live longer and more comfortably than our Stone Age ancestors. The traditional fairy tale that accounts for this progress is simple and effective: theoretical science develops an ever more accurate representation of reality *and on the basis of this accurate representation* produces recipes for practical behavior. Those recipes are effective *because* (and to the extent to which) the representation is accurate. Unless we find an alternative story concerning the relations between science and technology, and in general between theory and practice, insisting that traditional ideology is not humanitarian will just make us sound like sore losers.

Feyerabend's response is lame.[4] He reminds us that scientists often make mistakes, that there are more things under the sun than (Western, official) scientists can explain, and that people have developed successful practices outside of science. But this won't do. No scientist or layman thinks that the enterprise of (Western, official) science is complete, and hence any scientist or layman is ready to admit that there is room for improvement, that future scientists will correct the errors of past ones, and will be able to explain things we cannot explain today.

Also, until science is complete (which the current ideology is not bound to admit will ever happen), there is always going to be a chance that people may hit upon their best results by simply shooting in the dark.

What Feyerabend's criticisms can establish at best is the invalidity of any *argument* purporting to demonstrate a *necessary* connection between a successful technology and a science that provides an (at least partially) adequate picture of the world. But this is not what he needs to establish, for two reasons. First, if indeed what he is fighting is not an argument but a fairy tale, then even people who are convinced that scientists often make mistakes, and are often ignorant, will need *some other* fairy tale to explain to themselves the dramatic improvements that human life has experienced in the last twenty-five centuries or so. In the absence of competition, the fairy tale of a science that at least goes in the right direction, and does so mighty fast, will be accepted without much question. Second, even if theories are stories, fanciful narratives, literary fictions, still they seem to play *some* role in the progress of practices, so our new fairy tale must tell us what this role is—if the traditional one of providing rational guidance is ruled out. We need to use our imagination, "the most precious gift of the young,"[5] or maybe simply our perceptiveness with regard to the products of other people's imagination, to come up with as "reasonable" and convincing an account as the opposition has. Unless this effort is made (and is successful), the traditional story will continue to exercise all its rhetorical effectiveness, and we will be perpetually led to slip back into it, as Feyerabend himself does (not surprisingly, in view of the above) when, for example, he defends his anarchistic position by saying things like "*Variety of opinion is necessary for objective knowledge*" (p. 46)—that very objective knowledge that he spends most of his time ridiculing.[6]

Interlude: How Is the Shrink Supposed to Cure You?

Suppose you cannot go to bed unless you make an odd number of steps from your bedroom door to the bed, and if you happen to make an even number of steps you have to start all over again: go out the door, etc. You go to a psychoanalyst, lie on the couch, tell him about yourself, and after a while the symptom is removed. *How* was it removed? What did the trick for you?

During the fifty-odd years of Freud's contributions to psychoanalytic literature, he brought two factors to the foreground in his repeated attempts at answering this question. The first factor is knowledge, that is, finding out the reasons for your symptom and more generally the structure of your psychic life. The second factor is establishing, through the therapy, a new balance of (intra-psychic) forces, within which the symptom may fall off as useless. If the symptom was "*the patient's sexual activity*,"[7] it becomes superfluous when the patient develops a more "normal" sexual life.

By itself, the first factor won't work. If knowledge by itself cured,[8] then it would be enough to tell the neurotic straightforwardly why he is a neurotic, make sure that he gets the message, and thereby bring therapy to a successful end. But that does not happen: you can tell a neurotic all sorts of stories, and he may even believe them, but he will still worry about the number of steps from the door to the bed.

Enter the second factor. It is not the story by itself that does the curing: it is the force exercised by the transference relation that makes it possible to introduce an alteration in the patient's psyche. It is not enough for the patient to believe the story "in the abstract." He has to live by it, which becomes possible only through his entering into a passionate relation with the analyst. An "experimental neurosis" is thus induced in the patient to free him of his original one.

But there is a problem with this solution: the second factor makes the first one seem entirely redundant. If it takes a rearrangement of the psyche to cure, and if this rearrangement is effected by the transference relation, what is the point of the patient "finding out" the origin of his evils? At times, Freud expresses the sanguine conviction that, unless symptoms are accurately accounted for, transference by itself won't work, but he offers no credible grounds for this belief, and critics have justly crucified him for it.[9] Most often, he simply fudges the issue, lauding psychoanalysis for its therapeutic successes in some contexts and for its contribution to the knowledge of human psyche in others.[10]

One might have various reactions to this puzzle. Without argument, I will discount what may be the most tempting: psychoanalysis has never cured anybody. I will point out instead that Freud's embarrassment can be seen as a special case of the main problem discussed in this chapter: the lack of a suitable alternative to the traditional picture of the way in which theories and practices interact to make the latter evolve and become more successful. Unless we are able to explain how a story can help me feel better other than by telling me the Truth about myself, it will be just as well to shut up.

The background of the new story that I am to recommend is due to Konrad Lorenz's ethological work, and primarily to his (1973). Here is a brief review.

Say that a (human) culture is a system of relatively stable practices by which a community of individuals cope with a system of environmental problems. There is no limit on how wide (or narrow) these systems have to be: we may want to talk about the culture of a given nation, but it makes perfectly good sense to talk of the culture of the barristers, or the airline pilots, or the bank tellers of a given branch.

Two complementary problems arise concerning the development of human cultures: one is that of explaining their *continuity*, and the other that of explaining their *transformations*. The first problem is addressed by Lorenz by a variant of innatism. Humans, and animals in general, are genetically provided with *open programs*, that is, with tree-like structures that allow for a definite number of developmental options. The role of the environment is that of providing an input that will make the organism go a certain way up the tree. A typical example is the following[11]: some species of birds do not "know" their species-specific song at birth, but they are programmed to learn songs having a certain pattern. Since this pattern includes their species-specific song, and under normal circumstances they will hear instances of that song relatively early in their lives, they will normally learn the "right" song after all, but it is possible to so manipulate the environment that they will learn some other slightly different song instead. Similarly, we are programmed to ape other human beings who command our respect and attention, as is the case with parents, teachers, or friends, but this aping does not require an extensive study of the relevant person: what is needed is enough input to make us select a specific path up the open program, and from that point on we just "feel" things, all things, a certain way. It is primarily through this aping process—*not* through the construction of libraries or data-banks—that generational continuity is established. And note the similarity between this story and the Platonic idea of knowledge—and education—being a form of recollection: learning is the awakening of dormant faculties, not the impressing of data on a smooth surface.

So much for continuity. Our major problem, however, is that of explaining change, and here is where Lorenz's originality emerges most clearly. What he does is apply to the development of cultures the same mechanisms that determine biological evolution: mutation and selection. Cultures occasionally mutate, that is, some of the practices they consist of are occasionally modified, slightly or not so slightly, by one or more participants in the culture. Probably most of these mutations, in the cultural as in the biological case, are counterproductive: probably in most cases what cultural mutation produces is cultural monstrosities, in the form of crime, madness, or in general social deviance.[12] But in rare cases a mutant practice may prove more effective than the pre-existing variety, and then the new practice may be retained, by a cultural variant of natural selection. Either, that is, the mutant practice is integrated in (a novel form of) the culture, or a new competing culture comes into existence side-by-side with the old one, and eventually supplants it. It is this blind random chase for the competitive edge in survival value that the tradition rationalizes into the teleology of getting a better and better picture of the world.

This Lorenzian evolutionary model is a useful "theoretical" complement of Feyerabend's political view, in that it provides us with the new tale about technological progress we were looking for. And within the "logical space" defined by this tale, we can try to resolve our perplexities concerning theories and practices. How do the former contribute to the development of the latter? By suggesting (some of) those new moves that may (and sometimes do) bring about technological advances. But note that, in order to fulfill this role, theories need not be *true* or *accurate*, and once they have fulfilled it, they may well fall off as something whose time has passed.

In fact, one can go even further than this recognition of the occasional or perhaps even frequent relevance of theories to technological advance. One can, that is, encourage theoretical reflection and production, in exactly the anarchistic way in which Feyerabend recommends it, but with a little more story to tell. For one can say the following. The more cultural mutation there is, the more likely it is that the nonadaptive features of a culture will be phased out in the presence of significant opposition, hence the better the culture will work in the long run. So we must encourage mutation. But the anarchistic spread of diverse theories is probably the most effective and least dangerous mechanism that can promote large-scale mutation, certainly less dangerous than either bombarding people's brains with particles or maximizing social unrest. In conclusion, it pays for society to keep intellectuals in their think-tanks, but it does not pay to encourage conformism among them. The former pays because the intellectuals' onanistic games will produce more crazy ideas than the ordinary activities of ordinary sane people, and we can use those crazy ideas to get more things moving faster. The latter does not pay because when the crazies become professionals they will tend to defend their turf instead of regularly destroying it, and will put a premium on consistency instead of on excess and perversion.[13]

And in any case, let the intellectuals not delude themselves into thinking that it is their products — the theories — that contribute in this important way to technological advance.[14] The theories themselves are nothing but stories, and their content is as true as that of the *Odyssey*. It is the *fact* of their building theories, it is the peculiar ability they have of playing with words and with their memory-traces (or *ideas*), and most important it is the policies that they recommend on the basis of their (delusive) conviction in the truth of their stories that make the difference. For all this activity extends the field of alternative strategies on which to bring to bear the ax of cultural selection.

Reprise and Resolution of the Interlude

Look at the psychoanalytic situation again. From the traditional standpoint, the best way to set a practice straight begins with having a correct picture of what is going on. Then, of course, you also need some other things: a real desire to set the practice straight, enough energy to do it, and so on. Since the latter are inadequate when the subject is a neurotic, within this framework the only alternative is *constraint*: take someone who is not a neurotic and who has the correct picture and he will force you to be well, by first making you dependent on him and then threatening you with the loss of your new source of security. You will be blackmailed into normality, as countries are blackmailed into democracy or students into common sense in this happy age of ours. And you hope that at least that guy's picture *is* correct, or you might have the worst of worlds: domination but no cure.

Within the framework that I am recommending, on the other hand, an alternative account is available for what makes it possible for the analyst to make you feel well, and one that does not depend on the transmission (or the possession) of an accurate representation of the situation. The new account is based on the transmission of practices, of strategies for handling one's life. The patient's ordinary automatisms are broken down by his renewed childlike state, to some extent he reverts to the receptivity of his early years, and within this state is able to "pick up" behavioral structures from the analyst, showing the same capacity to generalize from a scanty observational basis that is ordinarily shown by a child. For the treatment to work, what matters is whether the analyst indeed has any useful strategy to share with his patient,[15] not whether any of his beliefs are true. Which does not mean that the stories told (by the analyst *and* by the patient) do not play an important role: they most certainly do, not, however, as faithful reconstructions of the patient's psyche but, rather, as a risk-free medium of exploration and play, as a relatively neutral ground where one can focus on the new strategies and try them out, or simply as an excuse to spend time together and check and see what (if anything) can be learned in the process.

Irrationality?

Proposals such as the one sketched here are often disqualified as flirting in a dangerous way (or perhaps, downright mating) with irrationality. But though in *some* sense the name of the rose may be irrelevant to its smell, hence the temptation arises to let the "rationalists" play with words as they see fit, I think that in the present case this temptation must be resisted. Words are not neutral, nor is the fact that a certain tradition has appropriated such value-ridden epithets as 'rational' or 'cognitive' to be made light of, or the opposing party will not be given a fair chance.

The fundamental move in resisting the temptation in question consists of pointing out that 'reason,' 'knowledge,' and 'wisdom' are ambiguous terms, and that, though the reading the conservatives give of them (and take for granted) has some coherence and plausibility, it is not the only one that does. When this point is appreciated, one may begin to realize that throwing accusations of irrationality at each other may have the same ideological significance (and the same intolerant effects) as did throwing at each other accusations of not being "enlightened" by the various parties involved in the struggle of the Reformation.[16]

I will illustrate the point by focusing on the word 'knowledge.' Insofar as knowledge is conceived as a relation of the mind with propositions, as knowledge *that*, the picture I drew above will be characterized as noncognitive, as not grounding technological progress on knowledge. But note that, in spite of how popular this conception is, and how much it has been legitimized by the establishment through the assignment to the verb 'to know' of the role of a propositional operator, it is not the only possible conception. An equally respectable, though by now largely underground, conception would see knowledge as primarily knowledge *how* (to do certain things).[17] It will be useful to contrast these two conceptions in some detail.

First, knowledge that (or, as I will also say, *propositional* knowledge) is typically a conscious experience, and one that shares with other experiences of awareness a *reflective* character. If one knows (in this sense), it seems inevitable to conclude that one also knows *that one knows*. Furthermore, the ideal of propositional knowledge involves distinguishing carefully between who knows and what is known. Even when I want to know (about) myself, I am best advised to try to find some external, neutral standpoint from which to look at me: my usual standpoint is impeded in reaching knowledge by all sorts of ego- and ethno-centrisms, which are especially bothersome and intrusive if the self is the object of my quest. And finally, propositional knowledge is typically something that can be put in words and communicated verbally.

On the other hand, knowledge how (or *practical* knowledge) is not necessarily conscious. If anything, consciousness seems to work against that effectiveness of moves in which this knowledge finds its expression. When you run down the stairs, you'd better not think of what you are doing, of the complicated tasks your muscles are performing: if you do, you are likely to trip and fall.[18] Also, practical knowledge is at its best when the distance between the knower and the known is reduced to zero, when the ability it consists of becomes part of the knower. You do not know how to swim when you know all sorts of propositions about swimming, propositions that you can carefully distinguish and distance from yourself (though it may be different with the practical abilities of saying or writing or remembering the relevant sentences): you know how to swim when certain moves become for you automatic responses to being thrown into the water, when, in a way, you cannot help making those moves upon being thrown into the water. And finally, practical knowledge is something that one is typically not able to verbalize and communicate to others by language: it is best "awakened" through practice and example.

So much for the sketch of a typology. Now, clearly, the two pictures of technological evolution I discussed are each based on one of these two notions of knowledge. The conservative picture sees that evolution as a by-product of our access to an increasing number of true propositions, whereas the radical one sees it as the accumulation of more functional responses to the environment. To call one or the other noncognitive (or worse, irrational) is simply to fail to recognize the dignity of an alternative reading of reason or knowledge. It is to attempt to transform the discussion about rationality (!) into a shouting match.

Coda

Both the traditional outlook and the one that I have been recommending here are self-referring in important ways. Supporters of the former will think that their story is a true account of the relation between theories and practices, and that *because* it is true those who base their practices on it will be more successful. I, on the other hand, think that the point about stories is not that (or even whether or not) they are true. The point about stories is that people like them, in fact even seem to need them to be reassured. On the basis of the stories that make them feel reassured—*and a great many other factors as well*—people will gradually develop their behavioral approach to the world. What works will be retained, what doesn't will be eliminated if better alternatives are at hand. If a particular theory has no alternatives, people will feel very secure about it, but to think that inertia will follow is once more to assert implicitly the primacy of theory. Inertia won't necessarily follow because there are many other factors that can promote mutation.

To be sure, my story gives definite suggestions for action. For example, it suggests that the best way to find a cure for AIDS is not to try to come up with an accurate representation of the behavior of human cells or antibodies or what have you, but, rather, to give a group of people who are skilled at these things (largely because they have done them often) a great deal of time to play with cells and tissues, and tools to look at them and take them apart. The more such people you bring in, the more time you make them spend on the matter, and the more tools you give them to play with, the more likely it is that one of them will hit upon a successful concatenation of moves. If that happens, you may be sure that a theory about it will be forthcoming shortly; in fact, probably more than one.[19]

And to be sure, insofar as I am committed to my story, I will recommend the policy indicated above. But I will not claim that that policy's only (or best) chance will come through the acceptance of *any* story, since practices can be (and often are) developed independently of stories. My new fairy tale belongs to the general practice of story-telling, just like the old one, and it is within this practice that its presence on the market may help, so long as while fighting traditional elitism with all its might it does *not* succeed in getting rid of it altogether.

Notes

1. Note that I will not take a position here on how far Aristotle, or "the Greeks," were committed to the view that (the translation of) this passage suggests to us. A whole story would need to be told in this regard about the significance of *phronesis* — or practical wisdom — and its relation with *sophia* (the notion mobilized here). But the passage (or its translation) is a clear formulation of the view that I intend to criticize in this chapter, and that (Aristotle or not) I consider dominant in the present cultural situation (though see notes 3 and 19 below).

2. Rorty (1979), p. 11.

3. Of course, the social hierarchy is not quite like that, at least not in contemporary America. In fact, decisions in this country are often left to practitioners of sorts, primarily on the basis of their practical sense. But the ideology I am talking about still plays an important role when the practitioners find it necessary (or useful) to justify their decisions by calling on "the experts" of various tricks and trades. Then the ideology reveals its mystifying power, and the political need is reaffirmed to find a suitable alternative to it.

4. See his (1978), pp. 300–309.

5. Ibid., p. 45.

6. It may be instructive to consider some other examples of such slipping. On p. 20 Feyerabend offers two main reasons for anarchism. The second one is "that the world which we want to explore is a largely unknown entity," so that "we must . . . keep our options open and . . . not restrict ourselves in advance." Thus, implicitly, the view is accepted that our task is that of exploring the world (a theoretical one), not that of coping with it (a practical one) — in perfect agreement with the opposition. On p. 25 he talks about the mistaken conception the tradition has of the relation between idea and action, and compares such a relation with the process by which children learn a language. He correctly emphasizes the practical, sensuous, manipulative aspect of this learning process ("They use words, they combine them, they play with them"), but then suddenly and unjustifiably throws a new character into the picture, which is going to give the whole game away: "until they grasp a *mean-*

ing that has so far been beyond their reach" (italics mine). Nobody is going to be talked out of the distinction between the contexts of discovery and of justification — *and of the primacy of the latter* — until such concessions to theory are made. Who needs a meaning here? Is it not enough to say that children become more and more skilled at playing with words, and can get more and more practical benefits out of their play?

Some of the negative impact of these *faux-pas* may be defused by remembering that Feyerabend's demonstrations and rhetoric "do not express any 'deep convictions' of [his]," and are "merely to show how easy it is to lead people by the nose in a rational way" (p. 32). But the (rhetorical) need remains, after showing people that they have been led by the nose, to tell them some other tale that they can compare and contrast with the one generating the trouble. Otherwise, they will just revert to the old tale and think of *you* as the spoiler and trouble-maker.

7. See Freud's *Complete Psychological Works*, vol. VII, p. 115.

8. In the terms to be introduced later in this chapter, 'knowledge' here means 'propositional knowledge.' When pressure is put on this (conventional) identification, it will be clear that in some (other) sense knowledge *can* cure.

9. Most vocally and thoroughly, Adolf Grünbaum (1984) in his analysis of the "Tally Argument."

10. See, for example, vol. XX, pp. 32–33, and vol. XVI, p. 255, of Freud's *Works*.

11. See Lorenz (1973), pp. 153ff.

12. I am not suggesting that there are no deviant cultures, with (in principle) the same dignity as the dominant one(s), but only that, as a matter of fact, the former tend to be less adaptive than the latter.

13. The reader will see that a delicate balance must be struck, according to the position I advocate, between the revolutionary import of the intellectuals' proposals and the control society is to exercise on them. Theirs must be storms, in other words, but they must be confined to teacups. At different times my specific rhetorical ends may lead me to stress different aspects of this dialectic (as is the case here), but then contexts must be played against one another to have the full picture emerge (for example, compare the present context with Chapter 8 below). In my (1987), I point out that there are analogous problems in reconstructing Kant's position (see pp. 137, 211).

14. Or perhaps, let them be deluded — they will probably fulfill their task better that way — so long as the public is not.

15. Near the end of his career, Freud said that the analyst "in certain analytic situations . . . can act as a model for his patient" (*Works*, vol. XXIII, p. 248).

16. See Popkin (1960).

17. Note — by way of example — that *knowledge how* is not even mentioned in the classic Hintikka (1962), whereas in Lehrer (1974) it is mentioned in the first two pages and then quickly put to rest with the following epitaph: "In our study, we shall be concerned with knowledge in the information sense. It is precisely this sense that is fundamental to human cognition and required both for theoretical speculation and practical investigation." (p. 3) On the other hand, the central significance of *knowledge how* has not escaped "edifying" philosophers. Thus Wittgenstein says in the *Philosophical Investigations*: "The grammar of the word 'knows' is evidently closely related to that of 'can,' 'is able to.' " (p. 59)

18. An additional element of contrast here is the following. If we agree that the analogue of knowing that one knows, in the case of practical knowledge, is the ability to use abilities one has for certain (second-order) ends, it becomes clear that this analogue does not hold. I may be perfectly good at swimming, and still not good at all at cashing in on my swimming ability in any way.

19. This, by the way, is how things ordinarily go, though not how one tends to *describe* them *in retrospect*. So, once again, it is the mystifying (and self-serving) ideologies promulgated by most intellectuals that I antagonize, not the (empirical) reality those ideologies (allegedly) apply to.

5

A New Paradigm of Meaning

Doing philosophy after Kant amounts to conceptualizing our ordinary empirical activities (including the ordinary empirical activities of the professional scientist). Within philosophy, we are not to challenge those activities, and we are not to add to them; for example, we are not to establish that there are more or fewer objects than ordinarily assumed, or that acts that we ordinarily judge right are, in fact, wrong. Rather, we are to ask ourselves how our ordinary activities can be *understood*; we are to tell ourselves a story (or many stories) in which those activities find a place. For some, the existence of such stories will give a *justification* or a *foundation* to the relevant activities; for others, no such justification is even conceivable, and all that the stories do is satisfy our need for stories, or soothe the anxiety that follows upon our being thrown into the world. But whatever their ultimate destination, some stories are better than others and make sense of the relevant activities in a more convincing, less strained way. In the end, those are the stories we would rather hear.

Because the stories are usually formulated in terms of (reference to) entities of which we have no immediate presentations — entities like minds or sets or properties or what have you — the language of the stories will largely be one of evocation and allusion. This language will use empirical notions in a metaphorical way, that is in a way that loosens their definite conditions of application and thereby transforms a number of questions ordinarily asked about them into pseudo-questions. Still, the fact that some empirical notions are used and others are not is important, since it is on the associations suggested by those notions that our understanding (or maybe our illusion of understanding) of the story and our interest in it are based. Thus development in this story-telling enterprise comes in two forms: there are times when the basic metaphors are articulated (to put it sympathetically, or stretched, if we do not want to be so nice) to cover cases to which they do not have a natural application and times when a suggestion is made to use different metaphors altogether. In Kuhn's language, there are times of normal science and times of revolution.

In this chapter, I want to propose a revolution in our conceptualization of the notion of meaning,[1] that is, I want to propose a change in the basic metaphor that we use in understanding this notion. As with every revolution, mine will be one that is very much "in the air." The anomalies of the classical paradigm I will point out have surfaced before, and suggestions for a change of paradigm (in something like the direction I will explore) are already present in the literature. But I will not even try to indicate my many (objective, if not subjective) debts[2]; my concern here is to make a clear statement of the new metaphor and of its (stylistic) advantages.

1. Apples

First of all, I want to identify my task. Part of our ordinary dealings with ordinary empirical contexts amounts to considering questions of the form

(1)   What is the meaning of X?

Considering such questions includes asking them (of ourselves or of others) and trying to answer them; call the collection of these activities *the language-game of meaning*. A conceptualization of the language-game of meaning would consist of a(n intensional) description that captures all the specific moves people ordinarily attribute to *that* game, and distinguishes them from moves they ordinarily attribute to other games, or to no game at all. This description should have the effect of making the game intelligible.

Given the nature of the task, the most promising way to approach it would seem to be the following: consider categories of people whose main professional concern is declared to be that of asking and answering questions of the form (1), professional players as it were, and try to draw some general moral from the moves they actually make. In this chapter, I will consider three such categories, on which I have some direct information: literary critics in the present section and psychoanalysts and historians of philosophy in the next. For various reasons, none of these categories is taken seriously by many analytic philosophers, who would probably claim that their members are not *really* concerned with meaning even if they *think* they are. The end result of this attitude is that the stories these philosophers tell about meaning are usually condemned either to propaganda use or to plain irrelevance. But, of course, this last value judgment is part of the revolution that it is my present job to account for, so without further anticipations of my conclusions let me return to the main train of thought.

The idea that the interpretation of a literary text is a process of psychological reconstruction goes back at least to the traditional hermeneutic theory of Schleiermacher and Dilthey. Recently, this idea has been revived by E. D. Hirsch. Here is how David Hoy (1978) describes the most basic of Hirsch's intuitions:

Hirsch [claims that] there is "no objectivity [of interpretation] unless meaning itself is unchanging." . . . [H]e is specifically fighting a skepticism
about objectivity that he sees in what he considers "radical historicism" in
Heidegger and Gadamer. Hirsch makes the counterclaim that while the *importance* of a work may vary with time and within different interpretive
contexts, the one underlying meaning of the work does not change. The
meaning of the text—which, on this account, is the author's willed
meaning—is said to be self-identical, determined, and reproducible (that is,
shareable rather than private). The understanding that grasps this deter-
minate and unchanging meaning is totally neutral and unsullied by the interpreter's own normative goals or his views of the work's importance. Only
on such grounds, Hirsch believes, is it possible to speak of the validity of
interpretation. (pp. 13–14)[3]

Thus searching for the meaning of a text is searching for the author's intentions.
On the face of it, this position has problems. We attribute a meaning to the Odyssey but have absolutely no way of establishing Homer's intentions, indeed, not
even a way of knowing whether he existed or not. And, more important, there
are literary critics (American New Critics, for example) who claim that the
author's intentions are simply irrelevant to the interpretation of a work.[4] To save
the position, we could go one of two ways (or maybe some combination of both).
We could distinguish the epistemology of meaning from its ontology and claim
that there is an objective meaning to the Odyssey (the objective intentions of whoever its author was) even though we may never know it, or we could think of "the
meaning" of the work as some kind of regulative ideal.[5] Either way, we would
still have many questions to answer, and much more explaining to do. For there
are cases (say Lukács's interpretation of Balzac) in which a critic interprets a text
in terms of things like the structure of society, of which it is plausible to think
that the author was not even fully aware (not, at least, in quite the same terms).
And there are critics (within the hermeneutic tradition, for example) who claim
that there are *many* (sometimes conflicting) meanings to most works.

Clearly, all this explaining could be done. As Kuhn points out, with enough
stretching and patching any theory could be saved, and to a person committed to
the theory such stretching and patching will probably look more like fine-tuning
the instrument and extending its use.[6] In the cases mentioned above, the "intentionalist" may have to postulate "ideal," or unconscious, or conflicting intentions.
Or he can just say that the critics in question have it wrong, that what they talk
about has nothing to do with the meaning of the text. On the other hand, it is interesting to notice that these difficulties are ultimately the consequence of adopting a particular metaphor of meaning, and that adopting a different metaphor
would make the difficulties go away, and eliminate the necessity of all the stretching and the fine-tuning. As with all conceptual revolutions, this observation will
not convince the believer, but might be suggestive for those whose faith is already
shaken.

A natural starting point to explore the old paradigm of meaning is Frege's notion of a sense (*Sinn*). For our present purposes, it will be sufficient to limit ourselves to considering senses of sentences, that is, what Frege calls *thoughts* (*Gedanken*). The primary function of a thought for Frege is that of being something that can be *communicated*. For example, in his (1918), he says: "But here I do not count exclamations in which one vents one's feelings, groans, sighs, laughs [as expressing thoughts] – unless it has been decided by some special convention that they are to communicate something" (p. 355). Or consider the following passage, from Michael Dummett's (1981):

> The exact ontological status of senses Frege found it embarrassing to describe: there is nothing that can be done with a sense save to grasp it, express it and thereby convey it to another, and, in the case of a thought, assert that it is true, or ask whether it is true, or the like. For all that, Frege did not want to say that thoughts, or senses in general, are mental entities: for he was afraid that that would make them too little unlike "ideas," i.e. mental images, and perhaps share with these the incommunicability he supposed them to possess. (p. 154)

This passage refers to Frege's controversial assumption that senses are part of a third realm of objects (in addition to the realm of physical objects and the realm of ideas), a realm such that anything belonging to it "has it in common with ideas that it cannot be perceived by the senses, but has it in common with things that it does not need an owner so as to belong to the contents of his consciousness" (1918, p. 363). And what Dummett suggests is that this controversial ontological assumption, which many have criticized as a "reification" or "hypostatization" of meaning, is ultimately due to Frege's conviction that language is *meaningful* only insofar as something is communicated through it.

Let us take this suggestion seriously, and try to conceptualize the use of language in terms of the metaphor of communication.[7] There are two parts to this metaphor: communicating is some kind of *giving*, and is a giving that results in all the parties involved *sharing* something. Let us examine the two parts separately.

First, communicating is some kind of giving. Therefore, a sentence like

(2) Tom says "It is raining outside" to Mary

is to be understood in analogy with a sentence like

(3) Tom gives an apple to Mary.

The following are general features of the event described by (3):

(a) the event is an (intentional) action, that is, Tom consciously intends to bring it about;

(b) this action consists in transferring some object (the apple) from Tom to Mary (call that object *the object of the action*);

(c) the object of the action existed before the action, it exists unchanged throughout the action, and it continues to exist (still unchanged) after the action.

When (2) is understood in analogy with (3), the analogues of (a)-(c) will apply to (our understanding of) (2). So the event described by (2) will be understood as the (intentional) action of transferring an object from Tom to Mary, where the object in question existed before the action and continues to exist (unchanged) throughout the action and after the action: this object is in general identified with the meaning of the utterance. Though this picture will have to be supplemented below, note how natural it is already to go from it to an "intentionalist" reading of literary texts such as the one suggested by Hirsch. Insofar as the literary critic is involved in the language-game of meaning, he is involved in the search for some *unique* entity *intentionally* conveyed by the text's author to his audience, and certainly the author's 'intention(s)' seems to be a good catchword for whatever this entity is. Also, note the similarity between Hirsch's concern with the objectivity of the critic's work and Frege's concern that thoughts be the vehicles of *truth*.

Consider now the second aspect of communicating, that is, the fact that what *A* communicates to *B* ends up (after the communication process is completed) being *shared* by *A* and *B*. Physical objects like apples cannot be communicated in this way; after Tom has given the apple to Mary, *he* is left with no apple. Of course, Tom and Mary could share an apple, but then Tom would not give *the apple* to Mary: he would give her a *piece* or a *slice* of the apple. When meanings are communicated, on the other hand, the full meaning is transmitted, and at the end of the process it is this full meaning that the parties involved share.

So let us complicate our metaphor a little. Suppose that Tom is the owner of an apple tree and that by signing a piece of paper *P* he agrees to have Mary acquire joint ownership of the tree. Now consider the sentence

(4) Tom signs *P*.

The following are general features of the event described by (4):

(a') = (a);
(b') the action consists in transferring the *ownership* of some object (the apple tree) from Tom to Tom and Mary (the object can still be called *the object of the action*);
(c') = (c).

If (2) is understood in analogy with (4), the event described by (2) will be understood as the (intentional) action of transferring the ownership of an object (the meaning of "It is raining outside") from Tom to Tom and Mary.[8] That this metaphor is an important driving force in Frege's conception of a thought is illustrated by the following footnote in his (1892):

By a thought I understand not the subjective performance of thinking but its objective content, which is capable of being the *common property* of several thinkers. (p. 162; italics mine)[9]

And much the same message is conveyed by the verb 'to grasp,' which corresponds to the major action one is to perform on senses; according to Webster's *Dictionary*, 'to grasp' (as a transitive verb) is primarily "to seize and hold," "to take possession of," and secondarily (that is, metaphorically) "to lay hold of with the mind."[10]

The ownership of a tree (as opposed to *the tree*) is an abstract object, but at least it is the ownership of something concrete. The ownership of a meaning, on the other hand, is the ownership of something that is itself abstract. So it becomes crucial, if we want to flesh out our metaphor, to say what kind of (abstract) entity we transfer ownership of when we communicate a meaning. There are two main ways in which this has been done. The first is to think of what is transferred as some kind of dispositional property, the ability or capacity to do something. This route is usually preferred by the ontological conservatives, since in general dispositional properties are seen as ontologically cheaper than full-blown abstract objects. Transferring to somebody the ownership of a tree amounts (among other things) to transferring to him the dispositional property of *being able to get apples from the tree at one's will without incurring the risk of having a suit brought against one*. In analogy with that, one might think that when the ownership of the meaning of 'It is raining outside' is transferred from Tom to (Tom and) Mary, Mary becomes able to do things she was not able to do before—and things that will often involve language in some way. It is along these lines that one is led to the Wittgensteinian suggestion that the meaning of a sentence reduces to its *use*.[11]

The second way of fleshing out the ownership-transferral metaphor (and the one that is closer to Frege's own) is by biting the bullet and allowing for *bona fide* abstract entities to be transferred from the exclusive possession of a speaker to the joint possession of several. The most likely candidates for this exalted status, at present (at least as far as the meaning of sentences is concerned), would seem to be *propositions*, variously described as sets of possible worlds or as functions from worlds to truth-values.

One concluding note: whichever of these two major avenues we decide to take, there will be *prima facie* difficulties in making sense of the language-game of meaning in the case of contradictory sentences. For on the one hand, it is part of (the ability of) using language correctly that one does not make incoherent utterances, and on the other, major formal construes of propositions agree that *all* contradictory sentences express *the same* proposition.[12]

2. Matches

Suppose that you and I are sitting in my living room, watching TV, and all of a sudden we hear a noise coming from the backyard. We throw a suspicious look at each other, and I exclaim, "I wonder what that means." Somewhat uneasily, you get up from your comfortable armchair and walk out of the room. A few minutes later, you come back and say: "Nothing to worry about. A pot fell off the shelf. It was the wind." Completely relieved, we return to our educational activity.

This episode seems to fall within the language-game of meaning. A question of the form (1) is asked, and an (apparently satisfactory) answer is provided. But it would be absurd to account for the episode in terms of the ownership-transferral metaphor articulated in the preceding section. The crucial problem is that that metaphor requires conceptualizing a winning move in the language-game of meaning as the uncovering of an (intentional) *action*, but no such move is involved in the present case. We ask ourselves what the meaning of the noise is, and the answer comes in terms of an *event* which is *not* an action: the event of the wind blowing and making the pot fall. Also, the (apparently satisfactory) answer is (in effect) an *explanation* of the (occurring of the) noise.

Extrapolating from this example, one could come up with the following tentative suggestion. A sentence like (2) is to be understood in analogy with a sentence like

(5)   The match m ignited (at time t),

or if you wish with a sentence like

(6)   There was a noise in the backyard (at time t).

When sentences like (5) or (6) are uttered, it is often natural to ask a question of the form "why . . . ?" ("why did the match ignite?," "why was there a noise in the backyard?"). An alternative way of asking this question consists often of asking "what is the meaning of . . . ?" ("what is the meaning of the match igniting?", "what is the meaning of there being a noise in the backyard?", or, more loosely, "what is the meaning *of the noise*?"). Satisfactory answers to such questions (in either form) are satisfactory explanations of the relevant events. Analogously, one can ask what the meaning is of *Tom saying "it is raining outside" to Mary*; in this case, too, a satisfactory answer (a winning move in the language-game of meaning) would be a satisfactory explanation of Tom's utterance.[13] (Of course, one could also ask what the meaning is of it being the case that it rains, but that would have nothing to do with asking for the meaning of utterances or linguistic entities in general.)

Later I will articulate this suggestion and address a major objection to it. But for the moment, it will prove instructive to look at more professional players. For such a digression will make it apparent that whereas the *practice* of the players is better understood in terms of the model I am proposing, the *ideology* of that practice is usually the traditional one, based on the traditional paradigm. And it will also be clear, I hope, that this (intellectual) bad faith is deeply counterproductive.

One of the major things Freud presents himself as doing is assigning meanings to previously uninterpreted occurrences. For our purposes, it will be sufficient to concentrate on his interpretation of dreams. The way this interpretation is supposed to work is as follows. There is a (deep-seated) meaning for each dream, which is centered around some unconscious, infantile wish. This meaning is distorted by various censorships, and made (in most cases) virtually unrecognizable. Since the distortion is obtained by disintegration of the original meaning and displacement of the resulting (minute) components of it through associative chains, the first thing to do to reconstruct the meaning is to break down the (manifest content of the) dream and then run the associative chains in reverse order. This first phase of dream interpretation is called dream *analysis*. Then a second phase is supposed to occur: the last elements of all the associative chains are to be put together, and thereby the meaning of the dream finally uncovered. This second phase is the dream *synthesis*.

There are some six hundred pages to the *Interpretation of Dreams*,[14] and dozens of dreams are analyzed in it. However, no dream is ever synthesized; in fact, in no interesting case do we even get a clear formulation of the infantile, unconscious wish that is the essential component of the *meaning* of the dream.[15] The reasons Freud adduces for this practice are all in the form of excuses.[16] Most of the dreams are his own, and he does not want you to know too much about him. But the only other dreams he has available for purposes of illustration are those of his neurotic patients, which would require him to enter into lengthy digressions on neuroses and could always be discounted by unsympathetic readers as the dreams of crazy people.

However, the excuses are not convincing. For never during the analysis of a dream is there any guarantee that the associative chains have been run through *completely*, that the *final* associations have been found, and thus that the meaning even *can* be expressed. Analysis, Freud convinced himself with the years, is likely to be an *interminable* process. But then what exactly is it that one does when one interprets a dream? What is it that people learn to do by reading the *Traumdeutung*? They do not learn to discover the meaning of a dream, in the sense of some unique entity associated with the dream in a canonical way; so what do they become able to discover?

Some of us will probably want to say: nothing at all. Psychoanalysis is not a popular subject within analytic philosophy, and a number of people will probably be happy to "find out" that the enterprise of dream interpretation makes no coherent sense. But here I ask you to try a temporary "suspension of disbelief." Try for a moment to consider psychoanalysts as people who are involved in the language-game of meaning, and see if you can learn anything from the kinds of activities that they get involved in, *and that they construe as relevant to their main concern*.

The activities they get involved in are explanatory activities. They consider the manifest content of the dream and try to determine what brought it about. In general, the explanation is given by connecting elements of the dream with mental contents that are emotionally charged in various ways, *and of course any such explanation is partial.* In fact, any explanation *whatsoever* is: explaining *A* in terms of *B* generates the further question "why *B*?", and so on forever. In this particular case, explaining the occurrence of an element in the dream in terms of its associative connection with some emotionally charged mental content generates (at least) the further question of what makes that mental content emotionally charged, and so on forever. But the impossibility of reaching the end of this activity does not make the activity impossible (or illegitimate), and in fact it is *this* activity that you find instances of in the *Interpretation of Dreams* – this is what you learn to do if you read the book and take it seriously. On the other hand, the activity of finding *the* meaning of the dream in the sense previously characterized is probably impossible to perform, hence you could not learn to perform it by reading the book or by any other means.

What is interesting in this example (as I suggested earlier) is not only that the psychoanalyst's practice is best understood in terms of the new model I am proposing, but that his ideology is best understood in terms of the *old* model. It is the classical metaphor of meaning as something uniquely associated with an utterance that makes him think of his work, insofar as that work is to be conceived as concerned with meaning at all, as the work of discovering some such unique entity. And it is the intentional nature of the ownership-transferral metaphor, one could argue, that ultimately suggests to the psychoanalyst that where there is a meaning there must be an intention, and so if there is no conscious intention there must be an unconscious one.

A similar predicament is what we encounter when we try to conceptualize the activity of the historian of philosophy. Like the literary critic, the student of Descartes or Kant claims to be primarily concerned with discovering the meaning of a text. An additional problem the latter has, however, is that most philosophical texts, *and in particular most of the most interesting ones*, are simply inconsistent, and hence according to (the usual articulations of) the old paradigm seem to have no meaning at all. So how are historians of philosophy to understand their ordinary practice within this paradigm?

An example will make things clearer. Suppose you take the first *Critique*, and find in it (either stated or implied) the following four sentences:

(7) Appearances are objects.
(8) Appearances are representations.
(9) Objects are not representations.
(10) There are appearances.

Since (7)-(10) form an inconsistent set, it seems impossible to think of the text as associated with some unique meaning that is conveyed through reading (and interpretation) from the author to the reader. So what is left to historians of philosophy to do with this text?

Apparently, the most natural thing would be to say that the text is nonsense, at best suggestive nonsense. If by analyzing it we are able to identify parts that can be elaborated into a reasonable philosophical position, then we will not be wasting our time; otherwise we will.

To be sure, some commentators do go this "natural" way. To remain with Kant, a notable example of such practice is Jonathan Bennett. But, interestingly enough, those who do are often apologetic about it,[17] and many prefer a more subtle, "sympathetic" approach. What this approach amounts to, in most cases, is discovering some tensions within Kantian intuitions that lead Kant to say (for example) sometimes (7) and sometimes (8). Thus Norman Kemp Smith will tell you that it is Kant the subjectivist who says (8) but Kant the phenomenalist who says (7) (and (9)). And what are these tensions supposed to do if not *explain* the text as we find it?

In his (1923), Kemp Smith says of the Transcendental Deduction: "The arguments of the deduction are only intelligible if viewed as an expression of the conflicting tendencies to which Kant's thought remained subject." (p. 272) That is (by paraphrasing the word "intelligible" in what seems to be a natural way), we can *understand* these arguments, or find out what they *mean*, only by referring to the "conflicting tendencies" that brought them about. But again, *once* these tensions are identified, the old paradigm shows its attractiveness by inclining people to single out some passages as expressing an author's "more considerate," or "genuine," opinion. In Kemp Smith's case, the "subjectivist" tendency, and with it a large portion of the *Critique*, is discounted as "unkantian," as not expressing "what Kant *really* meant."

3. Pragmatics

Consider (5) again, and suppose that we ask a why-question concerning it. Such a question could be interpreted as a request for *the* explanation of (5), and an answer to it could come in the form of something like

(11) Because *m* was struck.

But if this is how we think of why-questions, we have not really progressed a great deal in our search for a *new* paradigm of meaning. In particular, we cannot yet do justice to the intuition of psychoanalysts and (some) critical theorists alike that there is *more than one* meaning to an action or a text. For if *the* meaning of an utterance is to be conceptualized as *the* explanation of that utterance, we are still to think of it as something unique. In fact, when things are put this way, it may even be natural to think of this unique thing that supposedly explains the utterance as being the mythical "intentions" of the speaker (or writer).

Fortunately, there is a lot of work already done in the philosophy of science that I can utilize to develop my position further. What I have in mind is the account of scientific explanation given by Bas van Fraassen (1980). According to van Fraassen, there is no such thing as *the* explanation of a phenomenon. For one thing, science by itself does not explain *anything*: it is we who *use* science to explain. For another, what we are to accept as a successful explanation in a given context depends on the criteria that are relevant in that context; in particular, on what *other* contexts we have in mind as terms of comparison for the present one. So, for example, science establishes a connection between the igniting of a match, its being struck, *and many other circumstances*. In a specific case of a match igniting, we may ask

(12) Why did *m* ignite?

having in mind only cases of matches which were in exactly the same conditions as *m* except for their not being struck; then, of course, the factor of *m* being struck is what makes the crucial difference, and a reference to this factor is to be accepted as providing a successful explanation *in the context in question*. But if our terms of comparison were to be 999 other matches which were struck but were wet and consequently did not ignite, then we would probably feel that an adequate answer to (12) is

(13) Because it was dry.

Moving now to the language-game of meaning, a question of the form (1) will have different (adequate) answers in different contexts, depending on the criteria that are relevant in those contexts, in particular depending on what is and what is not taken for granted in those contexts. For example, if a number of stylistic or psychological factors are considered irrelevant, and the issue is (explicitly or implicitly) one of comparing Balzac's *La comédie humaine* with works produced within other social structures, one may well agree with Lukács that *the* meaning of that text is to be found in the organization of the nineteenth-century French bourgeoisie. And if one considers that criteria of relevance change with time, one may well agree with Gadamer that the meaning of a text, not just its importance or its impact, changes with time.

Van Fraassen describes his position as concerned with "the pragmatics of explanation," and sees his contribution as consisting primarily in moving the proper context for an analysis of explanation from semantics to pragmatics. Similarly, I could say that the proper area where the language-game of meaning should be conceptualized is that of language-use and language-users, not that of the alleged relation between "language" in general and extralinguistic entities. However, a qualification is necessary. People like Austin, Searle, and Grice have already articulated positions in which language is to be analyzed primarily at the level of speech-*acts*, not speech-*contents*, and hence have already intimated (one might say) that pragmatics, not semantics, is the proper context for such an analysis.[18] But my position is different in an important way. Emphasizing that an utterance is an act is ultimately emphasizing the role of the utter*er*, because the utterance is (conceptualized as) an act *of his* (or *hers*). On the other hand, my intuition is that the key figure in the language-game of meaning is the *audience*. It is the audience that asks questions of the form (1), and it is the audience that tries to provide answers for them, on the basis of the criteria that *it* finds relevant.

The difference between the account of meaning that I am offering and one that could be elaborated within the theory of speech-acts is that the latter is still committed to a view of language that underscores motives and intentions. The meaning of an utterance is what the utterer *meant*, what he *wanted* to communicate, hence there is an action involved, insofar as an action is an occurrence that can be legitimately accounted for by reference to a *will*.[19] Since only rational beings are usually granted a will, hence the possibility of acting, only rational beings can *mean* something, hence only of their (intentional) actions is there a *meaning*. I, on the other hand, want the notions of an action and a will (or of an intention, or a motive) to have nothing *necessarily* to do with meaning. Insofar as we admit such things, they could conceivably be mobilized in *some* successful moves in the language-game of meaning, but this game can be played with all kinds of *events*, whether they are actions or not, whether they have a will behind them or not. Whereas the old paradigm of meaning inclines those who are interested in the meaning of (apparently unintentional) moves to see physical behavior in analogy with language, and often postulate unconscious intentions to apply that paradigm to this "body-language," I have no such tendency. For me, it is not that behavior can be construed as a kind of language; it is, rather, language that is a kind of behavior.[20] If there is an analogy between saying "It is raining outside" and scratching one's head, it is not that in both cases one intentionally (though perhaps unconsciously) transfers ownership of some "meaning" to an audience, but, rather, that in both cases *the audience* can explain the occurrence in question, *and find such an explanation useful* for its further dealings with (*inter alia*) that person. And of course, in both cases the explanation can be different for different members of the audience, and teach them quite different things about the utterer (or scratcher). Think of a player in a poker game saying (before the betting is over) "I have seen such great cards tonight!" How many different (successful) explanations could such an utterance have for the various people around the table? That is, how many different *meanings* could it have? And how many different things could these explanations tell them about that guy? And about their next bet?

4. Meaning and Saying

It is time now to consider an objection that many may have had for some time, and that the preceding section may have offered a precise way of formulating. The objection goes as follows. I have assigned the language-game of meaning to the area of pragmatics—of language-use and language-users. But how could we use language effectively unless we understood what utterances *meant* in a more general sense, precisely in the sense in fact in which meaning is conceptualized within *semantics*, as an extralinguistic entity uniquely correlated with an utterance-*type*, *not* an utterance-*token*? To put it otherwise, what I said may be interesting as a way of bringing the role of the audience into clearer focus, but what of my insistence that this be the *only* way in which meaning is properly conceptualized? Is not that insistence virtually a proposal to *eliminate* semantics altogether, and reduce ourselves to having syntax and pragmatics only? And is not this proposal ultimately self-defeating, in that (an understanding of) pragmatics *presupposes* (an understanding of) semantics?

My first reaction to this objection is to point out that a conceptual revolution (as *any* revolution) is primarily a change of *standards*, of what is to count as important or not important. To use a relatively trite example, the Copernican revolution was not a revolution in how much more (or less) one was able to explain, but, rather, a revolution in the standards for a good explanation: conceptual and mathematical economy were to be preferred to adherence to the "natural standpoint." So in the present case, too, my concern is not with eliminating the general sort of considerations that go under the name of semantics, but, rather, with establishing a different order of (conceptual) priority between them and the considerations usually associated with the area of pragmatics. It is in the latter area, I would argue, that the *interesting* questions about meaning arise: semantics is a pale concoction of rough generalizations, of rules of thumb that are usually much less informative and helpful than a proper sensitivity to the individual characters of the multifarious games actually played with language. So, to put it briefly, it is not that semantics must necessarily be dropped; it is enough if pragmatics comes first and semantics is conceptualized *in terms of it*.

One qualification is in order here. When I talk about semantics, I refer explicitly to the classical Morris distinction, according to which semantics is concerned with the relation between language and extra-linguistic entities. Much of what goes under the name of semantics, and formal semantics especially, consists largely of translating from one language to another, usually from an arbitrary language into the (privileged) language of set theory. So-called completeness proofs, allegedly establishing the adequacy of a language to its "semantics," are probably best seen as establishing equivalence results between two (or more) *syntactical* strategies for defining classes of sentences. None of that needs to be conceptualized in terms of a relation between language and "the world," though of course some may *want* to conceptualize it this way.

Semantics in the classical sense enters the picture only when we conceptualize understanding a linguistic expression as laying hold of a meaning, knowing a language as knowing the meanings of (most of) the expressions of that language, or translating from one language to another as correlating expressions of the two languages which have the same meaning. For unless we can find an alternative way of thinking of such activities, semantics will continue to play a central role in our conceptualization of language. This is the basic challenge the present objection poses to the new paradigm.

To address this challenge, return to the issue of explaining (5). Depending on the contexts, a successful explanation might be given in terms of *m* being struck, *or* of *m* being dry, *or* of *m* being in the presence of oxygen, *or* of a number of other factors. Now suppose someone asked you what *the* explanation of (5) is. Is there any way of making sense of such a request *within the present understanding of what it is to explain*?

The following sounds like a reasonable answer. To be sure, there is no such thing as a *unique* (successful) explanation of (5), but there may be a *most frequent, most common* (successful) explanation of (5). For example, it may be that in general the matches we are interested in are dry, and in the presence of oxygen, and what have you, and hence that a reference to the match being struck is what is *most likely* to count as a successful explanation of a match igniting. And knowing these most frequent, most common explanations may be of pragmatic value, in that when we are puzzled by an occurrence we will probably begin by following Hercule Poirot's suggestion and looking for a culprit where we are most likely to find one.

The same strategy can be followed in the case of meaning. When someone says "It is raining outside," the meaning of such an occurrence (that is, its explanation) is very likely to include a reference to the fact that it rains outside, so much so indeed that we would tend to regard alternative accounts as somehow *nonstandard*. In fact, this regularity extends to more than just alternative explanations *of the same utterance*: it seems to characterize our general understanding of utterances of a certain sort. And it may be useful to bring out this regularity by saying that *the* meaning of the expression-*type* "It is raining outside" is or includes the presence of rain, as a helpful recipe for the construction of explanations of many linguistic occurrences.

One key aspect of this example is its great *simplicity*. The statistical relevance of cases in which an utterance of the form "It is raining outside" is *not* to be explained in terms of rain is extremely low, and by classifying such cases as nonstandard (and thereby passing a negative value judgment on them) we show an inclination to discount them in conceptualizing language, that is, to see them at best as evidence of a malfunctioning which is not to be taken seriously from a theoretical point of view. Of course, the great simplicity of cases like this entails that they are also (in general) not very interesting, that the search for a meaning here is one that does not (in general) require a lot of work or great ingenuity. And the way in which *within my paradigm* I would describe someone coming up *with the old paradigm* is that they would focus on such simple and relatively uninteresting cases too much and want to see *all* other cases, including the not so simple and not so uninteresting ones, in analogy with the former. That is, they would want to see the search for the meaning of a dream, or of the *Odyssey*, or of the *Critique of Pure Reason*, in analogy with the search for the meaning of utterances such as "It is raining outside."

There are analogues of such an oversimplified view and of its questionable consequences elsewhere in the same philosophical tradition in which we found the old paradigm of meaning to be active and influential. For example, that tradition first developed logical analysis at a very elementary level, limiting itself to systematizing the logic of a few conjunctions and pronouns, and maybe one or two adjectives. At that elementary level, the systematization could be done with great effectiveness, and all sorts of powerful and useful metatheoretical results could be established, but when the systematization moved to deeper levels of analysis, most of these results were lost. For example, within "classical" propositional logic the rule of substitution is an admissible one, but when we move to the most natural interpretation of modal operators, the so-called primary modal semantics of Leibniz, Kaplan, and Cocchiarella, the rule of substitution loses admissibility.[21] However, instead of just accepting the fact that deeper levels of analysis are likely to be more difficult to handle, most logicians and philosophers conceptualized "logic" on the basis of the simple case, frowned upon non-perfectly-manageable semantical treatments, and ruthlessly changed them around to extend to the more complicated formal languages those metatheoretical results which *happened* to hold for the simple ones.

We should resist such tendencies to oversimplification.[22] In the case of logic, this means seeing the metatheoretical results provable within, say, quantification theory as largely made possible by the limitations of expressive power that characterize that theory (and language), that is, as ultimately *negative* results.[23] In the case of the language-game of meaning, it involves beginning from the most complicated cases and seeing the simple ones as relatively uninteresting (though probably welcome) simplified versions of them, *not* forcing the interpretation of a philosophical text into the Procrustean bed of weather reports.

And now for some details. When somebody says "It is raining outside," there is no need to think of him as at the same time performing the action of *saying* something and the action of *meaning* something. All he does is speak, say whatever it is he says.[24] *Understanding* such an utterance is explaining it in terms of other occurrences, some of which may well be other utterances. *In general*, the explanation of utterances of this kind will be of a fairly standard nature; if we want, we may label such a *typical* explanation *the* meaning of the *linguistic expression* "It is raining outside." But such a labeling has a precondition of legitimacy; when a typical explanation does not exist, there will be no moving the operation of understanding out of the concrete, empirical, pragmatic contexts where it primarily belongs and where it primarily finds its dignity as an intellectual problem.

When we move from the local issue of understanding an utterance to the global one of knowing a language, the strategy is going to be analogous. The new paradigm has room for a notion of knowing a language as being able to explain all (possible or actual) utterances of a given community. But such a notion is at best a regulative ideal, and as useful as regulative ideals may be, they are probably not attainable, hence it would not be possible to say of anyone that he knows a language *in this sense*. On the other hand, a different notion may have a great pragmatic value, that is, the notion of someone being able to explain *most* of the *most common* (kinds of) utterances of a given community. Accepting and using this notion would have the advantage of making us regard most people raised in the Anglo-American community as knowing (or competent in) English, even if they cannot quite account for the text of *Finnegans Wake*.

Translation will be treated in the same way. An utterance *a* of a language *L* will be considered the translation of an utterance *b* of a language *L'* if *a* is what a member of the *L*-community would utter *in most cases in which* a member of the L'-community would utter b. And once again, this account allows for the possibility that a number of utterance of L' have no translation at all in L, if the precondition that such a most frequent utterance exists in L is not satisfied — a gap that philosophers have been more inclined to admit than (the corresponding ones) in the previous cases. Also, the account in question avoids the Quinean problem of the indeterminacy of translation altogether. For we need not think of the L'-speaker as *meaning* something extralinguistic that he cannot quite identify linguistically; all we need to admit is that he *says* something, and that his utterance(s) can be explained.

One further step in this pragmatically oriented "semantics" would be the pointing out of regularities in the explanation of utterances *containing certain words*. Insofar as such regularities can be identified, one can legitimately talk of *the meaning of* a word, though, of course, it is much more likely that a given word will be associated with various regular patterns, hence will be found to have *various meanings* — a case that presents some *prima facie* complications for the old paradigm but is perfectly natural in mine.

To conclude, there is an interesting structural similarity between my approach here and Freud's in *Jokes and Their Relation to the Unconscious*,[25] or Wolfgang Iser's in his (1978). Just as Freud finds it necessary to conceptualize jokes as something *that a hearer is told* (so that if there were no hearer, there would be no joke), and as Iser insists that "the meaning of a literary text is . . . a dynamic happening" (p. 22) that involves the reader in crucial ways,[26] so I have been proposing that meaning in general be conceptualized with an explicit and substantial reference to an audience, and specifically as something (that is, an explanation) that an audience is to produce. This similarity is not surprising, since my attitude was from the beginning one of taking seriously the people who construe themselves as interpreters of meaning, whatever we think of the *empirical value* of their results. If we do not take those people seriously, there is the risk of mistaking for conceptual impossibilities what are merely consequences of our limited perspective, and maybe ultimately of criticizing the very professional players we refused to look at as committed to the conceptual impossibilities thus "discovered."

Notes

1. Note that my proposal is self-applicable in important ways. For example, it will become clear by the end of the chapter that "conceptualizing the notion of meaning" reduces for me to accounting for (or explaining) people's use of the word 'meaning.'

2. I will, however, counterpoint my analysis here with textual references to Wittgenstein's *Philosophical Investigations*. For though Wittgenstein's most elaborate proposal in that work seems to be that of identifying meaning with use (see below), there are enough suggestions in it of the kind of view I recommend to be worth mentioning.

3. I have privileged this statement here because it most clearly and concisely summarizes Hirsch's view on the matter, though I must hasten to note that what Hoy calls "importance" Hirsch would rather call "significance."

4. To avoid confusion, it may be useful to point out explicitly that there are activities of three

different levels involved here. First, there is the activity of the writer or poet who composes the literary work. Second, there is the activity of the critic who studies that work. And third, there is the activity of the philosopher who conceptualizes the critic's activity as an example of the language-game of meaning. (Analogous distinctions apply to the other examples used below.) I take Hirsch to be making (at least in part) statements at the third level, and it is at that level that I disagree with him. To a large extent, this disagreement originates from the fact that my general metaphilosophical attitude (expressed at the beginning of this chapter, and located *at a fourth level*) makes me look unfavorably upon attempts at solving philosophical problems by passing value judgments on what happens at lower levels. On the other hand, I must recognize that this attitude is not generally shared and that philosophers (including Hirsch, insofar as his are philosophical concerns) have often passed such value judgments, usually by invoking the occurrence at lower levels of some kind of conceptual confusion.

5. Hirsch's position seems to result from a combination of these two approaches.

6. See Kuhn (1957), p. 75.

7. What follows is not intended as an exegesis of Frege, but only as the development of a theme which is at least implicit in Frege and in the philosophical tradition that begins with him—and that, incidentally, includes Hirsch, who defines (verbal) meaning as "whatever someone has willed to convey by a particular sequence of linguistic signs and which can be conveyed (shared) by means of those linguistic signs" (Hirsch, 1967, p. 31; later in the same book Hirsch refines this definition, but without in any way limiting the importance of communication (and sharing), and still later he refers explicitly to Frege's *Sinne*). In particular, I think there are more problems with Frege's notion of a sense than I am interested in discussing here. Note also that the origin of the communication metaphor is probably to be found in those ritual activities (analogous to the holy communion) through which a group of people reinforce their sense of themselves as constituting *one community*. If I were interested in the old paradigm per se, it would be useful to explore these connections in detail.

8. See *Philosophical Investigations*, p. 49: "Here the word, there the meaning. The money, and the cow you buy with it."

9. It must be noted that in his (1918) Frege was to insist that thoughts have no owner. But that claim is based on a very peculiar reading of the expression 'owner.' For what Frege wants to emphasize there is that thoughts, as opposed to ideas, are ontologically independent, and such independence is usually regarded as being consistent with being owned. I may own a car without it being the case that, were I to cease to be, the car would have to cease to be, too.

10. Analogous considerations hold for the original German verb *'fassen'* used by Frege and translated into English as 'to grasp.'

11. See for example *Philosophical Investigations*, p. 126: "Look at the sentence as an instrument, and at its sense as its employment." But an important qualification is added on p. 20: "For a *large* class of cases—*though not for all*—in which we employ the word 'meaning' it can be defined thus: the meaning of a word is its use in the language" (last italics mine).

12. To be sure, there are ways of getting around these difficulties. One can be found in Thomason (1974), and alternative ones have been proposed by David Lewis and George Bealer. As I pointed out earlier, with enough stretching and patching any paradigm can be saved. But it is still instructive to see how the difficulties evaporate if we take a different viewpoint.

13. See *Philosophical Investigations*, p. 146: "Can I not say: a cry, a laugh, are full of meaning? And that means, roughly: much can be gathered from them."

14. *Complete Psychological Works*, vols. IV–V.

15. The only exceptions are some dreams *of children*. At pp. 310–11, Freud promises a synthesis to be forthcoming in the *Fragment of an Analysis of an Hysteria* (*Works*, vol. VII, pp. 7–122), but even there the analysis is not complete.

16. See, for example, pp. 104–5.

17. See, for example, the following passage from the preface to Bennett's (1974):

The Dialectic is full of mistakes and inadequacies. . . . Still, there are doubtless fewer mistakes than I allege: my charge-list has gradually shortened as I have gained in understanding

of the work, and presumably it could be reduced further. But I have worked for so long as
I am prepared to . . . (p. viii)

18. See, for example, Austin (1962), Searle (1969), and Grice (1957, 1969). Note that I am not
committed to the claim that any of these authors would recognize what he does as "pragmatics"; whatever *they* call the object of their concerns, I am interested in distinguishing their position from mine,
and thereby bringing the latter into sharper focus.

19. In fact, Grice finds it necessary to isolate the phenomenon of "non-natural meaning" as the
subject of his study, thereby excluding by definition anything that is not an action from having meaning in the sense he accounts for.

20. See *Philosophical Investigations*, p. 146: "Words are also deeds." Note, on the other hand,
that it is precisely along these lines that I would distinguish my position from Wittgenstein's "official"
claim that meaning is use: it is not so much the use of language per se that matters for meaning, but
the way in which spectators of this use relate it to their own concerns.

21. See above, p. 43.

22. See *Philosophical Investigations*, p. 155: "A main cause of philosophical disease—a one-sided
diet: one nourishes one's thinking with only one kind of example."

23. The view that most results in contemporary (meta)logic can be seen as negative ones is suggested by Chang and Keisler (1973).

24. See *Philosophical Investigations*, pp. 8–9:

if you shout "Slab!" you really mean: "Bring me a slab."—But how do you do this: how do
you *mean that* while you *say* "Slab!"? Do you say the unshortened sentence to yourself? And
why should I translate the call "Slab!" into a different expression in order to say what someone
means by it? And if they mean the same thing—why should I not say: "When he says 'Slab'
he means 'Slab?'"

25. *Works*, vol. VIII, pp. 9–236.

26. See below, pp. 83–84.

6

Economy of Expression and Aesthetic Pleasure

> Virgil . . . loves to suggest a truth indirectly, and without giving us a full and open view of it, to let us just see so much as will naturally lead the imagination into all the parts that lie concealed. This is wonderfully diverting to the understanding. . . . For here the mind, which is always delighted with its own discoveries, only takes the hint from the poet, and seems to work out the rest by the strength of its own faculties.
>
> Joseph Addison, "An Essay on Virgil's Georgics," in *Works*, vol. II, p. 382

> As a rule . . . a certain degree of the enigmatical is not un-welcome in a book, since analysing the obscure into clear concepts makes the reader sensible of how clever he is.
>
> Immanuel Kant, *Anthropology from a Pragmatic Point of View*, p. 18

1. Economy

The last chapter of Herbert von Einem's (1973) is entitled "The Incomplete and the Uncompletable." In it, we read things like the following:

Would the agonized self-probing of *St Matthew*, the brooding melancholy of *Evening* and the dawning power of *Day* in the Medici Chapel, the silent

---

I thank Nuccia Bencivenga, Rob Content, and Jean-Luc Nancy for their comments on an earlier draft of this chapter.

meditation of Nicodemus in the Florentine *Pietà*, the otherworldliness in the expression of the Virgin in the *Rondanini Pietà* be one whit better if Michelangelo had made one more stroke of the chisel? Is there not a sense in which these works are in fact not incomplete at all, so that any addition to the explicit sculptural forms would detract from the significance of the work of art as a manifestation of spiritual value? Would we therefore have wanted Michelangelo to "finish" them? (p. 257)[1]

The other day I was watching a movie-review program on TV. Talking about a particular movie, the critic said: "The idea of the movie was very good, but the script writer kept hammering away at it. When we thought we had got it, he would repeat it once again, just to make sure. The result was unbearable. The movie should have been half an hour shorter."

Alessandro Manzoni's *I promessi sposi* (*The Betrothed*) is the greatest novel in Italian literature. One of its main characters is Gertrude, the nun of Monza. Most of Chapters 9 and 10 of the work constitute a digression, which tells the story of Gertrude from her birth through her entrance to the convent to her breaking the vows and committing murder. In an early unpublished draft of the work, entitled *Fermo e Lucia*, the digression was much longer. In particular, there was a long description of how young Egidio, after addressing Gertrude from a window overlooking the convent, ends up seducing and corrupting her. In the final version, all of this material was mercilessly cut, and almost two chapters of *Fermo e Lucia* were condensed into a single sentence of three words. When Egidio addresses Gertrude from his window, Manzoni simply says: "La sventurata rispose." ("The poor wretch answered him.") The following is a typical critical opinion on this passage of the novel:

> The whole story of the relation between Gertrude and Egidio, which in *Fermo* continued for pages and pages, is concentrated in that powerful abbreviation: "La sventurata rispose." Three words broken and suspended by the end of a proposition and a paragraph, by a violent break. The end of this paragraph opens as if into a void, into an anxious abyss, like a silence of unspeakable horror, more eloquent than any word. (Getto, 1964, p. 183; my translation)[2]

These three critical judgments—of a number of Renaissance sculptures, a contemporary movie, and a nineteenth-century novel—have something in common. The suggestion is made that in some cases economy of expression is aesthetically more valuable than its opposite, that an "incomplete" or at least essential formulation or representation is to be preferred to a highly detailed one, and that "completing" such a formulation or adding further details to it may "detract" from its significance. The critics I have quoted do not do much to make sense of this suggestion, to explain what exactly is so good about economy of expression. They would not have wanted Michelangelo to "finish" his works, they would have wanted the movie to be shorter, they are happier to contemplate an "anxious abyss" than a careful description of the events, but they do not say why it is so. In this chapter, I want to address this question, that is, I want to investigate the reasons why economy of expression is often found to be aesthetically valuable. In the last section I will suggest that, were my solution of this problem to be accepted, it might open a new perspective on the whole issue of aesthetic appreciation.

2. Activities

A promising starting point for our research is offered by the idea that the appreciation of a work of art is not to be understood as passive reception, that spectators or readers must be involved in constructive activities analogous to those of the artist or writer if they are to be able to meaningfully relate to the artist's or writer's production. This idea is an old one. In our century it has been expressed, for example, by such different authors as Dewey and Sartre. The following two passages come from *Art as Experience* and *What Is Literature?*, respectively.

> Everyone knows that it requires apprenticeship to see through a microscope or telescope, and to see a landscape as the geologist sees it. The idea that esthetic perception is an affair for odd moments is one reason for the backwardness of the arts among us. The eye and the visual apparatus may be intact; the object may be physically there, the cathedral of Notre Dame, or Rembrandt's portrait of Hendrik Stoeffel. . . . But for lack of continuous interaction between the total organism and the objects, they are not perceived, certainly not esthetically. . . . For to perceive, a beholder must *create* his own experience. And his creation must include relations comparable to those which the original producer underwent. . . . Without an act of recreation the object is not perceived as a work of art. (pp. 53–54)

> . . . reading is an exercise in generosity, and what the writer requires of the reader is not the application of an abstract freedom but the gift of his whole person, with his passions, his prepossessions, his sympathies, his sexual temperament, and his scale of values. Only this person will give himself generously. . . . And as activity has rendered itself passive in order for it better to create the object, vice versa, passiveness becomes an act; the man who is reading has raised himself to the highest degree. . . . When I am enchanted with a landscape, I know very well that it is not I who create it, but I also know that without me the relations which are established before my eyes among the trees, the foliage, the earth, and the grass would not exist at all. (p. 36)

A more elaborate formulation of the idea in question can be found in Ernst Gombrich's (1960). In this book, Gombrich (among other things) reacts against the Impressionists' claim that they painted reality as they saw it, a claim probably best expressed by Cezanne when he said, "Monet n'est qu'un oeil—mais quel oeil!" Gombrich characterizes this claim as "self-contradictory" (p. 393), and then goes on to say that

the Impressionists proclaimed that their methods allowed them to render on the canvas the act of vision with "scientific accuracy." The paintings that resulted from this theory were very fascinating works of art, but this should not blind us to the fact that the idea on which they were based was only half true. We have come to realize more and more, since those days, that we can never neatly separate what we see from what we know. A person who was born blind, and who gains eyesight later on, must *learn* to see. (p. 394)

In 1857 John Ruskin asserted that "[t]he whole technical power of painting depends on our recovery of what may be called the *innocence of the eye*; that is to say, of a sort of childish perception of these flat stains of colour, merely as such, without consciousness of what they signify."[3] To Gombrich, this anticipation of the Impressionists' doctrine is nonsense: there is no innocent eye to be recovered, "as soon as we start to take a pencil and draw, the whole idea of surrendering passively to what is called our sense impressions becomes really an absurdity." (p. 394)

But what then does explain the magic of Impressionist paintings, which certainly Gombrich does not want to deny? According to him, the Impressionists mastered more fully than their predecessors the art of giving hints to the beholder and letting him "complete" them.

[I]t is surely no accident that they limited themselves to the motifs and scenes of *la vie contemporaine*, where they could . . . rely on the beholder's knowledge. Perhaps we shall become increasingly aware of this need to supplement their hints from our own experience as their period recedes from ours. Impressionist paintings are of less documentary value to the social historian than are the paintings of conventional realists. When horse racing becomes a dimly remembered ritual and the horse is as extinct as the dodo, Manet's spirited sketch of a race certainly will tell the historian less about those bygone days than will that famous showpiece of Victorian realism, *Derby Day*, by Frith. (pp. 215–16)

So if Impressionist paintings are regarded (by some, or many) as more valuable than, say, Victorian realist ones, it is because "we enjoy nothing more than the demand made on us to exercise our own 'imitative faculty,' our imagination, and thus to share in the creative adventure of the artist." (p. 278) "We prefer suggestion to representation, we have adjusted our expectations to enjoy the very act of guessing, of projecting. And we rationalize this preference by fancying that the sketch must be nearer to what the artist saw and to what he felt than the finished work." (p. 385)

An interesting literary-theory counterpart to Gombrich's position is represented by Wolfgang Iser's *Wirkungstheorie*. In his (1978), Iser writes:

Central to the reading of every literary work is the interaction between its structure and its recipient. This is why the phenomenological theory of art has emphatically drawn attention to the fact that the study of a literary work should concern not only the actual text but also, and in equal measure, the actions involved in responding to that text. The text itself simply offers "schematized aspects" through which the subject matter of the work can be produced, while the actual production takes place through an act of concretization. . . . In literary works . . . the message is transmitted in two ways, *in that the reader "receives" it by composing it.* (pp. 20–21; italics mine)

Most of Iser's book consists of a painstaking and illuminating analysis of how writers stimulate the reader's constructive activities. It is this stimulation that in Iser's opinion ultimately accounts for the aesthetic value of a literary work:

author and reader are to share the game of the imagination, and, indeed, the game will not work if the text sets out to be anything more than a set of governing rules. The reader's enjoyment begins when he himself becomes productive, i.e., when the text allows him to bring his own faculties into play. There are, of course, limits to the reader's willingness to participate, and these will be exceeded if the text makes things too clear or, on the other hand, too obscure: boredom and overstrain represent the two poles of tolerance, and in either case the reader is likely to opt out of the game. (p. 108)

To sum up the results of this detour through various critical positions, we have now a first answer to our question about the significance of economy of expression: the fruition of a work of art usually involves a certain amount of activity on the part of spectators or readers. They are not simply to record data provided them by the author; rather, they are to construct situations and characters out of the skillful hints the author throws at them. Within certain limits (remember the reference to overstrain in the last passage quoted), the more spectators or readers are involved in these activities the more they enjoy themselves. So what makes many spectators or readers (or critics) find essential or even incomplete formulations aesthetically more valuable than highly detailed or complete ones is that they are more *pleasing*, and they *are* more pleasing because they get people more involved in the game of projecting and completing.[4]

This is all very well. But, in a way, it only carries our questioning one step further. For why are the constructive activities described above a source of pleasure?

3. Perception

On p. 49 of his (1960), Gombrich writes:

What a painter inquires into is not the nature of the physical world but the nature of our reactions to it. He is not concerned with causes but with the mechanisms of certain effects. His is a psychological problem – that of conjuring up a convincing image despite the fact that not one individual shade corresponds to what we call "reality." In order to understand this puzzle – as far as we can claim to understand it as yet – science had to explore the capacity of our minds to register relationships rather than individual elements.

But this "psychological problem" has a much wider significance than mere aesthetic considerations might lead us to believe:

> We were not endowed with this capacity by nature in order to produce art: it appears that we could never find our way about in this world if we were not thus attuned to relationships. (ibid.)

The suggestion contained in this last statement may be useful for continuing our discussion. Perhaps to understand the pleasure derived from the constructive activities involved in relating to a work of art we should pay attention to the fact that these constructive activities are involved in all cases of perception, not only of paintings and novels but also of tables, chairs, and letters from the front.

Gombrich himself reminds us that this theoretical model of perception "ultimately goes back to Kant" (p. 28), and in fact it was Kant who said that "intuitions without concepts are blind,"[5] that is, that without the mobilization of our conceptual and categorial apparatus we literally would not see any*thing*. In a Kantian theory of perception like the one that Gombrich advocates,[6] seeing (for example) a table can in no way be identified with the reception of a sense datum or a class of them. Seeing the table includes guessing how to complete the data I receive, forming expectations based on my guesses, and using these expectations to test the guesses and possibly revise them. It includes, in other words, "constructing" a three-dimensional and relatively permanent table out of a two-dimensional and continually flickering retinal image.

How can this generalization of our problem help to solve it? Suppose you are facing a painting by Turner, or a sculpture by Henry Moore. A great deal of activity is required on your part to "see" something in it (though to a large extent the amount of activity required may be lessened by your familiarity with the author's "style"), but this activity is not different in kind (though it may be in degree) from the activity that is required to see something in "reality." And if you think of how essential seeing is to "find our way about in this world," you will not be surprised that performing such a useful activity is felt as pleasurable. In the same manner, the child finds it extremely pleasurable to perform in the course of play all kinds of activities that later, in a "serious" context, will prove useful to his/her survival and success.

Well, maybe so. But note that the above still constitutes no real explanation.[7] In connecting the pleasure experienced in the course of the constructive activities required for the appreciation of an "economical" work of art with the usefulness of such activities in a more general context, I have only offered a reason why *it would be good if* those activities were also pleasurable. I have offered no reason why *in fact* they are. And the reference to play is nothing more than an analogy, since the pleasure experienced in playing is as much in need of an explanation as the pleasure we are presently concerned with.[8]

Still, the generalization is not without significance. For a more general question depends less on context than does a more specific one, hence it may be answered in terms of fewer and simpler assumptions. In particular, those who have followed me so far have seen the *aesthetical* question of what is valuable about economy of expression transformed into the *psychobiological* question of why activities that are often conducive to the organism's survival and success are felt as pleasurable.

4. Forepleasure

The simplest and most powerful model of the nature of pleasure in this century is probably the one proposed by Freud.[9] This model is based on a hydraulic metaphor. The psychic system is normally characterized by a certain amount of (psychic) excitation, derived to a large extent from endogenous sources of stimuli, that is, from the (instinctual) drives (*Triebe*). The dominating tendency of psychic life is that of getting rid of this excitation by discharging it outside,[10] and pleasure is the phenomenological counterpart of this process of discharge.[11] So the striving after pleasure on the part of an organism is just a manifestation of its general tendency toward discharge, which in turn can be seen as a special case of a homeostasis principle characteristic of all of nature.

This model seems to work very well with the pleasure of (male) sexual orgasm. Sexual abstinence generates a build-up of sexual excitation in the psychic system (corresponding to a build-up of sexual products in the genitals), which is experienced as an unpleasant tension. During orgasm the excitation is released, the tension decreases, and pleasure is felt.

However, even without leaving the area of (male) sexuality, problems arise as soon as we turn our attention from orgasm to foreplay. For the result of foreplay is not the reduction of sexual tension but rather its increase, not the release of excitation but rather a further build-up of it. So how can the pleasure usually experienced during foreplay (and called by Freud *fore*pleasure) be accommodated in the above model?

In *Three Essays on the Theory of Sexuality*,[12] Freud attempts to answer this question. Each of the foreplay activities is connected with a pregenital phase of sexual development, and thus with a specific *component* sexual drive (oral, anal, or what have you). Forepleasure is the pleasure resulting from the release of excitation associated with the component drive, and "[t]his pleasure then leads to an increase in tension which in its turn is responsible for producing the necessary motor energy for the conclusion of the sexual act." (p. 210) The way in which forepleasure—that is, a kind of *pleasure*, to be associated in the above model with a reduction of tension—can bring about an *increase* in tension is left by Freud utterly mysterious.

In *Jokes and Their Relation to the Unconscious*,[13] published in the same year as the *Three Essays*, Freud utilizes the mechanism of forepleasure to explain the genesis of tendentious jokes. Most of the pleasure of a tendentious joke is to be derived from the (sexual or hostile) repressed drives that find expression and thus release in them, but these drives would not produce pleasure if they were expressed directly. It is *when they are expressed in jokes* that they are found pleasurable. So the construction of the joke is necessary for the release of the drive, and in its turn this construction is possible because it, too, produces a (more modest) pleasure. Here is how Freud sums up the explanation:

> A possibility of generating pleasure supervenes in a situation in which another possibility of pleasure is obstructed so that, as far as the latter alone is concerned, no pleasure would arise. The result is a generation of pleasure far greater than that offered by the supervening possibility. This has acted, as it were, as an *incentive bonus*; with the assistance of the offer of a small amount of pleasure, a much greater one, which would otherwise have been hard to achieve, has been gained. I have good reason to suspect that this principle corresponds with an arrangement that holds good in many widely separated departments of mental life and it will, I think, be expedient to describe the pleasure that serves to initiate the large release of pleasure as "forepleasure," and the principle as the "forepleasure principle." (pp. 136–37)

The conceptual confusion surrounding Freud's notion of forepleasure reappears here, from a different angle. If the construction of a joke were just a way of expressing and thus releasing sexual or hostile drives, there would be no difficulty in applying the model of pleasure as (the phenomenological counterpart of) discharge. But if this construction is characterized as independently pleasurable, then there is a difficulty. For it is not *prima facie* clear what kind of tension the construction releases, to what kind of drive it gives expression, or how it contributes to reducing tension at all.

There is a very good reason why Freud must accept the existence of a pleasure independent of the satisfaction of repressed sexual or hostile drives. The reason, quite simply, is that not all jokes are tendentious. There are *innocent* jokes, and though Freud tends to underplay their frequency or the amount of pleasure they generate,[14] he cannot deny their existence. It is the pleasure to be found in innocent jokes that acts as forepleasure for the expression of sexual or hostile drives, but what accounts for the existence of this (fore)pleasure?

Freud addresses the question with characteristic openness:

> If we do not require our mental apparatus at the moment for supplying one of our indispensable satisfactions, we allow it itself to work in the direction of pleasure and we seek to derive pleasure from its own activity. I suspect

that this is in general the condition that governs all aesthetic ideation, but I understand too little of aesthetics to try to enlarge on this statement. As regards joking, however, I can assert, on the basis of the two discoveries we have already made, that it is an activity which aims at deriving pleasure from mental processes, whether intellectual or otherwise. No doubt there are other activities which have the same aim. (pp. 95–96)

So there is such a thing as deriving pleasure from the mind's own (purposeless) activity, and probably aesthetic ideation is conditioned by this pleasure. But, once again, this flies in the face of Freud's "official" model of pleasure. For if the mind's activity is not required "for supplying one of our indispensable satisfactions," the pleasure derived from its activity cannot be connected with any kind of discharge.

5. Birds

It is for reasons like the above that many authors have criticized Freud's model of pleasure in general and his contributions to aesthetics in particular. Thus D. W. Winnicott (1971) says:

the phenomena that I am describing have no climax. This distinguishes them from phenomena that have instinctual backing, where the orgiastic element plays an essential part, and where satisfactions are closely linked with climax. . . . Psychoanalysts who have rightly emphasized the significance of instinctual experience and of reactions to frustration have failed to state with comparable clearness or conviction the tremendous intensity of those non-climactic experiences that are called playing. Starting as we do from psychoneurotic illness and with ego defences related to anxiety that arises out of the instinctual life, we tend to think of health in terms of the state of ego defences. We say it is healthy when these defences are not rigid, etc. But we seldom reach the point at which we can start to describe what life is like apart from illness or absence of illness. (p. 98)

To put it simply, activities such as playing are "non-climactic," that is, do not involve discharge, hence their "tremendous intensity" (which seems to include the pleasure connected with them) cannot be accommodated in the model described above. If (as seems to be Freud's own opinion) artistic ideation is an activity of this kind, then artistic ideation, too, falls largely outside that model. And if (as I have been arguing in this chapter) artistic appreciation is to some extent the result of analogous activities, then the discharge model will not be able to explain it either. Shall we then just discard Freud's association of pleasure with discharge, and conclude with Pribram and Gill (1976) that "Freud would have saved himself and everyone else a great deal of confusion if he had from the beginning separated the quantitative concepts of drive, energy and effort from the qualitative concepts of unpleasure and pleasure" (p. 90)?

Maybe not. Consider the following passage from Konrad Lorenz's (1970):

I once had a hand-reared starling which, although it had never trapped a fly in its whole life, performed the entire fly-catching behavioural sequence *without* a fly — i.e. *in vacuo.* The starling behaved as follows: It would fly up to an elevated look-out position (usually the head of a bronze statue in our living room), perch there and gaze upwards continuously as if searching the sky for flying insects. Suddenly, the bird's entire behaviour would indicate that it had spotted an insect. The starling would extend its body, flatten its feathers, aim upwards, take off, snap at something, return to its perch and finally perform swallowing motions. The entire process was so amazingly realistic, particularly with regard to the bird's convincing behaviour before take-off, that I always took care to see whether small flying insects which I had previously overlooked were in fact present. But there were really no insects to be seen. (vol. I, p. 93)

Lorenz's account of this and other cases of animal *in vacuo* activity can be found in the following passage:

the elicitation of genuine "instinctive motor patterns" becomes easier with the length of time since the last elicitation. This *lowering of the threshold* for releasing stimuli can proceed to such an extent, with certain instinctive motor patterns which are normally employed frequently, that after a long period of "damming" they will be performed *in the absence of* any demonstrable external stimulus. In this "vacuum activity," the entire motor sequence is a truly photographic replica of the normally performed pattern, though of course the species-preserving function is not fulfilled. The phenomenon of continuously increasing motivation in the interval between two elicitations of the instinctive motor pattern was itself suggestive of internal *accumulation processes.* (1970, vol. II, p. 204)

Note the structural analogy between this explanatory model and the one used by Freud for "climactic" activities. In both cases, the initial metaphor is a hydraulic one: a certain amount of drive excitation is accumulated, retained, and finally discharged. But note the differences, too. Freud's model is ultimately teleological: a drive is *the drive to attain a certain goal* (orgasm, satisfaction of hunger, or what have you). For Lorenz, on the other hand, a drive is simply *the drive to perform a certain activity,* which will *in general, but by no means always,* be conducive to the attainment of a goal. So for Freud, the excitation connected with the hunger drive would be released when a bird actually swallows a fly. For Lorenz, the release involved in such a case would have to be directly associated *with the moves* of chasing, catching, and swallowing. Hence for Lorenz, but not for Freud, there would be release associated with such moves *even if there were no fly.*

Lorenz himself is quite clear about this peculiarity of his view. Thus he says:

According to the vitalistic-teleological view, a spontaneous, goal-directed behaviour pattern aimed at a specific "drive goal" must *ipso facto* have a constant biological end-result. . . . But . . . in the extreme case, the pattern will erupt explosively, in the absence of demonstrable external stimuli, as a so-called *vacuum activity*. Naturally, in such a case the species-preserving "purpose" of the pattern is in no way fulfilled. (1970, vol. II, p. 133)

How is all of this relevant to our problem? First, note the similarity between *in vacuo* activities on the one hand and aesthetic performance on the other. In both cases, we have something performed *for its own sake*, with no tangible attainment of a goal distinct from the activity itself.[15] This similarity is suggestive, and my proposal results from fleshing it out. What I propose is to combine Freud's model of pleasure with Lorenz's understanding of the nature of a drive. The result of such a combination is as follows:

A drive is the drive to perform a certain activity. With the drive is associated a certain (kind of) psychic excitation, which is accumulated throughout the life of the individual and (periodically) released through the performance of the activity. The phenomenological counterpart of such a release is pleasure.

In general, certain internal and external conditions must be satisfied for the activity to be performed. They constitute a threshold for the release of the drive. For example, the activities of chasing and swallowing are normally performed in situations that include a low level of sugar-content in the blood and the presence of a prey. But a high level of accumulation of the drive excitation can bring about a lowering of the threshold and consequent performing of the activity even in the absence of the relevant internal and/or external conditions. *In vacuo* activities and other deviant behavior patterns (for example, overeating) may result from such threshold lowering.

Under normal circumstances, drive activities are functional to the organism. This is a simple consequence of the general adaptiveness of (most) animal species. In fact, the converse is probably the case, too: any adaptive activity is probably controlled by one or more such drives.[16] But the adaptive character of the drive and of the attending activity *is extrinsic to the drive itself*: the relation between the performing of a drive activity and the attainment of its "goal" is that of a highly frequent concomitance, not of an analytic equivalence. Therefore, under non-normal circumstances, drive activities may have results that are entirely superfluous or even counterproductive for the organism. Even in such cases, however, their performance causes the same release, and consequently the same pleasure, as in normal cases.

6. Conclusions

Our investigation has taken us far afield, so it may prove useful to sum up the results in a compact way. The original question was

(1)   Why is it that incomplete or economical works of art are often judged more valuable than complete or highly detailed ones?

The answer to (1) was

> (2)   Because spectators or readers get more involved in constructive activities, and these activities give them pleasure.

(2), however, generated a further question, that is,

> (3)   Why do constructive activities give pleasure?

In answering (3), I first noted that

> (4)   Analogous constructive activities are involved in normal perception,

hence that, given the usefulness of normal perception for the individual's survival and success,

> (5)   These constructive activities are in general of great utility to the individual.

But (5) was no answer to (3) yet. For

> (6)   Why do generally useful behavioral patterns give pleasure?

In addressing (6), I decided to adopt (and possibly adapt) the Freudian model of pleasure as resulting from the satisfaction of a drive and a consequent reduction of psychic tension.[17] The model, however, had no direct application to activities like perception or art appreciation (or, for that matter, art ideation), which do not have the appearance of consummatory, climactic activities in Freud's sense. Comparative ethology came to the rescue, allowing us to reconceptualize drives as *drives to perform certain (largely adaptive) activities*. My final answer to (6) was then the following:

> (7)   Generally useful behavioral patterns give pleasure because (and to the extent to which) they release (à la Freud) drive excitation (à la Lorenz).

So, once again, why do I enjoy Michelangelo's incomplete works (for example, his unfinished Boboli *Slaves*) more than his complete ones (for example, more than the finished *Slave* to be found at the Louvre)? Because the incomplete works allow me to release my drive for completing visual images, a drive that proves in general very useful for me to successfully adjust to the world.

But, to play the devil's advocate now, why is it that I do not derive the same pleasure from perceiving tables and chairs, if in fact the same constructive activities are involved there? The answer, quite simply, is that they are not involved nearly as much. To a large extent, we live in a very predictable world, in which things appear to us in predictable ways. To stretch the metaphor a little, these things by and large have already been constructed, hence do not require as much collaboration on our part as do Michelangelo's sculptures. In Kant's words, "the pleasure appeared in due course, and only by reason of the most ordinary experience being impossible without it, has it become gradually fused with simple cognition, and no longer arrests particular attention."[18]

Does this mean then that if I had one of Michelangelo's unfinished *Slaves* as constantly before my eyes as I do this table I would eventually grow as bored with it as I am with the table? I dare say I would. I wonder how much pleasure the *Slaves* could have given to the Boboli *gardeners* of years past.[19]

A few final remarks. First, some might object to the very formulation (1) of my problem. The fact that some economical works of art are found to be valuable, they might say, is *in itself* not of aesthetic significance. For *other* works of art are found valuable *precisely because* of how rich and detailed they are, so it is likely that no real aesthetic issue can be captured along the economy-richness axis, that the generalization(s) truly relevant to aesthetic judgment must be found in some other dimension(s) of expression. In other words, here I have carved out an area within the general field of aesthetic appreciation, concentrating my attention on some cases of appreciation and discounting many others, but it is not clear that this discounting (and the carving out process that is based on it) is legitimate. My response to this objection consists in pointing out that it seems to be based on a simplistic view both of aesthetic experience (and pleasure) and of the person doing the experiencing (and having the pleasure). If one conceives of this person (as I do) along the general lines of Freudian theory, that is, as a *complex* of different and partly conflicting tendencies, one has no problem accepting and understanding the fact that the system may offer different (and sometimes conflicting) possibilities for pleasure, and that different people, or even the same person at different times, may exploit the system in different ways, and derive pleasure from different components of it.[20]

My second remark is to some extent a corrective of the first one. Whereas in the preceding paragraph I defended my right to be concerned here with a *limited* issue, now I want to point to one way in which my conclusions could be generalized. Most works of art require "constructive" activities of some sort. Even the Louvre *Slave* is after all made *of marble*, and slaves normally are not. No matter how faithful the representation is, it is nonetheless always a representation, which in most cases involves at least a change in the *matter* of the thing represented.[21] Representation is never complete recreation: even the splendid (and highly realistic) *Moses* sculpted for Pope Julius's tomb did not talk back to its artificer. Therefore, appreciation of a representation always involves some (perhaps minimal) degree of *recognition* (that is, in the view of perception advocated here, reconstruction) activity.

Third, a connection has often been drawn between children's play and works of art. If my suggestions are accepted, they can offer a new way to understand and justify this connection. For it is by one and the same drive that a child "completes" a broom into a horse and I "complete" Cezanne's "hints" on the canvas into an image of France's mountainous landscape.

Notes

1. A different view on this matter is to be found, for example, in Robert Liebert's (1983), where the incompleteness of Michelangelo's sculptures is often traced back to unresolved psychological conflicts. Here is a statement by Liebert on the *St Matthew*: "The change in Michelangelo's art marked

by the *St Matthew* raises certain issues concerning aesthetics and the creative process. It has become axiomatic to regard all artistic production as containing, in varying degrees, projections of thoughts and feelings of the artist that are not even conscious in him. Art, however, is only 'art' when the creator is able to express his hidden mental life with such technical skill, as well as sublimation of the unconscious roots and generalization of the content, that the creation is transported from the limited province of dreams and fantasies to a realm of human experience which the beholder can recognize and share. The artist, therefore, must steer a course between the sterility of being too programmatic and the sentimentality of undisciplined personal statement" (pp. 135–36). In connection with this judgment, see the reference to overstrain in Section 2, as well as note 20 and the attending text.

2. For a dissenting view on the relative value of the early and the final draft of the work, see Paratore (1972).

3. Quoted by Gombrich, p. 296.

4. Of course, I am not committed here to suggesting that there be a general (even less, necessary) connection between "aesthetically valuable" and "pleasing." For my present purposes, I may admit that there are many things or activities that are found aesthetically valuable but give no pleasure at all (or perhaps give pain). All I am interested in here is to find an explanation for *a particular class* of aesthetic judgments, or, to put it more provocatively, to tell a story in which these judgments (appear to) make coherent sense. (But see the first two remarks at the very end of this chapter.)

5. *Critique of Pure Reason*, p. 93.

6. The psychologist to whom Gombrich refers most often is J. J. Gibson. For example, in his *Note for the 1969 Printing*, Gombrich writes: "the conclusion of my central chapter, 'The Analysis of Vision in Art,' for which I quoted an 'aside' by Professor J. J. Gibson, can now rest on the solid support of a closely reasoned book by that great student of perception [Gibson, 1966]." (p. xiii) But the constructive character of perception is emphasized in other recent works as well – for example in Marr (1982), where perception is characterized as "the construction of a description" (see p. 354).

7. Or perhaps it does, if we think that final explanations are "real" explanations. A convincing strategy for "cashing out" final explanations in causal terms is offered by the theory of evolution. To a large extent, my procedure in the next three sections can be seen as an attempt at applying evolutionary considerations to the final explanation implicit here.

8. I will return to play at the very end of the chapter.

9. See, for example, the *Project for a Scientific Psychology* (*Complete Psychological Works*, vol. I, pp. 295–387).

10. See *Works*, vol. XVIII, pp. 55–56.

11. "Pleasure would be the sensation of discharge." (*Works*, vol. I, p. 312)

12. *Works*, vol. VII, pp. 130–243.

13. *Works*, vol VIII, pp. 9–236.

14. Thus consider the following quotes: "Jokes, even if the thought contained in them is nontendentious, and thus only serves intellectual interests, are in fact never nontendentious." (p. 132) "The pleasurable effect of innocent jokes is as a rule a moderate one; a clear sense of satisfaction, a slight smile, is as a rule all it can achieve in its hearers." (p. 96) On the other hand, Freud was lucid enough to recognize that "[f]rom the point of view of throwing theoretical light on the nature of jokes, innocent jokes are bound to be of more value to us than tendentious ones. . . . Innocent and trivial jokes are likely to put the problem of jokes before us in its purest form." (p. 94)

15. It might not be stretching things too far to connect this Lorenzian construe of *in vacuo* activities with the "finality without an end" discussed by Kant in the third *Critique*.

16. That Lorenz would agree on this statement is suggested for example by the following passage: "all cognitive functions with which we are endowed indubitably are, like all other adaptive life processes, the function of organic systems evolved in age-long interaction between the organism and its environment." (1970, vol. II, p. 255)

17. One may wonder why I made this decision. Why, that is, go through the trouble of revising Freud's model in what certainly is a substantial way instead of adopting a different model altogether? The reason goes well beyond the limits of the present context and has to do with my general belief

that psychoanalytic theory and comparative ethology each possesses exactly what the other lacks and needs to produce a satisfactory comprehensive explanation of human behavior.

18. *The Critique of Judgment*, p. 28.

19. Since 1980 the Boboli *Slaves* have been displayed in the Florentine Academy. Note, however, that (many) works of art have enough complexity to sustain this game longer than (most) ordinary objects.

20. I would follow an analogous strategy to explain conflicts of opinion among critics such as those mentioned in Section 1.

21. There are apparent exceptions to this generalization in some contemporary works of art, where physical objects such as chairs are themselves part of the work. But I conjecture that in these cases what is "represented" is not so much the physical object as perhaps art itself, or some social convention, or some decontextualization process.

7

That Obscure Object of Desire

Tis pity . . .
That wishing well had not a body in't
Which might be felt; that we, the poorer born
Whose baser stars do shut us up in wishes
Might with effects of them follow our friends,
And show what we alone must think, which never
Returns us thanks.

(*All's Well That Ends Well*, Act I, Scene I)

In the fifties, Quine sounded a call to arms against all kinds of creatures of darkness: propositions, meanings, nonexistent objects, and the like.[1] Since then, many of those creatures have found safe haven in other possible worlds or in Meinongian appendages of the actual one, with one notable exception: objects of desire. The anomaly has gone largely unnoticed; I want to focus on it here, and make it into an Archimedean turning point for a conceptual revolution of the Kantian variety.

1. Unicorns

Consider the two sentences:

(1) I am looking for a unicorn
(2) I am eating an apple.

I thank Richard E. Aquila for his comments on an earlier draft of this chapter.

In spite of their grammatical similarity, (1) and (2) are different in an important respect: (2) has, but (1) does not have, existential import in the object position. That is, though I can rewrite (2) as

(3) There is an apple that I am eating,

I cannot rewrite (1) as

(4) There is a unicorn that I am looking for.

In fact, I cannot even infer

(5) There is something that I am looking for

from (1).

The problem is not specific to sentences of the form (1). For example, it is also the case that

(6) I am thinking of a unicorn

cannot be rewritten as

(7) There is a unicorn that I am thinking of

and that

(8) There is something that I am thinking of

cannot be inferred from it. The moral Quine drew from such examples is that (1) and (6) – in contrast with (2) – cannot be read *de re* (if, as we may safely assume, they are taken to be true). Their truth does not establish the existence of a *relation* between two objects: the occurrence of "unicorn" in them is no more "referential" than, say, the occurrence of "nine" in "canine,"[2] and it would be more perspicuous to rephrase them as

(9) I am-looking-for-a-unicorn

(10) I am-thinking-of-a-unicorn,

respectively, thus emphasizing that the truth of these sentences proves nothing more than that I have a certain (complicated) property.

But this radical solution runs against a number of intuitions. First, I can expand (1) into

(11) I am looking for a unicorn, and when I find it I am going to cut its horn,

and it is hard to see how "it" and "its" are to be understood if (1) – and consequently the first half of (11) – is read as in (9).

Second, consider the inferential pattern instantiated by

(a) I am eating an apple
(b) Apples are fruit

(12) _____ .

(c) Therefore, I am eating a fruit

The validity of this pattern seems to depend on "apple" receiving an independent interpretation within (a), and not being simply an incidental component of a predicate expression. But essentially the same pattern can be applied to (1):

(13)

    (a) I am looking for a unicorn
    (b) Unicorns are animals
    _____ .
    (c) Therefore, I am looking for an animal

Third, consider the sequence of sentences:

    (14) I am looking for Pegasus

    (15) I am looking for Ronald Reagan

    (16) I am [or, perhaps better, I was] looking for this.

Since apparently the difference between (1) and (2) has to do with the verb, all of (14)-(16) should receive an analysis similar to (1). But as we move through the sequence, it becomes increasingly difficult to deny that a genuine relation is established by the truth of the relevant sentence.

Analogous problems arise with the analysis (10) of (6), and to address such problems in the case of (6) two (for our purposes, essentially equivalent) strategies have been proposed. The first consists of admitting a bunch of alternative possible worlds and letting the relation *thinking of* range across different worlds. Then (6) can be taken as stating a relation between me and an object (a unicorn) inhabiting a nonunicornless world. The second consists of adding to the actual world a bunch of nonexistent objects and taking (6) to state a relation between me and one of these ghostly entities. Either way, (6) can be read *de re*—even though nothing prevents us from *also* reading it the way Quine would favor. And as for the problematic (7) and (8), they would be considered ambiguous; for example, (7) would indeed be false if read as

    (17) There *exists* a unicorn that I am thinking of

or as

    (18) There is *in the actual world* a unicorn that I am thinking of,

but it would be *true* if read instead as

    (19) There is a *possibly nonexistent* unicorn that I am thinking of

or as

    (20) There is *in some possible world* a unicorn that I am thinking of.

Now the important bit, as far as we are concerned, is that neither of these strategies has a straightforward application to (1). For, as noted, for example, by Roderick Chisholm (1967, p. 201), when I look for a unicorn I look for an *existent* unicorn, or for a unicorn that inhabits the same (possible) world as I do. If someone was able to pull out a unicorn from the Meinongian or counterfactual joints where they lead their shadowy life and ask me, "Is this the (kind of) thing you were thinking of (when you uttered (6))?" I would probably answer "Yes," but if the corresponding question was asked relative to (1), the answer would be a resounding "No." Hence the perplexing conclusion is: whereas the problems listed above suggest that it should at least be possible to read (1) as *de re*, the *res* (1) is supposed to be *de* (that is, the object (1) is supposed to be about) cannot be an existent one (since there exist no unicorns) and cannot — *contra* what happens in the case of (6) — be a nonexistent one either (since that is not what I am looking for). But an object must be one or the other, so even with the most liberal attitude with respect to the admission of (non)entities we seem to make no progress in accounting for the object-directedness of desire.

There may be ways of complicating the analysis suggested above that take care of (some of) the problems I mentioned. And there may be further problems with such complications. But I will not get into any of this. My intent here is not critical: it is constructive. I want to suggest a whole new way of thinking of the issue. Specifically, I want to suggest that what we are facing in the case of verbs of looking for, desiring, wanting, and the like is an anomaly in Thomas Kuhn's sense, whose awareness implies "the recognition that nature has somehow violated the paradigm-induced expectations that govern normal science,"[3] and whose resolution requires a paradigm shift. Most often, scientists (and philosophers) are not anxious to get down to such a shift: they are "perfectly willing to wait, particularly if there are many problems available in other parts of the field."[4] Which seems to be what has happened with the verbs I am presently concerned with: philosophers were busy enough generating logics of belief, obligation, causality, and what have you, to be justified in forgetting the problem of generating a logic of desire, or, in Kuhn's terms again, to be justified in *waiting* that the problem go away. But the problem, I suggest, may never go away unless we take drastic measures. It is to these measures that I now turn.

2. The Copernican Revolution

In the *Critique of Pure Reason* Kant points out that metaphysics has not been able to give a satisfactory account of the relation between (*a priori*) knowledge and objects.[5] The reason, he urges, is not to be found in a lack of ingenuity on the part of workers in the field, but, rather, in the fact that they were looking at the matter in the wrong way. So he proposes to look at things differently: this operation has gone down in history as Kant's Copernican revolution.[6]

It is far from clear what exactly the operation in question consists of. In my (1987) I have offered and defended an interpretation of it; here I will simply rehearse the main points. First of all, the revolution occurs at the conceptual (or "transcendental") level: it is not to concern *what there is* (or why what there is is that way), but, rather, *what it is to be assigned certain denominations* (among which 'object,' 'knowledge,' and the like). Specifically, whereas in the traditional paradigm experiences were taken to be cognitive (or constitute knowledge) insofar as they fit objects in certain ways (knowledge conformed to objects), in the new Kantian paradigm experiences are cognitive insofar as they fit *together* in certain ways, and their ostensible (or, as we can also say, *intentional*) objects[7] are real (or objects *simpliciter*) if the experiences they are objects of are cognitive (objects conform to knowledge).

Second, the revolution is to remain *only* at the transcendental level, and not to infect our ordinary, "empirical" life, so whatever counted as an object (or as knowledge) before will still count as such: the difference will only be in *why* it thus counts, in what is (conceptually) prior to what, or in how we are going to begin our (philosophical) story to explain what makes the world (and experience of it) possible.[8]

Consider the liberalization induced by the new paradigm. Traditionally, objects were the conceptual starting point, and everything that was not an object had to be assigned the status of either a property of, or a relation among, objects *before it could be put on the map* (and, possibly, become the subject of study). Experiences, in particular, and among them desires, were to be assigned such a status, which created the (at least *prima facie*) difficulty that if a desire is construed as a property then no account is given of its *de re* character, if it is construed as a relation with existent objects only then no justice is done to the fact that what we desire often does not exist, and if it is construed as a relation with possibly nonexistent objects then no justice is done to the fact that our desires are—virtually without exception—desires for something existent.[9] But now the conceptual starting point are experiences themselves, hence experiences need not be assigned a status in terms of anything else: specifically, it need not be decided in advance whether, say, representations or desires are properties or relations or whatever *of objects*. Some experiences, of course, will have objects, and some possibly will not[10]; additionally, all experiences will have a subject. But these will (conceptually)[11] be features of experiences, not the other way around: they will come *after* experiences in our philosophical accounts, and failure to ever come to them will no longer mean that the account cannot get started.

Thus, what the liberalization ultimately means is that it will be possible to go a long way in studying the structure of experience without having to study, or even to worry about, the structure of the *objects of* experience, not because there are no such objects or because they do not exist, and not *simply* because in some cases (for example, in the case of desire) we often do not know whether these objects exist or not, but, rather, because we are not *conceptually committed* to taking a position on the structure of objects in order to explore the structure of experience: conceptually, experience is independent of (its) objects. In studying the ways in which experiences are related, we may eventually hit upon those relations that make it possible to say that the relevant objects exist, but much of interest will be said before that point is even raised. It is time now to see what of interest we can say about the theme that we are specifically concerned with.

3. On Experiencing Desire

Return to (1), and suppose first of all that I utter it, and that you ask me:

(21) Are there any unicorns?

My answer is probably going to be: I do not know. I have not *found* any unicorns yet, hence I cannot be sure that any exist. On the other hand, since I am looking for one (and assuming that I am not simply putting up a show), it is clear that I was not convinced by the repeated failures on the part of others (and myself) to find unicorns, or by the persistent rumor that there are none to be found, hence I am not sure that they do not exist either. I can certainly imagine my experiences to develop in various ways, which would eventually convince me of the existence or nonexistence of what I was looking for, but at that point I would in general no longer *be looking for* it, and I would be having a *different* kind of experience. *As long as I am looking for an object*, the issue of its existence is in general open.[12]

This account is quite natural, and it finds a natural place within the new (Kantian) paradigm. For there the issue of the existence of the object *of* a given experience can arise—and possibly be settled—only after that experience has been put in relation to *other* experiences[13]: that issue is conceptually *posterior* to this relation, hence it is perfectly possible to say that the object of a specific activity of looking for is indeterminate with respect to existence or nonexistence, *not* because the object has some kind of unclear intermediate status between the two but because the question of whether it exists or not can only receive, at this stage of the game (where not all that is conceptually presupposed by it has been mobilized yet), a *corrective* answer. A corrective answer which—I find it useful to repeat once more—would not be legitimate within the *old* paradigm; for if we *start* with objects, then all that is relevant to them must be decided in advance (though we might not be aware of it).

Second, the sense of the remark by Chisholm noted earlier is that any (serious) utterance of (1) is true if and only if the corresponding utterance of

(22) I am looking for an *existent* unicorn

is true. So the question arises whether this equivalence contradicts the conclusion reached above that what I am looking for when I utter (1) is in general—as long as I keep looking for it—indeterminate with respect to existence. But the answer to this question is a negative one. To understand why, it will be useful to make a digression.

Consider the experience of *assuming* that something is the case. What I assume may well turn out to be false, but this means that there was something wrong with my assumption, and that the assumption has been refuted. Assuming, that is, is more than simply entertaining in thought: part of what makes this experience what it is is that what is assumed (the intentional object of the experience) is taken to hold.[14] So, though a judgment about the truth of the assumption can come only in terms of its relation to other experiences, there is a truth claim *internal* to the experience. In fact, it is precisely because such a claim is made *within* the experience that a judgment can be passed on the veridicality of the experience.

Much the same is true of visual experiences. What I see may well turn out to be nonexistent, and the experience of seeing it may well be judged in the end to be a hallucination, but undeniably a visual presentation includes a presumption of veridicality, in a way in which, say, an experience of daydreaming does not. Again, this is precisely why the latter cannot be sensibly said to be veridical (or nonveridical): since it makes no claim (and hence raises no expectation), it cannot be right (or wrong).

The point of these examples is one that I conjecture Meinong was trying to express with his distinction betwen nuclear and extranuclear properties,[15] that is: if experiences are the conceptual starting point, and objects are conceptualized as objects *of* experiences, then qualifications such as 'true' or 'existent' may attach to objects from the inside — as properties of the relevant experiences — or from the outside — as ways in which those experiences relate to other experiences. Thus suppose that I think of an existent unicorn, that is, that it is true to say that

(23) I am thinking of an existent unicorn.

Within the Copernican viewpoint, at least the following two alternative construes of (23) are possible:

(24) I am thinking of a unicorn, and there are other (for example, visual) experiences that could be related to the present one in such a way as to convince me of its veridicality.

(25) I am thinking of a unicorn, and expecting that there are other (for example, visual) experiences that could be related to the present one in such a way as to convince me of its veridicality.

Since (24) is false — hence the expectations expressed in (25) are not going to be satisfied — the situation might be summed up with the following paradoxical sounding statement:

(26) The existent unicorn I am thinking of does not exist.[16]

But note that the paradox is only apparent: (26) means nothing more than

(27) The claim made by my experience (construed as in (25)) cannot be vindicated.

Within the traditional paradigm, on the other hand, where objects enter the (conceptual) picture first, we do not have this much freedom, and statements like (26) may turn out to be more than paradoxical *sounding*.[17] In particular, no natural analysis of (23) is forthcoming there. For what is it of which it is true to say I am thinking of it? It must be either an existent or a nonexistent object. But if it is existent, it cannot be a unicorn, since there aren't any; and if it is nonexistent, again it cannot be what I am thinking of.

The digression is now over, and we are ready to understand that (22) is not supposed to contrast the experience of looking for an existent unicorn with the experience of looking for a nonexistent one, but, rather, to bring out a fundamental feature of the kind of experience that looking for is, and a feature that is only implicit in (1) — much the way that

(28) I am assuming that *A is true*

brings out a fundamental feature of the experience of assuming that is only implicit in

(29) I am assuming that *A*

or

(30) I am seeing a table *out there in space*

brings out a fundamental feature of the experience of seeing that is only implicit in

(31) I am seeing a table.

More specifically, it was pointed out earlier that some experiences contain claims within themselves, and consequently raise expectations: in general, claims and expectations about what other experiences are to follow. Such claims and expectations can be verified or falsified, confirmed or disconfirmed. For example, the experience of hitting the wall when trying to pet the pink elephant I see in the corner may be taken as disconfirming the claim of veridicality implicitly made by this (as by any other) visual experience, and the experience of inspecting the details of a mathematical proof may be taken as satisfying the claim of veridicality made by the experience of assuming a given mathematical conjecture. Similarly, looking for a unicorn *includes, as part of the (kind of) experience it is*, the expectation that there are unicorns to be found, and this expectation would be satisfied if I had a visual experience (which I judged to be veridical) of an animal with one horn and some other characteristic features, whereas it would not be satisfied, say, by experiences of thinking of a unicorn, or telling a story about a unicorn, or writing a philosophy paper about one. That there is such an expectation is what (22) brings out, and, of course, I may well conclude after a while that

(32) The existent unicorn I was looking for does not exist,

but this paradoxical sounding statement is in fact no more paradoxical, within the present paradigm, than (26) was; in analogy with (26), (32) is to be construed as equivalent to

(33) The expectation raised by my (earlier) experience of looking for a unicorn has been disconfirmed.

I think the above may give enough evidence that the conceptual net I have been articulating here (and elsewhere) does allow one to catch the elusive objects of desire and search. I will close with three remarks.

First, it may be worth insisting on the most delicate point of the Copernican revolution (as I understand it) — a point that has crucial relevance for our present concerns. The revolution is not supposed to change the fact that we know, desire, or otherwise experience *objects*: for example, it is not supposed to establish that what we know or desire are *experiences*. It is an animal that I look for when I look for a unicorn, not an image of an animal, or a thought of an animal, or any such, just as it is Juliet that Romeo desires, not her ghost or the memory of her. *As it turns out*, the object I look for when I look for a unicorn does not exist, but this does not make it less an object, *that is*, does not make the experience of looking for it less a directional, targeted experience. The gist of the revolution – what the revolution *is* supposed to change – has to do with *the concept of* an object and *the concept of* an experience: specifically, as already indicated, the former concept is posterior to the latter, or, to put it otherwise, that there be an object (of a certain kind) *means* that there are experiences (of certain kinds).

Second, much of what I said sounds like phenomenology, and rightly so. Kant's Copernican revolution did not end with Kant, and was supplemented in important ways by Brentano and Husserl; but it did not end with them either. At least they did not give (what I would consider) a clear formulation of the conceptual operation involved here, and many of their statements acquire a new significance when looked at from the point of view I am recommending. Thus, for example, Husserl's proposal to bracket ontological considerations and concentrate on the structure of experience amounts (for me) to a proposal to discount *the way ontology was traditionally conceptualized* and to base a new conceptualization of it on the notion of experience. So whereas I am sympathetic to many of phenomenology's suggestions, I am not sympathetic to its claim to be a radically new discipline: I think of it as a(n important) step on a path that goes back (at least) to Kant, and I see my own work as an additional step in the same direction.[18]

Third, one of the things that contribute the most to making it difficult to understand Kant's conceptual revolution is the fact that there is a close affinity between the epistemological concerns dominant in the first *Critique* and the traditional paradigm. The point of knowledge – its ideology, one might say – is that of effectively mirroring an independent world. Indeed, even after the Copernican revolution, to capture what is essential to knowledge (and its objects) one must still mobilize the traditional priority of objects in an instrumental way.[19] On the other hand, a similar affinity exists between the new paradigm and conative attitudes. To be sure, desires and the like are directional attitudes, they are directed to an object, but they need not be successful to be the attitudes they are. An experience of knowledge cannot be an experience *of knowledge* if it does not fit its object (however that fit is construed conceptually), and hence *a fortiori* if such an object does not exist, but an experience of desire does not cease to be the experience it is on the basis of the ontological vicissitudes of its object. Given how opposite the two paradigms are, and how germane cognition and desire are, respectively, to them, it is not surprising that complications should arise when one of the two kinds of experience is studied from the point of view it is *not* germane to. But aside from such complications, moving from one paradigm to the other is also moving from assigning a central, "paradigmatic," status to one kind of experience to assigning it to another, hence changing what we think is most crucial to human life. Which means that the revolution may not be empirically harmless after all, insofar as it makes us think of human beings no longer as mirrors that are out to reflect as adequately as possible an image of an independent (and largely indifferent) world, but as appetitive creatures that want the world to be(come) fit to their needs.[20]

Notes

1. For a useful summary of Quine's arguments, see his (1960).

2. This way of putting the matter was originally suggested by David Kaplan (1969).

3. Kuhn (1962), pp. 52–53.

4. Ibid., p. 81.

5. It is often noted that Kant's characterization of his work as centering around the question "How are synthetic *a priori* judgments possible?" is unjustifiably reductive and that the first *Critique* aims (implicitly, at least) at revolutionizing our views about knowledge in general.

6. It has been pointed out occasionally that Kant never used the expression 'Copernican revolution.' But this is exceedingly pedantic. Kant did propose a conceptual revolution, and one that people usually refer to as Copernican: this is all that matters.

7. It will become clear later that talk of intentional objects is simply talk of the directionality of (some) experiences and is supposed to have no ontological implications.

8. But see the last paragraph of this chapter.

9. In Chapter 2 above I argued that nonexistent objects are an absurdity in the traditional paradigm. Here I can take a more liberal attitude, since even with the admission of nonexistent objects that paradigm would allow for no natural analysis of conative attitudes.

10. Among the experiences *not* having an object, for example, one might count experiences of pain.

11. This qualification is important, in view of the empirical conservatism emphasized above. From an empirical point of view, experiences will still be *of a subject* (or still relate subject and object(s)); it is only within philosophical reflection that the order is reversed. See my (1987), pp. 63–70.

12. It is not when my looking for is what Quine (1956) called *relational* (exemplified here by (15)-(16)). But note that there may be less (conceptual) room than expected for this kind of looking for; even if I knew at one point that *a* existed, when I look for *a* I may not know that it *still* exists.

13. Specifically, with experiences that are often *in principle* not accessible while the experience of looking for is being had (see the preceding paragraph). So from the Copernican viewpoint it is inevitable that desire should create an anomaly to the traditional paradigm, since it brings out a conceptual clash: to be understood by a realist, desire must be analyzed in terms of objects, but there are cases in which the experience of desire would cease to be the experience it is as soon as that analysis becomes possible.

14. Frege, of course, was well aware of this difference, and in his symbolism distinguished the sign of content from the sign of judgment (the two of them together constituting the ordinary turnstile).

15. Much recent discussion of this distinction is still conducted on the basis of the traditional conceptual priority of objects over experiences and as such does little justice to the philosophical import of the distinction. But for this defect Meinong himself is to blame: as I pointed out in Chapter 2 above, he was not clear about the revolutionary significance of his proposals.

16. A similar paradoxical sounding statement is made by Meinong, and in that case, too, the issue of whether the statement is *really* paradoxical depends on which paradigm one adopts. See above, p. 23.

17. Incidentally, this diagnosis explains why many authors have tried to reduplicate the distinction I am suggesting, hence to face the problem at the level at which I am suggesting it should be faced: the level of experience, or of *some specific kind* of experience – most notably, discourse. (An obvious

reference here is to the various distinctions of scope that have been repeatedly proposed since Russell.) These positions clearly go in the same direction I propose here, but since they ordinarily do not take the major step of reconceptualizing objects themselves, they can apply only to our *discourse of* objects (not to objects *of discourse*).

18. In fact, partly because of the lack of clarity mentioned in the text, discussions of intentionality have recently moved one or two steps backward (from my point of view), in the direction of an uneasy compromise between phenomenological intuitions and transcendental realism. Such is the case, for example, in Smith and McIntyre (1982) and Searle (1983).

19. See Chapter 4 of my (1987).

20. Of course, if we could limit ourselves to just *thinking* of humans this way, the revolution would still be empirically insignificant. But it is natural for such thoughts to "spread" into action; see the next chapter.

8

Metaphors and the Transcendental

This chapter is self-applicable. In it, I present a view of conceptual analysis, or the "transcendental" level of discourse, which makes it consist of the straining of words and phrases outside their ordinary contexts. The straining occurs through seeing those words and phrases as *examples* relevant to other contexts, which is a first step toward a mixing of the contexts and ultimately the creation of new linguistic practices. But to introduce this talk of conceptual enterprises is to some extent to engage in a straining of the existing philosophical context,[1] hence it stands to reason that I should proceed exactly in the way I thematize. So in the first two sections "examples" are offered, and they are used to build a new practice of expression which is then articulated in the central Section 3. Section 4 draws a moral from the preceding "theoretical" proposal.

1. Pure Reason

In the preface to the first edition of the *Critique of Pure Reason* (pp. 12–13), Kant admits to a peculiar source of embarrassment. "I have been almost continuously at a loss," he says, "during the progress of my work, how I should proceed in this matter." The "matter" mentioned here is whether or not to give the reader something that he "has a right to demand," namely, "*intuitive* (aesthetic) clearness . . . through examples and other concrete illustrations."

In the end, Kant reports, he has decided not to satisfy the reader's need in this regard, and he lists three reasons for his decision. First, the book was already large enough without examples, and it would have gotten totally out of hand with them. Second, examples "are necessary only from a *popular* point of view; and this work can never be made suitable for popular consumption." Third, intuitive clearness does not harmonize, but is in competition, with the discursive variety, that is, clearness through concepts—which he judges more essential here. For what we get through examples is "assistance in regard to details," which "often interfere[s] with our grasp of the whole," insofar as "the bright colouring of the illustrative material intervenes to cover over and conceal the articulation and organisation of the system."

The first reason sounds unconvincing. Not only is the *Critique* very long, it is also very repetitious. The Dialectic especially would benefit from substantial pruning, and it seems unfair to penalize the reader for such an inefficient use of space. The second reason is more interesting. In my (1987) I defended the view that Kant's "revolution" was addressed to professional philosophers and was supposed to leave the general public alone – in fact, to defend it from the attacks some of those professional philosophers had conducted on the legitimacy of its practices. If this view is accepted, the claim that the *Critique* will never be suitable for popular consumption acquires an interesting dimension, though the rest of our discussion here will have the effect of questioning and to some extent undermining the easy distinction this claim presupposes between ordinary and philosophical activities.

But it is the third reason I want to concentrate on. First, because it is the only one that sounds decisive (if, indeed, there is a conflict between the two kinds of clearness, then you *have to* give up one if you want to attain the other); second, (and more important) because some of the things Kant says later in the *Critique* seem to contradict what he says here. Consider the following passages:

> Now how it is possible that from a given state of a thing an opposite state should follow, not only cannot be conceived by reason *without an example*, but is actually incomprehensible to reason without intuition. (p. 255; italics mine)

> If we here wished to resort to the usual subterfuge, maintaining as regards *realitates noumena* that they at least do not act in opposition to each other, it would be incumbent on us *to produce an example* of such pure and non-sensuous reality, that it may be discerned whether such a concept represents something or nothing. (p. 290 footnote; last italics mine)

> Thus the object of a concept to which no assignable intuition whatsoever corresponds is = nothing. That is, it is a concept without an object (*ens rationis*), like noumena, which cannot be reckoned among the possibilities . . . ; or like certain new fundamental forces, which though entertained in thought without self-contradiction are yet also in our thinking *unsupported by any example* from experience, and are therefore not to be counted as possible. (p. 295; last italics mine)

Some of the themes brought out by these passages I have discussed elsewhere,[2] so I will begin by recapitulating the results of those discussions. According to Kant, possibility cannot be established at a purely conceptual level. He would agree with Frege (1980, p. 43) that the possibility of a conceptual model (or, in more contemporary jargon, its consistency) can be established only by providing an instance, *an example*, of it. Otherwise, one can never be sure that contradictions that have not yet surfaced will not surface later; one cannot be sure that when one speaks (or thinks) of something one is really making sense. Two interesting consequences follow from this claim.[3] One has to do with understanding: if understanding entails being aware that what one understands is coherent, then one cannot really understand things at a purely conceptual level (though one can think — or delude oneself into thinking — that one understands): this much seems suggested by the first passage above, at least in the specific case of the notion (or concept) of alteration. The second consequence has to do with knowledge: if knowing involves understanding, then knowledge is not possible at a conceptual level, either. Kant seems to agree with this conclusion,[4] but does not fully realize the devastating implications the conclusion has for his own practice in the *Critique*. What he is supposed to be doing there is transcendental philosophy, but according to his definition on p. 59 transcendental philosophy consists of transcendental knowledge, which is (a kind of) purely conceptual knowledge, that is (a brand of) a nonexistent article.

In light of these considerations, the diagnosis of Kant's case is obvious. He wanted philosophy to be a cognitive enterprise, and he wanted it to be "purely conceptual," not infected by empirical considerations and by that sensibility which so often "deceives" reason (p. 531). But nothing could be both of the above: concepts in isolation from sensible material have no knowledge, no wisdom, not even any understanding to offer. The only knowledge is empirical knowledge, which Kant himself realizes when he moves from the programmatic statements in the preface to concrete problems.

Once this diagnosis is formulated, and one appreciates how much confusion there is in the system, one can take any of a number of increasingly radical attitudes. One can say that Kant has misdescribed philosophy, and then either collapse philosophy into "science" or turn it into a noncognitive enterprise. Or one can turn the spotlight onto the very distinction between "concepts" and "intuitions," or the very notion of a "purely conceptual" activity, on which the tension identified here depends, in the hope that both will turn out to be ghosts and the tension will thus be resolved.[5] Though the second attitude is the one that would save the most of Kant's own work,[6] the third holds the most promise for those who would want to go beyond Kant, and consequently it is the one I will adopt here. But in closing this section (and before turning to another "illustration"), it is useful to notice that a great deal seems to be at stake for Kant in that distancing of philosophical activity from its empirical counterparts which I intend to question here: a moral significance that may appear to coexist uneasily with his declared (and seriously meant)[7] respect for ordinary people.

> Whoever would derive the concepts of virtue from experience and make . . . what at best can serve only as an example in an imperfect kind of exposition, . . . would make of virtue . . . an ambiguous monstrosity not admitting of the formation of any rule. (p. 311)

the following out of these [rational] considerations is what gives philosophy its peculiar dignity. (p. 313)

2. Paradigms

By far the most important word in Thomas Kuhn's (1962) is 'paradigm,' but there is hardly any systematic articulation on Kuhn's part of how the word is to be used. The only thing close to a definition of it is contained in the preface (again!),[8] and reads as follows:

These [paradigms] I take to be universally recognized scientific achievements that for a time provide model problems and solutions to a community of practitioners. (p. x)

But that this statement is not enough (or is not taken seriously enough in the book) is proved by Kuhn's later acknowledgment that "no aspect of the book is so much responsible [for its excessive plasticity] as its introduction of the term 'paradigm.' " (Kuhn, 1974, p. 459) So in 1969 he went back to work, and in "Second Thoughts on Paradigms" tried to remedy the looseness of his earlier formulations.[9]

The remedy took the following form. What communities of scientific practitioners share is primarily *disciplinary matrices*. These include at least three kinds of elements. First, there are *symbolic generalizations*, that is, "those expressions, deployed without question by the group, which can readily be cast in some logical form" (p. 463). Second, there are *models*, which "provide the group with preferred analogies or, when deeply held, with an ontology" (ibid.). And, finally, there are *exemplars*: "concrete problem solutions, accepted by the group as, in a quite usual sense, paradigmatic" (ibid.). Now 'paradigm' can be understood as referring to the whole of a disciplinary matrix or as referring only to an exemplar: it is this second sense that, according to Kuhn, is the most fundamental. And he proposes to drop the vague word 'paradigm' altogether, and replace it with the new terminology.

In his commentary on Kuhn's paper,[10] Frederick Suppe remarks:

The fact that in (1962) Kuhn repeatedly says that paradigms (*qua* disciplinary matrices) supply the scientist with a perspective for viewing the world, and so forth, strongly suggests that Kuhn views disciplinary matrices *inter alia* as *Weltanschauungen*, and since Kant it has been common to construe *Weltanschauungen* as conceptual frameworks. All of this strongly suggests that disciplinary matrices centrally contain conceptual frameworks—or at least something closely analogous to them. (p. 495)

Kuhn's response to this observation is largely perfunctory. He acknowledges that the notion of a conceptual framework, "when [he] first encountered it, was a source of great liberation from the confines of [the] 'received view,' " but then quickly points out that this notion is infected by plasticity and vagueness, and that, significant and fruitful as it may be, "it provides no resting point" in the philosophy of science (p. 503). I want to argue now that there are good reasons why Kuhn could find no resting point in this notion, for more than simply developing it (as his response suggests he is interested in doing) he was in fact undermining it.[11]

The most substantial part of "Second Thoughts on Paradigms" is devoted to a criticism of the role that is played in the "received view" by correspondence rules. "These," Kuhn says, "have ordinarily been taken to be either operational definitions of scientific terms or else a set of necessary and sufficient conditions for the term's applicability." (p. 467) Either way, correspondence rules sound close to (formulations of) what Frege would have called the *senses* of the relevant terms, and of what we might ordinarily refer to as the concepts associated with them. And in fact, the association of concepts with rules (of precisely the character Kuhn has in mind) has a long tradition. Thus Kant says in the first *Critique*:

> a concept is always, as regards its form, something universal which serves as a rule. The concept of body, for instance, . . . serves as a rule in our knowledge of outer appearances. . . . The concept of body, in the perception of something outside us, necessitates the representation of extension, and therefore representations of impenetrability, shape, etc. (p. 135)

To associate with the term 'body' the relevant concept is to come to expect certain things of the objects to which the term is attached, that is, it is to impose certain necessary and sufficient conditions on those objects, that is, it is to associate the term with a correspondence rule.

But "[v]ery few correspondence rules are to be found in science texts or science teaching" (p. 469). What is to be found there instead is the acquiring of "an arsenal of exemplars" (p. 471) and of an "ability to see resemblances between apparently disparate problems" (ibid.), much the way in which a child learns "to find the animal shapes or faces hidden in the drawing of shrubbery or clouds." (p. 472) *After* this training has had its effect, the philosopher may want to study the examples that did the trick "and derive correspondence rules which . . . make the examples superfluous" (p. 478), but in doing this "he will alter the nature of the knowledge possessed by the community from which his examples are drawn. What he will be doing, in effect, is to substitute one means of data processing for another." (ibid.) And in any case, there is going to be no guarantee that the set of correspondence rules thus generated has anything more than the function of rationalizing *past* experiences.

> Examining the collected examples of past community practice, the philosopher may reasonably expect to construct a set of correspondence rules adequate . . . to account for them all. Very likely he would be able to construct several alternate sets. Nevertheless, . . . though each of his sets of rules would be equivalent with respect to the community's past practice, they need not be equivalent when applied to the very next problem faced by the discipline. (p. 468)

The "received view" thinks that terms "hook up with the world" more or less as follows. Through its association with a concept, a term acquires necessary and sufficient conditions of application, and it applies to whatever satisfies those conditions. Learning the conditions may happen through the mobilization of examples, but once the conditions are finally apprehended, examples become immaterial and so in a way does application itself. By then, one must be able to talk about the conditions themselves, at a "purely conceptual" level, thereby exhausting all there is to the meaning of the relevant term.

According to Kuhn, on the other hand, there will never be a time when this purely conceptual, and at the same time perfectly adequate, talk is possible. What we gain by training is not access to a transcendental level of discourse, but simply the capacity to see some things as similar to others, that is, ultimately, to successfully apply to some things modalities of treatment that originated with other things. When we leave this practical, empirical context, no certainty is left that the words we utter, or the thoughts we think, will ever capture "the essence" of our moves.

Up to a point, this is to reiterate what Kant said (or implied). Independently of examples and illustrations, there is no guarantee that our language makes any sense. But note that there has been a slippage here, in the use of the word 'example,' and one that has central importance for the present discussion. The way Kant uses that word is in the sense of 'example of a concept,' that is, in the sense in which an individual table is an example of the concept *table*. And what he means by insisting on the necessity of examples is that concepts are realized only through their instances, hence without instances there is no guarantee that they are (or can be) realized. In Kuhn's discourse, on the other hand, concepts have no role. A commitment to a symbolic generalization like $f = ma$ is simply the commitment to raising no difficulties to writing these four symbols consecutively on a line, or to manipulating them in certain ways. Models only provide for analogies, and as for exemplars, they are examples in the sense in which, say, Henkin's completeness proof became an example to follow, that is, a (quasi-)concrete object on which to pattern one's practices and which to subject to a number of minimal or not so minimal modifications as the case requires.

3. Spreading the Word

What the "examples" given in the previous two sections suggest is that there are serious problems justifying the legitimacy of an activity of conceptual reflection. One cannot establish that the "results" of such an activity make sense (Kant), or that they have any application to empirical concerns (Kuhn) *if not* by correlating them with a set of practical skills, to be acquired and fine-tuned through proper training.[12] What those examples do *not* bring out, however, is the fact that conceptual reflection is itself a practice, and that no final judgment on its legitimacy can (or should) be passed until we investigate the modalities of its functioning.

Probably no philosopher has devoted more concentrated attention to "philosophical practice" than Ludwig Wittgenstein. The conclusions of his analysis are quite negative; it will be enough to illustrate them with a few quotes.

> When we do philosophy we are like savages, primitive people, who hear the expressions of civilized men, put a false interpretation on them, and then draw the queerest conclusions from it. (*Philosophical Investigations*, p. 79)

> So in the end when one is doing philosophy one gets to the point where one would like just to emit an inarticulate sound. (ibid., p. 93)

Wittgenstein's "official" recommendation, in light of these conclusions, is essentially to quit doing philosophy:

> To the *philosophical* question: "Is the visual image of this tree composite, and what are its component parts?" the correct answer is: "That depends on what you understand by 'composite.' " (And that is of course not an answer but a rejection of the question.) (ibid., pp. 22–23)

> To repeat: don't think, but look! (ibid., p. 31)[13]

And I am not ready to follow his "therapeutic" suggestion.[14] But I think a lot can be learned from this analysis, and in trying to learn from it I want to focus on a suggestive (though obscure) part of it: the statement that philosophy (or the philosopher) ends up being *inarticulate*.

What is it to be (or not to be) inarticulate? What is it to provide an articulation of something? It is to do exactly what Wittgenstein fails to do after the statement in question: to relate it to other statements, to get it involved in a network of linguistic practices, to show (by example) how to handle it so that it is no longer a(n incomprehensible) threat. Beginning students tend to lack this articulation, and consequently to feel insecure about their use of words (or symbols, or tools in general, like arguments). And one helps them overcome these difficulties by "going over" things, by illustrating how tools are applied, by making words on paper "connect" with their everyday activities.

Now what Wittgenstein is suggesting is that philosophers are always in the condition of beginning students. This is why the comparison with primitive people—that is, with people who do not master the ways in which our language is ordinarily articulated—is appropriate; and this is why the "cure" for such a condition consists in reverting to the ordinary use of language and the ordinary state of grown-ups. But is the picture suggested by Wittgenstein credible? Aren't philosophers supposed to be wise, and isn't Wittgenstein ultimately making them into fools?

What I have been calling (by a contamination[15] of Suppe's and Kuhn's terminology) the "received view" will probably find Wittgenstein's picture objectionable. There is an area in which philosophers should feel perfectly at home: the area of conceptual reflection. Just as mechanics are supposed to know a great deal about cars, be skilled at handling them, and make them work when they don't, so philosophers should know a great deal about concepts, and possibly help you find your way in the conceptual universe. Of course, mechanics might be ambitious and want to know more (or more deeply) about (more) cars, but the fact that they can expand their knowledge has no relevance to their being mechanics: they are mechanics insofar as they know (about cars), not insofar as they don't. Similarly, philosophers may continue to research the field, but by such an activity they will (be likely to) find more things, not (necessarily) forget the things that they already know, and that *make* them philosophers.

The rhetorical strategy I have been pursuing so far has had the effect (or at least the intent) of undermining this objection, through the suggestion that there is no (meaningful, independent) conceptual realm for philosophers to inspect and become expert in. So perhaps if we explore this suggestion further, we will be able to "articulate" Wittgenstein's statements in a more plausible way.

Words "make sense" by being correlated with empirical practices, I concluded in the last section. Which means: you get into the habit of using certain words in the context of making certain moves, you come to expect the words when the moves are made, or the moves when the words are uttered. (In fact, one could be even more general, since words are moves, too,[16] and say that one comes to expect certain moves in conjunction with other moves, but in the present discussion I prefer to remain at a lower level of generality.) For example, one is likely to utter (or hear) the word 'table' in connection with the presentation of a spatial object of a certain shape, and in connection with activities of eating or writing or conferring. But now suppose you are suddenly struck by the observation[17] that one can think of language as a table, or perhaps the surface of a table: each point on this surface is a word, and connections of all kinds can be "traced" among points. Then you might begin to use the word 'table' in new (and strange) contexts: you might say "the table is shrinking" when talking about the progressive lack of linguistic sophistication of the new, TV-addicted generation, and possibly few will understand "what you mean." How shall we describe what you are doing in this case?

Begin with the received view once again. You have noticed the fact that language and tables (or their surfaces) fall under a common concept, and lacking a name for this concept you have decided to use 'table' in a metaphorical way to refer to it. Now suppose you give up the received view. What you may be left with is the fact that there are (distinct) linguistic practices associated with 'language' and 'table,' and you are experimenting with mixing them, that is, with using 'table' when one would expect 'language' and vice versa. Note that the slippage from the first to the second construe mirrors the slippage reported earlier between two senses of 'example': in the first construe, tables and language are instances (examples) of a (higher) concept, whereas in the second one tables — or rather, our linguistic practices centered around the word 'table' — are concrete models (examples) on which to pattern (references to) language.

If you are lucky (?), your metaphor will stick and a new context will emerge, one that people will become able to handle as efficiently as they did the old ones. There might even be a new brand of professionals who beat on the metaphor until it dies, acquires "literal meaning," and becomes a source of livelihood. What the professionals will do to achieve this goal is to explore all the resources the metaphor offers: they will talk about the texture of language, and the smoothness of language, and the splinters of language, and perhaps even the legs of language. After some time and effort, there will be no more surprising moves one can make in the area.

But before we get to that stage, before the metaphor is fully *articulated*, even its creator will be in a strange condition of impotence, worse indeed than the condition of a child or a savage, in that he is not simply incompetent to perform an already established system of practices: the system does not exist yet, and may well never exist. Wittgenstein's remarks about philosophical practice can be understood if we think of philosophy as what happens at this primitive stage, before the metaphor dies, before the new practice gets entrenched.

We are used to hearing that all scientific disciplines came out of philosophy. Given that by now we have enough scientific disciplines to cover the universe, the question often arises what is left for philosophy to do? At one point, philosophers were supposed to worry about the structure of the earth and the structure of the mind and pretty much everything else; but now that we have physicists and people in A. I. and all kinds of other experts, what do we need philosophers for? Repeatedly, answers to such embarrassing questions have come in the form of some reference to an activity of conceptual, or logical, or transcendental analysis. Then, when people become disenchanted with the latest answer of this kind, they often tend to put the question on the back burner and continue to do whatever they enjoy doing. Ultimately, there is nothing wrong with that, but since part of what I enjoy doing is to ask myself what philosophy is, I find it interesting to propose the following alternative construe of the genetic role of this "discipline." Philosophy is the exploration of new linguistic practices: when one of them becomes entrenched, and a community of practitioners is established that make a habit out of it, the practice grows out of philosophy. If this picture is accepted, it won't be necessary for philosophy to continue to exist that there be "aspects of reality" yet uncovered by scientific disciplines: it will be enough if there are puns that do not yet fall flat.[18]

One way of summing up my proposal so far might be the following: philosophy is an essentially metaphorical activity. I may accept this (fairly popular)[19] description (which by the way explains the title of the present chapter), but only as provisional, as a step toward what I would judge a more satisfactory formulation. To make one further step in the same direction, I will now indicate what is wrong with the description in question.[20]

Talk of metaphors suggests talk of meanings. The significant battle to be fought in the neighborhood of the word 'metaphor' has to do with the possibility of metaphorical meaning and/or of its counterpart: nonmetaphorical, or literal, meaning. Now, as it turns out, I do not think that there are any meanings, metaphorical or otherwise, hence I think this battle is much ado about nothing.[21] But in the present context I can remain independent of such a thesis and simply point out that, whether or not there are meanings, they have nothing to do with what I am saying, hence, insofar as 'metaphor' is connected with 'meaning' – that is, insofar as the former suggests the use of a word or phrase to *mean* something different from what is normally meant by it – it is best for me to use other terms instead.

What I am saying is that language has a tendency to spread: words resonate in other words, or are "associated" with them. *A posteriori*, it is often possible to find a rationale for the associations: to justify them in terms of resemblances or experiential connections. But the bottom line is: these associations spin in all directions, and they make it possible to "reach" virtually every word from every other word. To a large extent, a successful utilization of language depends on resisting this tendency to spread, on integrating specific linguistic practices into nonlinguistic ones, on making sure that when one says 'slab' a slab is brought to him. But total fixation would be sterile: if the integration and rigidity of practices is defended on the basis of adaptiveness and pragmatic success, then we must remember that a certain amount of mutation is in general desirable, and even necessary, for adaptiveness. So there must be room for experimenting with language, for letting it spread under carefully controlled conditions, since it is from such experiments, from such spreading, that mutant linguistic practices may be occasioned, and eventually become entrenched.

A first step toward this kind of experimenting consists in decontextualizing words, in taking them out of (that is, abstracting them from) the associations they are stuck with, thereby freeing them to manifest all their connecting power. Through this operation of decontextualization we stop paying attention to the standard ways in which a word is used, or at least we stop considering it decisive for the word that it be standardly used in those ways. We sever (some of) the strings the word is attached to, in the process of possibly creating new strings. And the way the new strings are created is by modeling some linguistic practices on other linguistic practices, or, more specifically, by using linguistic practices involving a word A as examples (exemplars, paradigms) for (new) linguistic practices involving a word B associatively linked with A.

Most of the philosophical tradition has described this process of abstracting a word from its ordinary context(s) and utilizing it in deviant ways as moving from an empirical to a conceptual, or transcendental, level of discourse. But we have noticed that the significance, even less the autonomy, of this conceptual level could not sustain Wittgenstein's insistent questioning, and we have discussed a few authors who, maybe not self-consciously, gave unorthodox suggestions about what this talk of "concepts" might ultimately come down to. After words are abstracted from their ordinary contexts – if that is all we do with them – words are good for nothing: what we need to do then is to bring in other words and adapt our ordinary use of them, that is our practices insofar as they involve these words, to those other words that we left hanging in the air. We need to use other words and the practices associated therewith as *examples* for the "abstract" words we

have created; independently of these examples, "reason" cannot "conceive" anything, and no "understanding" is forthcoming.[22]

4. "Normal" Philosophy?

The proposal made in this chapter must face an important objection, which might
receive the following Kuhnian formulation. Even assuming that philosophy has
the "revolutionary" role I assigned to it, why make that its *only* role? Why deny
that there is normal philosophy as much as there is normal science, that is, that
philosophical games can stabilize and be played according to definite rules? Isn't
academic philosophy constituted by precisely these stable games?

My answer to this objection is a natural application of my general position.[23]
Words like 'philosophy' and 'philosopher' are correlated with a number of different linguistic practices, and there certainly is a(n academic) practice in which they
occur in association with clear standards for what counts as a successful argument, an insightful objection, or a valuable paper. But I think that this practice,
in and by itself, is a blind alley,[24] and that pursuing it will have the effect of making people more and more embarrassed to refer to themselves as philosophers,
and more and more willing to replace this characterization with a more "respectable" one; in the first two sections above, I have indicated some of the reasons
for this belief. On the other hand, I also think that a different use of the same
word(s) can perform an important function. This use is not new; in fact, it is nothing more than an explicit articulation of a traditional practice. After all, most of
the philosophers we still find it worth remembering today were not academics,
and/or became known for their new and different ways of looking at things, rather
than for how successfully they solved well-defined problems. So in essence I am
proposing that a linguistic practice involving certain words be preferred to alternative practices involving the same words, and that language be allowed to spread
in one direction rather than another.

However, this is not the whole story of academic philosophy, and to explain
why I find it useful to return to (and properly emphasize) a phrase that I used
above almost in passing. I said there must be room for letting language spread
"under carefully controlled conditions." The qualification is important, in view
of the revolutionary consequences the spreading process is likely to have. Engaging in this process is engaging in letting down the barriers that ordinarily define
our lives, in finding out that things we ordinarily judge necessary (or impossible)
are not. An important reason why humans are so successful, I surmise, is that
they have a medium where they can engage in this process without *necessarily*
suffering its negative impact. Experimenting with language (or with the internal-
ized language of thought) is cheaper and easier than experimenting with things
(or other humans). But note that the distinction between linguistic and other activities, and linguistic and other experiments, does not come as a matter of course:
once the spreading begins, it will not stop by itself in the way we use words.

Most of my adult life I have been perplexed by the following anecdote, which

I read in a newspaper some twenty years ago. In the days of student protest, on one occasion a group of students interrupted a lecture by Theodor Adorno, and some of the female students began stripping to manifest their revolutionary intent. Adorno, one of the foremost proponents of that revolutionary thought which was then finding immediate application in the student movement, left in disgust, claiming that the students were misunderstanding him and that the revolution was a theoretical matter. I do not know to what extent the story is true, but it has acquired a great significance for me, and over the years I have had mixed and conflicting reactions to the various characters in it. The reflections made here give me a better way of sorting out my reactions than I have found before.

There is nothing necessarily wrong with political revolutions or revolutionary violence, but they are not things to be made light of. As much as I believe that the essence of philosophy consists of (the practice of) revolutionary thought, I would not want that thought to be directly and immediately translated into political action. Much more can be said, and probably must be said, than can be done. But given how easily the spreading of language can become a spreading of moves, playing with words in this way is like playing with nuclear energy: a potentially very useful, but also very dangerous, activity. In both cases, you want to play with a great deal of care. And occasionally intellectuals display less than that amount of care. Eager to find their conclusions "relevant" to everyday life, they go straight into preaching; even worse, the people receiving their homilies are not skilled enough at the game to realize that it is only "theoretical," that is, that it is supposed to remain largely at the level of words. So there is a point after all to isolating philosophers in academia and having a long technical training instill in them a deep sense of their deficiencies. We need no such kings or king-makers: what we need from them is a few jokes, and then, when the laughter has subsided, we may think that there was after all a grain of truth—only a grain, though—in what the clown said.

Notes

1. On the other hand, this particular straining process does not begin here. Some of its important precedents will be utilized below.

2. In my (1987) and in Chapter 3 above.

3. In the texts mentioned in note 2 I have concentrated on the second consequence. But it is the first one that is most significant here.

4. See, for example, p. 93 of the *Critique*.

5. Or transformed into another kind of tension, say, one of a *political* nature. See the last section below.

6. This point (irrelevant for present purposes) is argued in detail in my (1987). Note also that one consequence of adopting the *next* attitude is that of questioning the most common use of the expression 'cognitive' (see Chapter 4 above), so these attitudes are more strictly related than it might seem.

7. See, for example, p. 31 of the *Critique*. At the very end of the chapter a suggestion will be offered concerning the practical and moral significance of the distancing involved here (though a suggestion Kant might have resisted).

8. It is not by chance that revealing statements occur so often in the "margins" of the text, as I noted in the preface(!) to my (1987).

9. To be more precise, Kuhn never really ceased to work on his position and described "Second Thoughts on Paradigms" as work in progress. But this paper represents an important step in the progress, partly because it was offered in the context of a symposium (on the structure of scientific theories) which, in Suppe's words, "occurred in the midst of . . . disarray, and thus provides a particularly vivid account of a discipline in search of a new direction." (Suppe, 1974, p. 618)

10. See Suppe (1974), pp. 483–99. See also Kuhn's response on pp. 500–506.

11. It is interesting to note that in his earlier (1957) Kuhn made many of the points that later became central to his (1962) in terms of the notion of a conceptual scheme. I am suggesting here (and will argue for below) that the move from talk of conceptual schemes to talk of paradigms is itself a revolutionary one.

12. The emphasis on practical skills is relevant to Kant, too — in particular to his comments in the *Critique*, in the *Anthropology*, and elsewhere on the faculties of *judgment* and *wit*. I have discussed this issue in my (1987), pp. 201ff.

13. Of course, this official recommendation flies in the face of Wittgenstein's own practice. And occasionally he seems to think that philosophy is not simply to be disposed of. Consider, for example, the following passage from *On Certainty*:

> I believe it might interest a philosopher, one who can think himself, to read my notes. For even if I have hit the mark only rarely, he would recognize what targets I had been ceaselessly aiming at. (p. 50)

14. See Chapter 3 above.

15. 'Contamination' is an interesting word to use here. The sense in which it occurs is that of a blending of linguistic, literary, or mythological traditions. (It was first used in this sense by the Romans, who "contaminated" Greek literature and religion.) But the primary sense of the word, of course, has to do with spreading a disease, that is, with getting something dangerous (which might be useful within the narrow confines of a laboratory) to roam freely about. And the association between these two senses resonates with the major claims of this chapter.

16. See *Philosophical Investigations*, p. 146: "Words are also deeds."

17. One might think that this "representational" metaphor is out of place here, but its presence is inevitable for those who think that the forcing of a new "point of view" (that is, of new linguistic practices) can only be a *gradual* happening. See also note 20 below.

18. When the pun does fall flat (or the metaphor is beaten out of its wits), a new "aspect of reality" may well crystallize, but one that will no longer be the specific competence of philosophy.

19. Derrida (1971) reminds us how popular the connection between metaphysics and metaphor has always been, and then proceeds to deconstruct this connection in a direction analogous to the one I take here. The fundamental difference between such a strategy and mine (as I pointed out in the introduction and Chapter 3 above) is that I think something more can (and should) be done than illustrate the limitations of *other* positions: I intend to *state* a position, though fully aware that it, too, has limitations — that insight requires blindness, as Paul de Man would say (or Wittgenstein for that matter: "Is my understanding only blindness to my own lack of understanding? It often seems so to me." (*On Certainty*, p. 54)) — and that perhaps even I in the future might want to go beyond those limitations. I do not "try to keep myself at the *limit* of philosophical discourse" (Derrida, 1972, p. 6), but well within it. My statements are part of the game (even *this* statement is), perverse and delusive as the game may be.

20. It will become clearer later that the strategy of employing imperfect descriptions at first and then progressively refining them is the only one that offers any hope of success here. For, in the terms to be introduced shortly, language can only spread gradually. I made a similar point in Chapter 1 about the title of *that* chapter.

21. A partial development of this claim can be found in Chapter 5 above.

22. It may be useful to indicate what has become of Kant's notion of "intuitive clearness" after the moves made here. The way in which examples and illustrations make it possible for us to compre-

hend "abstract" notions is by allowing us to anchor dislocated words onto existing practices, thus giving us a sense of how at least to begin to use them. So clearness in the end reduces to familiarity — in Wittgenstein's words again: "Only the accustomed context allows what is meant to come through clearly" (*On Certainty*, p. 31).

23. Or, more in line with my style of expression here, it results from patterning my reaction to the objection to the linguistic practices explored in the rest of the chapter.

24. The qualification "in and by itself" is crucial. It will become clear in the next three paragraphs that the academic practice is not (for me) something independently valuable, but it is an important corrective for a mechanism that might otherwise get entirely out of hand.

9

Free from What?

The phrase 'free logic' was introduced by Lambert (1960), and has come to be used as shorthand for 'logic free from existential assumptions with respect to its singular terms.'[1] The need for such a "liberation" is usually articulated as follows. Natural language contains non-denoting singular terms: empty names like 'Pegasus' and improper descriptions like 'the round square.' Classical logic, on the other hand, allows for no such terms: semantically, this exclusion is sanctioned by the definition of a model as a structure in which every term is to receive an interpretation, and proof-theoretically by the provability of the theorem-schema

(1) $\exists x(x = t)$,

which "says" that, no matter what singular term t is, there is an object which is the denotation of t.

Consistent with this motivation, free logicians have proceeded in the last thirty years or so to revise both the classical semantics and the classical proof-theory of first-order logic.[2] As is usual with nonstandard logics, this activity has resulted in a proliferation of systems, but some of them have proved more stable than others and by now free logic has become a respectable part of the logical landscape. Quantificational modal logics often have a free nonmodal basis,[3] and technical tools originally developed within free logic (most notably, supervaluations) have become popular in many other areas of research. However, in spite of the fact that free logic is a solid citizen of the commonwealth of "philosophical logic," and that the original motivation for the enterprise resonates of classical philosophical themes (truth in fiction, the ontological argument, etc.), philosophical discussions of the foundations of free logic and of the significance of the debate between free and classical logic have been preciously few and often quite superficial,[4] thus possibly generating the impression that the attending problems are marginal, and in any case no longer current. But this impression would be mistaken. The debate concerning nondenoting singular terms is a symptom of a fundamental chasm between two general thinking strategies that have been opposing each other more or less overtly for centuries, and whose significance is bound to emerge again, even from under the veil of the symbolic jargons that many thought could be used to resolve philosophical issues but that, on the contrary, have often ended up hiding them. It is not the only symptom, but it is possibly the clearest; here I want to explore it and show its affinity to another major symptom.

1. Two Paradigms

In his (1892), Frege says:

> Now languages have the fault of containing expressions which fail to designate an object (although their grammatical form seems to qualify them for that purpose) because the truth of some sentence is a prerequisite. (pp. 168–69)

The factual point made in this passage is an important one: essentially, Frege is indicating that there are in natural language relations of (existential) presupposition, and that, consequently, many nominal expressions are not to name anything (and the sentences containing those expressions are not to receive a truth-value, given that this truth-value would have to be a function of the *Bedeutung* of the sentences' components) because of the falsity of (some of) their presuppositions. And I need not elaborate on the fruitfulness of this notion of presupposition in contemporary logic and linguistics. But then why is this important statement of fact accompanied by a negative value judgment? Why is this *feature* of natural languages referred to as a *fault*—and one that, I should add, Frege proceeded to "remedy" in his own "logically perfect" idiom?[5]

The beginning of an answer to these questions can be found in a passage from another of the founding fathers of contemporary logic. In his (1919b), Russell says:

> If ['Romulus'] were really a name, the question of existence could not arise, because a name has got to name something or it is not a name, and if there is no such person as Romulus there cannot be a name for that person who is not there, so that . . . if you think of ['Romulus'] as a name you will get into logical errors. (pp. 208–9)

It is on the basis of this argument that Russell claims that the grammatical form both of 'Romulus' (and all other "grammatically proper" names) and of the sentences containing it is deceptive, that 'Romulus' and the like are *really* "truncated or telescoped description[s]" (ibid.), and that his theory of definite descriptions is necessary to bring order and transparency within the delusive world of grammatical appearances. In the course of our discussion, we will eventually reach a new understanding of this philosophical program, but for the moment I am interested in showing how far the crucial argument brought out in the passage above depends on the adoption of a specific point of view on the relation between language and world, in the following precise sense: that the argument sounds quite reasonable if that point of view is adopted, but entirely unconvincing if we look at things from a different perspective.

To begin with, a qualification. The two points of view—or "paradigms"—to be discussed here are not directly relevant to what is true or false, to what exists or doesn't, or to what is or is not a proper name. All those are factual matters, which I presume to be beyond the scope of the present discussion. The two paradigms are directly relevant to *what it is* to be true or false, *what it is* to be a name or an object, and *what it is* to exist. *Prima facie*, it is entirely possible that supporters of the two paradigms agree on all the same facts and factual judgments, since their disagreement invests only the *concepts* of (among other things) a fact and a factual judgment, not the *extensions* of those concepts. On the other hand, it is also possible that such conceptual debates have factually relevant consequences, if one party or the other is forced to admit that something that could and perhaps does ordinarily pass as a fact *cannot* possibly (that is, analytically) be one: it is usually at this point that the deceptive appearance ploy is thrown into the contest.

So consider the first paradigm, that I will call the transcendental realist's. There the concept of an object is the (conceptual) starting point, which means that it is not (necessarily[6]) to receive any analysis or elaboration. We may want to say, à la Aristotle, that an object is what exists in the primary sense, but such an account takes us only one station further around a circle, since within the paradigm in question *existing (in the primary sense)* is precisely *existing as an object*. Objects have properties and bear relations to one another: on the basis of which properties they have and which relations they bear to one another, they can be classified. An especially important class of objects is that of *subjects*, which are intelligent, reflective beings, and an important property subjects have is that of *experiencing*. To some extent, this experiencing mirrors objects, and a fundamental philosophical project, within this paradigm, is that of finding the conceptual conditions (if any) at which such mirroring is successful.

Switch now to the other paradigm, that of the transcendental idealist. Here the starting point is experience(s): we need not (and *can*not) explain what an experience is because we have nothing conceptually prior to it in terms of which to carry out the explanation. Experiences have a subject, that is, they are always experiences *from a point of view*; in addition, some of them have an (intentional) object, they are directional as it were. And experiences are related to one another: on the basis of such relations—specifically, of relations like mutual consistency and connectedness—some of them qualify as *veridical*, and their objects, if they have objects, as *existent*. Thus a long conceptual story must be told here before the notion of an existent object—or object *simpliciter*—can be introduced, and then this notion has received through the conceptual story a detailed analysis, just as in the other paradigm a long conceptual story is needed to introduce (and, simultaneously, explain) the notion of (an) experience.

Before we can show the relevance of this contrast to the subject at hand, an additional step is in order. I introduced the two paradigms, in line with their most important historical source, by using the psychological jargon of the relation between experience(s) and objects (or world). In the linguistic jargon that is so popular these days, it would be natural to present it instead in terms of the relation between *language* or *discourse* and world, that is, to think of subjects as primarily involved (not so much in experiencing but rather) in *talking about* objects. Instead of the (intentional) objects of experience(s), then, we would be concerned with the (intentional) objects of discourse, and the existence of such objects would be conceptualized in terms of the consistency and connectedness not of a set of experiences but of a set of *sentences*. Since the contrast between free and classical logic is located within a linguistic horizon, from now on I will adopt this more fashionable jargon; in particular, this means that in the transcendental idealist's paradigm I will take *language*, not experience, to be the conceptual starting point.

Take now the first paradigm, and ask yourself how we can think of a *name* in it: how, that is, we can explain what a name is by starting out with the notion of an object. There are two basic options, which for our purposes come to the same thing. On the one hand, we can think of a name as a property of an object: for example, we can think of 'Alexander the Great' as a property of Alexander the Great. On the other, we can think of a name as an object in its own right, say, a series of sounds or marks on paper, but then to qualify this object *as a name* we must require that it have a relation of *nomination* with an object; otherwise, it would remain a series of sounds or ink blots. And here comes the important consequence of it all. For properties and relations are conceptually dependent on (their) objects: we cannot even begin to explain what a property or a relation is without referring to the object(s) of (or among) which it holds. We cannot even begin to explain how the *property* 'Alexander the Great' could belong to no object at all, or how the *relation* of nomination could hold between the *object* 'Alexander the Great' and nothing else. So what if there were no object Alexander the Great? Then 'Alexander the Great' could not *possibly* be a name, for *conceptual* reasons; in Russell's words again, "a name has got to name something or it is not a name." In general, it is a conceptual (analytical, logical) truth within this paradigm that names denote, and if a language allows for expressions that look and (seem to) work like names but do not denote, that language is at fault. To repair which fault, we have two major options: the Fregean one of defining another, more "perfect" language, and the Russellian one of claiming that grammatical appearances do no justice to true "logical form."

On the other hand, consider the second paradigm, and ask yourself there what a name is. The difference is that your answer must not begin by mobilizing the notion of an object: it is not the world but language that constitutes the conceptual starting point. Thus the following would be (a good approximation to[7]) a reasonable answer:

(2)   A name (or nominal expression) is an expression that can occur as sub-
      ject in a singular sentence.

At this point, we may want to say that every name "purports to" name an object
and that some succeed in doing so, but no conceptual problem is going to arise
concerning those that do not succeed *because names are no longer conceptualized
in terms of properties of objects or relations among them.* We may decide that
some of them are properties of, or bear relations with, (other) objects, but now
this is going to be a *factual* matter, which has no influence on what it is to be a
name. A name has *not* got to name something in order to be a name; rather, it
has to have a certain role in language.

We are ready to draw a first conclusion from our investigation. Classical and
free logic go hand in hand with two opposing conceptual frameworks. Within
one, language is thought of as an appendage of the world, and parts of language
are identified on the basis of how they fit parts of the world. Specifically, names
are names *of objects*, and empty names are not simply useless or awkward or dis-
pensable: they are an absurdity. Within the other, the world is thought of as one
of many possible objectives of language, and parts of language are identified on
the basis of their mutual relations. Thus, whereas nothing prevents a name from
being the name of an object, there is no analytical necessity that this be the case:
empty names are a respectable component of logical space.

2. Semantics

The most serious problem in the development of free logic has been that of coming up with a semantics for it. It is not that this enterprise per se was especially
difficult, but, curiously, the solutions that proved the simplest and most powerful
from a technical point of view left workers in the field somewhat dissatisfied and
inclined to favor instead more cumbersome and less effective developments. We
are now in a position to understand the reasons for such dissatisfaction and inclination.

There are three major avenues in free semantics, which in my (1986) I labeled
outer domain, conventional, and supervaluational, respectively. Briefly, outer
domain semantics assigns nonexistent objects as denotations to empty names,
whereas the other two leave them empty. Conventional semantics proceeds then
to assign truth-values to sentences containing such names on the basis of some
convention or other, whereas supervaluational semantics assigns a truth-value to
one of these sentences if (and only if) that is the truth-value the sentence would
have *were the names occurring in it not empty* (and no matter what they were the
names of). A strong completeness theorem is provable for outer domain and conventional semantics. Supervaluational semantics, on the other hand, cannot go
beyond weak completeness: the set of supervaluationally valid arguments is not
recursively enumerable. In spite of this limiting result and of its many complications, this semantics is considered by many the most philosophically satisfactory

of the three, and apparently researchers held back from pursuing or publishing completeness results utilizing alternative approaches because of philosophical worries about their significance.[8]

Consider now this rather confusing situation from the point of view of the philosophical discussion in Section 1. Take conventional semantics first. In it, no logical analysis of atomic sentences containing non-denoting singular terms is provided, whereas one is provided for atomic sentences *not* containing such terms: truth-values are assigned to the former sentences by *fiat*, and then these truth-values are combined according to the usual truth-conditions for complex sentences. Why this invidious treatment? Clearly, there must be something strange or defective in non-denoting singular terms and in predications containing them, something that prevents us from looking into the structure of these predications to find there the basis for whatever judgment we intend to pass on their truth-value, and requires us to utilize instead a different, more superficial *sort* of truth-condition – which ultimately means: a different notion of truth. But from the point of view of (the paradigm germane to) the free logician there is nothing strange or defective about non-denoting singular terms, at least nothing *logically* strange or defective: it is a simple matter of fact that some singular terms do not denote, and one that should have no impact on logical investigations, and in particular on our search for a unified truth-theory.[9]

On the other hand, consider outer domain semantics. Formulating a semantics ultimately means *explaining* why one takes certain forms of argument to be correct and certain sentences to be logically true, and there is no denying that an explanation is better if it can be understood by a larger audience. So suppose that you are a free logican, and that you want to use outer domain semantics to explain to the classical logician why a certain sentence *A* containing some empty names is logically true. You start out by saying something like: "Well, take any possible world whatever, and consider its existent and its nonexistent objects." Insofar as he is committed to the transcendental realist's paradigm, your interlocutor should stop you right there, and ask you: "What do you mean by 'nonexistent objects'? What are you talking about?" Insofar as he is a realist, he *cannot* understand what you are talking about,[10] for (as I have argued in Chapter 2) about the notion of a nonexistent object much the same battle is fought as about that of an empty name: the former, too, is a notion that makes perfectly good sense within transcendental idealism but becomes an absurdity within its realist counterpart. Which explains two things at once: first, why it is that outer domain semantics for free logic is so easy (they express the same point of view, hence one fits the other quite naturally), and second, why its very originators were often not happy with this semantics. Because it is conceptually very close to the paradigm on which free logic is based, outer domain semantics will not help explain to supporters of the alternative paradigm what free logicians are after. Whereas the strategy of conventional semantics can be understood only from the realist's point of view, hence from a point of view that vanifies the enterprise of *free* semantics, the strategy of outer domain semantics is unintelligible to the realist, hence its outcome is not much of a free *semantics* after all.

Finally, consider supervaluational semantics. It does not require us to add nonexistent objects to any model, and the way in which it accounts for the truth (or falsity) of a given sentence is ultimately the same as in classical logic: by means of a "correspondence" with reality. Of course, not all is the same as in classical logic; otherwise, the result would be classical logic once again. But the "deviant" steps one is required to take in order to generate this new tool are minimal, and familiar ones as well. First, when well-formed parts of a sentence A receive no truth-value because they contain some empty names, we look for the other models (or "possible worlds") in which those names are not empty,[11] and combine the truth-values the well-formed parts in question have there with what we already know about A.[12] Then, we simply extend to (the general case of) truth application of a device whose use is common with *logical* truth: that of taking the logical product of a number of alternative possibilities. The result of all this may look exceedingly complicated, but the important point is that the *conceptual tools* used, though they are *combined* in new, perhaps even revolutionary ways, are essentially the same as in classical logic, so that the classical logician can understand what you are talking about. In the same way, you can ordinarily understand a new, perhaps even surprising, sentence if you know the words it is composed of.

Thus, ultimately, the superiority that many attribute to supervaluational (free) semantics over its competitors is due to the fact that it allows one to *translate* one point of view into the other better than its competitors do. For people who already espouse the transcendental idealist perspective that free logic reflects, outer domain semantics is a natural tool, though perhaps there are even more natural ones.[13] But given that classical logic and the transcendental realist perspective *it* reflects are still the more popular alternative, a semantical account that makes the enterprise of free logic understandable to the opposition is to be preferred. For after all, the point of semantics is that of *interpreting*, and an interpretation is always, more or less, a translation into a different jargon, which is more useful the more extensive the use of this jargon is.

3. Necessity

Within the semantics of modal logic, there are two major ways of conceiving possible worlds. One, that goes back at least to the *Tractatus*, thinks of possible worlds as alternative ways *these objects*, the objects existing in *this world*, could have evolved: call it the *counterfactual* conception. The other[14] thinks instead of possible worlds as structures our language could be used to describe: call it the *descriptive* conception.

According to the counterfactual conception, another possible world might be such that in it *this table* is red instead of brown, oval instead of rectangular, or not in this room, but it would be silly to ask, concerning such a world, *which* of the objects existing there is this table, for the answer is as clear as it is trivial:

it is *this table*. According to the descriptive conception, on the other hand, another possible world might well contain tables and rooms and people, but it is not at all clear whether it even makes sense to ask which (if any) of these objects is (the same as) this table, this room, or me. A whole range of possibilities is open here: according to an extreme one[15] no two things in distinct possible worlds are ever the same, not even if they are totally indistinguishable, whereas a number of milder options try to come up with reasonable "conditions of identification through possible worlds."

There is an interesting connection between these two conceptions of a possible world and the two paradigms discussed in Section 1. The counterfactual conception is a natural extension of the transcendental realist's point of view. The starting point there is objects, *the* objects that there are, and there is a limit to how far thought can play with them and devise "mental experiments" involving them. It can reclassify them, redistribute conceptual specifications among them, but cannot lose its grip on them or it will end up hanging helplessly in the air. Logic has a solid base in ontology. The descriptive conception, on the other hand, is just as naturally associated with transcendental idealism. For there we begin with language, and a world is simply an intentional structure to which (some) language is directed. And just as a long story must be told to explain how a member of one of these intentional structures (an object) can be taken to *exist*, a long story is necessary to account for the *identity* of such an object with itself.

This mutual connection can instructively illuminate a technical issue and a historical curiosity. We know by now that classical quantification theory is the logic of the transcendental realist, and free quantification theory the logic of the transcendental idealist. Thus we would expect that classical quantification theory *forces* one to accept the counterfactual conception of possible worlds, and free quantification theory makes it possible instead to go with the descriptive conception.[16] And this is exactly what happens. If propositional S5 – the system that more than any other is taken to express analytical necessity – is superimposed on classical quantification theory, both Barcan formulas become provable, which amounts to saying, semantically, that the domains of all possible worlds must be identical: what can exist, exists necessarily. On the other hand, neither Barcan formula is provable within free quantified S5: in both proofs, a crucial role is played by the Schema of Specification

(3) $\forall x A \supset A(t/x)$,

whose rejection is (proof-theoretically) the first and major step in the move from classical to free quantification theory. Semantically, this means that the possible worlds of free quantified S5 are entirely open regarding what they contain, that is, regarding whether the same or distinct objects occur in them.

And now for the historical curiosity. In 1963, while looking for a way of blocking the proof of the Barcan formulas, Saul Kripke called in question the Schema of Specification, which he formulated as

(4) $\forall x A \supset A(y/x)$.

He did not go all the way to claiming that the presence of this schema in classical logic meant that there was something wrong with this logic, however. What he did claim is that (4) was not being "interpreted" correctly. According to him, the correct interpretation of (4) was the "generality interpretation," which read 'y' not as a free parameter — a place-holder for any singular term — but as a universally bound variable. In other words, he meant that the correct reading of (4) was

(5) $\forall y(\forall xA \supset A(y/x))$.

As it turns out, neither Barcan formula is provable if (4) is "read as" — or, more properly, replaced by — (5). But the interesting thing is that the substitution of (5) for (4) is a crucial step in the construction of a "pure" free quantification theory, that is, a free quantification theory without identity and without a special existence sign. Now the first few systems of free logic were formulated in a language with either identity or the existence sign,[17] but in the same year, 1963, Karel Lambert, in total independence from Kripke and from modal considerations, gave the first pure free logic by proposing precisely the substitution in question. Working in different areas and with (apparently) different problems in mind, these two authors arrived almost simultaneously at the same system. The discussion carried out here shows that it was no coincidence. Their problems were not really so different, since they were but aspects of one and the same conceptual tension: the same tension essentially that existed between the before and the after of what has gone down in history as Kant's Copernican revolution.

Notes

1. Lambert's original intentions included an (existential) analysis of *general* terms as well. Some moves in this direction have been made recently by Lambert and myself in our (1986).

2. For an account of these developments, see my (1986).

3. See, for example, Fine (1978).

4. Among the few exceptions to this superficiality, I will mention at least Lambert (1981, 1983).

5. See his (1893).

6. The reason there is often such an elaboration, I surmise, is that the two paradigms are ultimately theoretical constructs, and every individual philosophical system is to some extent a compromise between them. See also note 10 below.

7. A more precise answer would require (among other things) a characterization of singular sentences, with special regard to the fact that many sentences with the verb in the singular are, in fact, universal. But all of this can be done, in terms (for example) of which transformations of a given sentence are legitimate.

8. This seems to have been the case for Belnap and Lambert. See my (1986).

9. In this sense, a semantics that simply left all sentences containing non-denoting singular terms truth-valueless because it judged that they were missing a(n empirical) component of a truth-value would be preferable to one that assigns truth-values to (some) such sentences on the basis of a special treatment. But, of course, the former would have a hard time extending to non-denoting singular terms *any* logical law, which is a major reason many try the uneasy compromise generating conventional semantics.

10. But probably nobody is *only* a transcendental realist (or idealist): the struggle I am describing is one often fought with oneself.

11. In view of the developments in the next section, it is important to emphasize that these other models need not contain any additional objects: it is enough if more of their objects have (more) names.

12. Note that sentences not containing non-denoting singular terms are trivial, vacuous cases of the application of this procedure, but still the same procedure is applied to *all* sentences: there are no preferential treatments here.

13. Such is the case, I believe, for semantics that utilize the framework (not of set theory but) of category theory, since the latter does not begin with the notion of an object (as set theory does, especially in the popular "cumulative" conception), but, rather, defines an object as a (degenerate) kind of arrow.

14. It is more difficult to associate this conception with any one definite author, though its origins are unmistakably related to the origins of model theory (hence, to the formalist school).

15. See Lewis (1968).

16. To make the parallelism clearer, note that making it possible to go with the descriptive conception is also in a way forcing it on us, for it is hard to see on what other *logical* grounds (i.e., other than their derivability in classical quantificational logic + S5) one might defend adoption of the Barcan formulas.

17. See Leblanc and Hailperin (1959), and Hintikka (1959). Incidentally, Kripke (1963) mentions these papers, but then goes on to assert that "the difficulty can be solved without revising quantification theory or modal propositional logic." (p. 68 footnote)

10

The Phantom of Liberty

Caesar de his causis quas commemoravi Rhenum transire decreverat.

(*De Bello Gallico*, IV 17)

Mr. Smith has just been hypnotized, and told that upon waking up he will have to go to the window and close it. He wakes up and is asked a number of questions about his experience. As he answers them, he becomes restless and distracted, until finally he can no longer resist the urge he feels: he gets up, goes to the window and closes it. The hypnotist asks him what the matter is; Mr. Smith answers that he was getting cold. He is undoubtedly sincere, has no notion of the post-hypnotic suggestion he is under, and is truly shivering.

There are three major points of view on this incident. One is Mr. Smith's: for him, what happened (*what he did*) is a typical instance of planned, deliberate, purposeful behavior on his part. He was getting cold and uncomfortable, considered carefully the pros and cons of making a move in that unfamiliar and somewhat threatening environment, and finally decided in favor of the preservation of his health. Another point of view is the hypnotist's: for him, there is nothing *Mr. Smith* did. He was used as an instrument, virtually as an extension of the hypnotist's arm; it was the hypnotist who decided what was to be done, so the action belongs to him. And then there is the third point of view: that of the hypnotist's hypnotist, who predetermined all of this a long time ago, in a galaxy many light years away. . . .

A number of questions are suggested by this example. Most of them I am not interested in. Specifically, I am not interested in which (if any) of the characters is right (or justified) in thinking the way he does, I am not interested in whether or not we have any reason to believe that what *we* take to be cases of deliberate, purposeful behavior on our part could turn out instead to be the progeny sprung up in full armor from somebody else's head, or in whether or not we are ever going to be in a position to prove that some such behavior is really ours. For my present purposes, I will simply concede that the (evil?) hypnotist's hypnotist has arranged it all from day one, and that all we (believe we) do is nothing but the mechanical spinning out of that primordial design. On the basis of this (depressing?) hypothesis, I will then proceed to raise a different, quasi-semantical query: what is it for all of us Smithlike characters to consider ourselves free agents, behaving in accordance with *our* plans? What is the role played by the phantom of liberty in the scheme of things? What difference does it make?

1. A Place in the Sun

Thomas Nagel (1976) says that, under the pressure of deterministic considerations, "the area of genuine agency . . . seems to shrink . . . to an extensionless point." (p. 35) The problem of free will, then, is the problem of whether and how this area can be extended, or, in other words, whether and how one can find *room* for oneself in the world. I find this metaphor suggestive, but must hasten to point out a crucial ambiguity in it. When my friend Scrooge gave me an old, monumental couch for my birthday, the problem presented itself of finding room for it in my one-bedroom apartment: it is not in this sense that our search for freedom is a search for space. It is, rather, in the sense in which Scrooge later told me that one must find room for entertainment in life: as opposed to that of dealing with his cumbersome furniture, the latter task requires not only inventiveness but also interpretation, for as part of it one must determine *what* entertainment *is* and *what it is* to find room for it. I for one would not be satisfied with contemplating my gold pieces.

But let us go one step at the time and begin with what happened last Sunday at the pizza parlor. I had my mouth open, ready to take another juicy bite, when all of a sudden I thought of all the small universes pulsating on the top of my fork, of their planets and orbits and energy levels. The thought was so vivid that for an instant I literally did not see the crimson red of the tomato juice and the fluffy white of the bread, but photons crossing the micro-sidereal world and hitting colorless particles. I experienced nausea of the Sartrean variety, quickly switched from eating to heavy drinking, and by the end of the night I had gotten into the other kind of disturbance, the one that induces vomit. I had probably overworked myself in thinking how best to get promoted, I concluded later, but as an unintended result of such improper self-administration I had finally *felt*, not simply (and vainly) chatted about, the fact that it takes considerable if usually subterranean work to keep ordinary things from falling apart. Descartes recommended God as the exorcist of this Grand Obliteration, whereas Kant preferred to put it in the more respectable chemical terms of a transcendental synthesis, and both ended up sending their followers the wrong way. But once we get rid of noise in the channel, their message sounds loud and clear: to conceptualize the possibility of saying that there is a pizza in my plate, rather than (or, if you prefer, in addition to) its atomic or subatomic parts or their parts etc., one must mobilize reference to the *action* of *choosing* this manner of speaking, among the indefinitely many alternative ones that would be equally justified by the available data. Where reference to an action is reference to the possibility of *beginning* a course of events without being necessitated to do so by the current state of affairs.[1]

Mind you: nothing would necessarily *happen* if we denied the reality of this action. Tragedies like the one on Sunday are rare, and their significance probably misunderstood by a frustrated, buzzing intellect: more likely than not, my stomach was upset to start with, say by the department meeting, and *it* caused the visions, not the other way around. Whatever I want to call what is on my plate, whatever I want to call the plate, and whatever I want to call what I do to it, I would still do it, and the same consequences would follow. In the end, what I call things makes no difference to what they are. It makes a lot of difference, however, to how I *tell the story* of what they are and what happens to them, for it provides me with the nouns and the verbs that are the basic elements of my description.

Shall we go one step further and say that, since an action is required, an *agent* is required, too? Not so fast: the logical possibility is still open of causal chains that have beginnings but no beginners, that begin *randomly*. This important possibility will be addressed in a moment; as a preliminary to that move, we need to ask now who the agent would have to be *if* there were an agent. The manducating embarrassment who could not hold his alcohol? Not directly, and not necessarily (but see below). If the action demanded here is the action of telling a story, one of many stories that could be told about the same facts, then the agent required is a story *teller*, someone who decides in favor of a certain level of analysis and then proceeds to analyze the events at that level. This narrator need not be *aware* of his decision, or of its being a decision: what I am talking about is conceptual, not phenomenological necessity. And there need be no event of deliberation or determination that occurs (consciously or unconsciously) *before* the telling of the story: the priority I am discussing is logical, not chronological (the kind of priority a given *choice* of axioms has on the theorems deducible from them, even though the axioms are ordinarily chosen long after (some of) the theorems are proved). In short, what I am saying is that, for it to be possible to give a philosophical account—within philosophical reflection—of the fact that a certain description of the data is "synthesized" (and leaving chance aside for the moment), one need refer to the synthetic activity of a narrator, and to his act of (freely) choosing the vocabulary of the description.[2] This act adds nothing to the universe, but finds "a place" for something, in the sense of drawing the map where places are to be found.

2. Reflections in an I

In the Refutation of Idealism and elsewhere, Kant makes the all-important point that self-consciousness per se is not a form of knowledge. It provides certainty of the existence of *something*, but no notion of *what* that something *is* and consequently no evidence that it is *the same something* at different times. The possibility of self-consciousness is part of the structure of experience: it makes for the fact that experience has a subject, that it is always experience from a point of view. But this subject has no privileged cognitive status with respect to the (other) things experience is experience *of*: it does not immediately translate into an *object* of experience.[3] To make self-consciousness objective the same moves are necessary as with consciousness of what is not self: spatio-temporal coordinates must be brought to bear upon the issue, a *body* must be identified, and this body inserted in a network of causal interactions with other bodies. In the more deviant, quasi-literary terms favored here, the narrator is in no better shape than the (other) characters of the story vis-à-vis the predicament discussed in Section 1: it, too, has no "absolute" place in the story, and for it to be something there one must postulate the same act of "primordial" choice which is vital to pizzas and other paraphernalia.

Turning to details, consider two different ways of telling the same (?) story.[4] One goes: "Mr. Smith got up and closed the window." The other: "*I* got up and closed the window." In both cases, the story teller describes the wanderings of a given human body, and in both cases, were it not for that body, or if you will for that aggregate of water and assorted minerals, he would be talking about nothing definite, and could not be said to *know* what he is talking about. But the second way of telling the story adds something crucial to it, since the use of 'I' establishes an identification between the story teller and a character. They are one and the same: the same body, the same aggregate of water and minerals, or whatever. It is the story teller who closes the window; the story is his own, it is the story of *his* closing the window. In the vocabulary of the story, the narrator is describing (hence has constituted, has found a place for) himself—*the self.*

If identifications like this are possible, then there *must* be a story teller with whom to identify, the story must be told by someone, and the option of letting blind chance (that is, nothing at all) direct the proceedings is ruled out. A form of life expressed by a language in which there is room for the pronoun 'I' is forced by the logic of that pronoun to find room for narrators, too. Which, of course, does not mean that there is something wrong with randomness or (God forbid!) with quantum physics; it means, rather, that the generalized application of randomness to the specific problem of initiating world descriptions would eventually bring about the obsolescence of first-person pronouns, and the development of a *different* form of life. *How* different that would be, that is, what is the role that the subject plays in *our* scheme of things, is a problem I leave for another day.[5]

So there must be a story teller as things (or rather, words) go, and it must be conceptualized as a free agent: more precisely, his selection of a code in which to phrase the story must be conceptualized as an act of choice. He must "construct" the narrative universe by bringing certain things together and keeping others apart, and unless it is so constructed, unless it is "gone through in a certain way, taken up, and connected,"[6] the universe will remain an undetermined "manifold," to which no member of an indefinitely large set of descriptions is more adequate than any other. Also, since the story teller recognizes himself as one of the characters of the story, by the indiscernibility of identicals that character must be assigned the same freedom.[7] And here we (by the way, we *who*? – or shall we say, more safely, "reason"?) precipitate in the darkness of an antinomy. For insofar as it is the behavior of an ordinary, middle-sized object, the I's behavior must be conceived as susceptible of explanation, that is, one must be able to ask why-questions about it and answers to them must be considered possible (which, one question after the other, will eventually take us beyond the spatio-temporal scope of any character in any story – unless what we are telling is the Bible or something of the sort, more about this later). And on the other hand, insofar as the nature of a free agent is attributed to it, that is, insofar as it is not any old object but is *the I*, this character must be conceived as capable of absolutely initiating a series of events.

The result of this tension is oscillation. One moment this body is the actor and nothing forces it to do what it is doing: witness the absence of chains and manacles and rope. Another moment there are invisible chains in society and education pulling it with the same effectiveness of the iron ones, and it would be impossible for it to move any differently. And then nothing could force you to accept the rules of society and education, to make them *yours*, if you didn't *want to*, and then again how could you *not* have wanted, given the way you are? One moment there is pain in my tooth and nothing could be more mine than that; another "this body is not really me," and I am ready to ally instead with a social class, or a psychic compartment, or absolute spirit.[8] And there will even be times when I say, "I have not chosen my vocabulary (or my world), it's been forced on me," but still this sentence is part of a story (maybe the last one before endless silence), a story that is what it is and not something else, that uses certain words and not others, and a story that is told by someone, by a narrator, an I, just like those other more conventional ones, hence poses exactly the same problems, and *im*poses exactly the same conditions, as they did. Which conditions, in any case, are not the end of the matter. In the Kantian universe where the present discourse takes place, necessities are no consolation and no resting point. Knowing that we must find a reference for the first-person pronoun does not mean that we can, and to prove that we can it is not enough to put words together: *real* possibility requires the establishing of a correlation between those words and empirical structures, that is, in the end, a proof of *actuality*.[9] With the result that, when the conditions imposed by the words are in direct conflict with the rules dominating (or indeed: defining) the scope of the empirical – and the present is a case in point, in view of the tension between freedom on the one hand and that causal necessity which is a crucial coordinate of objectivity on the other – what we are left with is an endless dialectic and a perpetual puzzle, and the alternative between living with it and changing the rules of the game (if indeed we can!).

Nor is this the *only* dialectic in the vicinity. According to Kant, a necessary condition of any description of an object is that it be possible that more than one object receive that description.[10] An object is categorially different from its properties, even from the complex property which is the sum of all of them: it cannot reduce to that property – or any property – without ceasing to be an object. Even if there is in fact only one object of a certain kind, it must be possible that there are other objects of the same kind, or the object would be nothing but a kind. So, if there is a free object, it must be possible that there are several of them; if there is a true agent, an object which acts and is not just acted upon, it must be possible that there are several such agents. But such agents are subjects of experience, narrators, primordial originators of a vocabulary in which to tell the world. Then it must be possible that there are other experiences just like this one, other stories, other primordial choices, other points of view. The identification between the story teller and a character implies not only the problematic injection of freedom into the story, but also the necessity of an equally problematic postulation of the existence, and the freedom, of the Other. To put it in a slogan, *my* freedom could not be my *freedom*: my freedom can only be conceived within a community of free agents. And here is another unsolvable problem – indeed, if possible, an even more serious one.

For consider: where shall I find this Other whose existence and freedom I need to give significance to my own existence and freedom, how shall I make it concrete and real? If I decide, at a certain stage of the first dialectic, to identify the narrator of my story with a certain human body, it will be natural to look for bodies much like that one, to reflect myself in something similar to me. But who tells me what the criteria of likeness must be? Who decides what the *relevant* similarities are? Is it necessary and sufficient to have a physical structure comparable to mine and to utter intelligible sounds? What if some of the limbs are missing? What if the color of the skin is different, or the sexual apparatus? And what if roughly the same behavioral functions can be performed by something very *very* different, say a bee, or a computer? Also, in my own case I have both sides of the problem: the inside and the outside, the narrator and the story, and it is only(!) a matter of matching them. Here, on the other hand, all I have is the outside, and it is always possible that there is *no* inside to match. No matter how similar another body is to mine, even if it is an exact replica of it, there is no way of establishing that a soul inhabits it, that it is not a mad scientist's ingenious creation. And if that ever proves to be the case, I must have some other candidate ready, some other community of which I can be a part, so I must continue to search. I must, that is, provided I can.

3. The Will to Power

With all its complications, the (meta)story I told so far is a good-natured one, and one that encourages hope for continuous, healthy progress. Toil and sweat will be needed on our way West, but the land there is fertile and the water clear, and there is more of both than you can imagine. Perhaps so, but, aside from the little problem of the Indians (which we can solve by adopting the bear's attitude toward a hive), there is less of either than we need. The Pacific Ocean is getting near, and lands across it are not so hospitable (those people think of themselves as the bears); regrettably, we have hit upon the villain of the story and the spoiler of our hopes.

The "construction" process we have contemplated in the first two sections looks like a (paleo?)-capitalist's dream: indefinite "room" can be found in it for new building and new profiting, the ways of the ego are infinite, and everyone is going to get richer and richer, *that is*, happier and happier. We know by now that these dreams easily turn sour, and we know why: the pyramid game cannot work on a finite supply of participants. *Finitude* makes the game a fraud.

If experience were (conceptualized as) infinite—the experience of (a) God— every act of choice would have only a positive significance. For the specific choices we are interested in, it would consist in the bringing to life of new, not yet actualized, possibilities of "reading," and making sense of, the world, and it would be natural to think that the more the merrier, that a general confusion is very creative, or some other such amenity. When time and resources are conceived as limited, on the other hand, every choice is also to be thought of as an act of negation and repression: the unactualized possibilities are in competition for realization, and those that win make it harder for the others to find their place. If experience is finite, it becomes necessary to conceive every (free) act of selecting a level of analysis of reality (and a vocabulary appropriate to that level) as also an act of favoring such a level (and vocabulary) *against* all the alternative ones that did not carry the day.

But this finite character is precisely what the search for a community of agents brings with it. I will never be able to experience the death of *this* body, *my* death is beyond my horizon, it is what defines the horizon, the ever receding boundary that *I* can't cross, but I am a witness to the death of others, of (some of) those others that I labeled relevantly similar to me, that I included in the range of subjects—and this happens often enough to convince me that it is no accident. I am a witness to their death and to their birth; I must admit that their experience is bounded on both sides, that it has a beginning and an end, and if theirs does, mine does, too. So my experience must be conceived as finite. Not that I understand what it means, but still grammar requires I do: it requires that I try to find some empirical significance for the new "transcendental" condition thus uncovered—in the fading of forces and attention maybe, in nightly slumbers, in the unfathomable depths of memory.

In the presence of finitude, the narrative appropriation of the world becomes entangled with issues of struggle and with conflicting evaluations—just as economic appropriation does in the presence of scarcity. A necessary connection is established between *being* and *power*: what I (decide I) am forces out all other things I could have been instead, for the time being, and since my time is not boundless, some of these things are forced out for good. Consequently, a political problem is posed, in the sense in which politics is the art (and the tragedy) of the acquisition and administration of power, and the logical space is opened for the application of political strategies to its solution: strategies of dividing and conquering, or of invoking unification, or of utilizing scapegoats and traditional values. Where the object of all such maneuvers, it will be recalled, is in the first place the population of possible me's, and then also that of the (possible) characters that have enough of a relevant resemblance with the possible me's.

Thus, inevitably, my choice comes to involve blame, justification, and responsibility: the blame of those who didn't make it, the responsibility of being the one (or one of the few[11]) who did, and the desire to prove that in some sense I had to—not a causal, physical sense, of course, or it wouldn't be a choice anymore, but still a sense in which the choice was the one to make, the sense in which we speak of *moral* necessity and moral justification.

This story is usually told in reverse, by saying that moral evaluation presupposes freedom because no one can be held responsible unless he could have done otherwise, etc. Part of the reason it is told that way, I think, is that one wants to use it to prove that something is the case: typically, that freedom is real, which is more likely to follow from as dignified a premise as morality is than from the "optional" characters of our grammar and our form of life. I, on the other hand, have no such use in mind. I don't know whether in fact Mr. Smith is free, or the hypnotist, or the hypnotist's hypnotist, and presently I don't care either. What I care about is what Mr. Smith or the hypnotist or whoever are doing when they reconstruct their behavior in terms of *their* intentions and their *freely* carrying them out. I care about a conceptual issue, that is, ultimately, a verbal one: how certain words put other words in motion, and paragraphs that include the former are likely to include the latter, in some form or other. I care about the tasks that those words set for us, about the tensions that the tasks produce when they prove unfeasible, and about how these tensions rule our experience and make it into the mess it is.

In terms of such concerns, I have gone a little way here in deciphering the logic that underlies the behavior of Smith and all those others. What they do to appropriate the world is select one of the many tales that could be told—which feat can be accounted for only, given the indeterminacy of the data, by making the selection somewhat arbitrary. Then, insofar as they reflect themselves in one of the characters of the tale, the same capacity to act and select somewhat arbitrarily must be assigned to that character, and to others like it. And because such arbitrary selections do not happen in a vacuum, but compete for the light of day with many alternative voices, these narrators—as well as their spokesmen in the tale—will have to carry the weight of the struggle, and of winning it.

Notes

1. This reading of synthesis (and argument for its necessity) is articulated in the last two chapters of my (1987).

2. It is important to emphasize the level of abstraction at which my discourse is situated, or one could move irrelevant criticisms of the following sort: though indefinitely many descriptions are ade-

quate to a (single) set of data, a given subject (or narrator) can only give one of them, as a sieve can only let grains of a certain size go through. This hypothesis may certainly hold of the empirical individual body with which the subject is (often) identified (see below), and, consequently, may well be good (empirical) psychology, but the identification itself is already part of a story which has precisely the conceptual presuppositions I am exploring here.

3. At least, not an object *simpliciter*, an object in the full (Kantian) sense, though we may want to extend the (realist's) language here and talk of it as an *intentional* object. See the introduction above.

4. Of course, there is a sense in which the same story could not be told in different words—if the story consists of words. Then my hypothesis should be reformulated as follows: consider two sentences belonging to the same story *and equivalent in that story*. (It may be useful to note, in this regard, that the stories I discuss here are potential, "theoretical" ones, including *all* that *can* be said from a given point of view—a feature that will play no further explicit role in this chapter.)

5. I deal with this problem in my book *The Discipline of Subjectivity*, forthcoming by Princeton University Press.

6. See the *Critique of Pure Reason*, p. 111.

7. I know that the freedom discussed here is not the only thing that goes under that name in the literature. But such controversies are irrelevant to my discussion, since I am not interested in proving that human freedom is either actual or absurd (hence in defining it in such a way that it can be one or the other). It is, rather, that, while pursuing conceptual analysis within a definite philosophical program (broadly Kantian in nature), I have hit upon the necessity of something which I find it natural to call "freedom," and which has often been called that, whatever *else* people have found it profitable to use this name for.

8. Note that some of these alliances are dangerous, insofar as spirit and the like are not in space and time, hence end up being a name for the problem rather than a solution to it (even one as temporary and revisable as we can have).

9. See Chapter 3 above.

10. See Chapters 4 and 5 of my (1987).

11. For remember: there are many who are not always faithful to the same (choice of an) I.

11

Whither Moral Philosophy?

For a long time, I have been dissatisfied with most current discussions in moral philosophy. No matter how ingenious the points made, and how carefully argued, I have felt that somehow they were missing the boat. But it is only recently that I became able to articulate my dissatisfaction, and specifically on the occasion of teaching a course in "Contemporary Moral Problems." (The relevance of this occasion will be apparent later.) I offer my articulation here, in the hope that it might prove useful to others.

1. Intuition

The present discussion is not conducted within moral philosophy proper, or normative ethics: it is a meta-ethical discussion concerning how to do normative ethics, or if you will (if you judge my position destructive for the field) what *else* to do instead. The issues usually discussed in normative ethics are things like: Shall we keep our promises? Shall we maintain our loyalties? How far shall we go in helping our fellow humans? Here I will not be taking a stand on any of these issues, but I will suggest a point of view from which to look at them. The plausibility of this point of view depends on a number of general philosophical tenets for which I will provide no defense.[1] I intend only to give a clear statement of my proposal, and as for its philosophical presuppositions, I will limit myself to offering an exposition of them, in the present section and the next two.

The first presupposition has to do with the structure of discussions in normative ethics, concerning issues like those indicated above. Two factors are mobi-

I thank George Draper and Sally Haslanger for their comments on an earlier draft of this chapter.

lized in these discussions. On the one hand, there is the painstaking logical articulation of some basic beliefs (or perhaps I should say, in light of what follows, of some basic reactions). On the other, there is the way in which the basis for the logical articulation is to be found, and here I see no credible alternative to moral intuition. Attempts to justify basic moral claims on, say, utilitarian grounds may have an important meta-ethical significance (in fact, my own position here could be described as rule-utilitarianism with a twist), but they have no significance at the object level, where moral behavior and moral justifications are ordinarily characterized by an immediacy and an emotional value that are in sharp contrast to the calculating attitude required by rationalization.

The appeal to intuition can be misunderstood. For there are two ways of construing this appeal: one that was more popular in the old days and one that is becoming current now.[2] According to the old conception, moral intuition is the infallible access to self-evident truths; according to the new one, moral intuition is the result of being educated in a certain tradition and of having certain behavioral modes become automatic and unreflective. The old conception runs into all sorts of problems with the existence of moral conflicts within a person, within a society, and between different societies; and besides (which may be the ultimate argument for a philosopher) it can easily find a theoretical place within the new conception (which thus appears as a generalization of the old), insofar as if the education was successful, then you would expect precisely that it made one judge the required practices of one's tradition to be self-evident truths.

When intuition is taken (as I would take it) in the new sense, the most natural way of addressing normative problems is the following. Either you already have forceful gut reactions to them, in which case your intuitions are (that is, your training is) enough to handle the matter, or you don't, in which case you have to think the case through, try to identify its key aspects, react to each of them individually (perhaps by bringing in simpler examples), and then use logic to put the whole picture together. This is a valuable enterprise, in that on the one hand it may make us aware of bad faith on our part, and on the other may extend our training process, thus making us more effective members of whatever tradition we are members of.[3] But as useful as this enterprise is, and as much as I would want to have everyone devote some time to it, I think there is something else intellectuals (philosophers, for example) should also do: something that may even have to take precedence for them *qua* intellectuals on sorting out their moral intuitions. And that is, plain and simple: what kind of moral intuitions do we want *future* people to have? How do we want *them* to be educated, given what the world already looks like and what we may expect it to look like for them? That these questions are crucial for intellectuals depends on the one hand on my conception of the role of morality and on the other on my conception of the role of intellectuals. I will now consider these two issues in turn.

2. Morality

My conception of morality is based on the ethological studies of Konrad Lorenz, primarily his (1963). A brief review of Lorenz's position is in order.

According to Lorenz, some fundamentally useful behavioral traits may have negative secondary effects. For example, intraspecific aggressiveness, besides fulfilling the useful purposes of establishing territoriality and breeding stronger defenders of the family and herd, may also bring about the destruction of a number of healthy specimens. Or, I might add, a tendency to accumulate goods, besides promoting an improved capacity to tolerate sudden downward swings in one's fortunes, may also bring about a degree of unequal distribution of goods that proves hurtful to the survival and well-being of many conspecifics.

In such cases, the mechanism of evolution will tend not so much to breed out the potentially dangerous behavioral trait, but, rather, to retain it on account of its utility while injecting into the system some safety devices which make it impossible – or at least highly unlikely[4] – for it to display all its negative potential. Among animals, ritualizations, personal bonds, and specific reflexes inhibiting injury-inflicting moves fulfill these safety functions. Among humans, in addition to all of the same means, there is morality. Thus morality is one of the means by which evolution has succeeded in blocking the negative consequences that some otherwise useful behavioral traits – primarily, but not uniquely (I would say), aggressive ones[5] – may have for the species as a whole and for portions of it (that is, for individual communities). The point of the commandments of not killing, stealing, and so on is to be found in their adaptive value.[6]

What one usually forgets in discussions of these themes, however, is that adaptiveness is a relative concept. You are not adapted, period; you are adapted to a specific environment – natural and cultural – or, more accurately, to a limited range of (similar) environments. So if the environment changes in drastic ways, your organs or behavioral modes – however useful they were originally – might suddenly become obsolete, with possibly lethal consequences for you as an individual and for the community of which you are a part. And the problem with human communities is how fast they change, in particular how much technological advances keep on making it easier to do things, thereby rendering our behavioral traits as outdated as the appendix or the wisdom tooth. Among the behavioral traits that are likely to become obsolete are moral intuitions.

A few examples may help. Only a few generations ago, there was little you could do about people starving in Africa. You could, of course, leave and go to Africa, but (1) this would probably make you desert your other (for example, familial) duties, and (2) it could not be generalized, or your own place would quickly become as derelict as Africa. So there was not much significance in having strong moral urges about the starving people in Africa, and if most people shrugged their shoulders about them they probably did the best they could, since worrying more would only have had the effect of impeding their work wherever they were. Now, however, technology has changed matters, and it is possible for you – because there are planes and freezers and other such miracles – *not* to desert your other duties, not even to leave home in fact, and still help. It is enough if a small number of people leave – too few for it to make a difference here – and the others just contribute money. Shrugging your shoulders *now* is evidence of the tyranny that our (moral) heritage has on us; it is a manifestation of the fact that, while our technology has made us planetary people, our morals have not caught up with it yet.[7]

A second obvious example is nuclear power. Not long ago, it did not matter much for the world at large if two nations decided to have a fight, or one decided to carry out a little experiment inside its borders. And insofar as survival was essentially survival of and within a (partial) community, it proved effective if the community instilled sentiments of loyalty in its members. Now, however, survival is a global matter. What happens anywhere may well have destructive consequences everywhere, hence those sentiments and the strong feeling of national self-determination that traditionally goes along with them have become counterproductive for the future of the species. But once again we have no moral intuitions adequate to the new situation, and we still reason (dangerously) with the mentality of a child in the grips of the Oedipus complex who suddenly finds himself endowed with the strength and skills of an adult.

What many may find difficult to accept is that it is already too late for *our own* moral intuitions. They have been shaped by the education we received: an education that, useful as it may have seemed to those who imparted it to us, did not and could not make us adapted to the many perplexing changes technology has brought about.[8] And maybe it is too late for everybody: maybe the technological clock is simply too fast for the biological or cultural ones *ever* to catch up with it. But if there is a chance – and I think we should operate as if there were one – it can only be found in shaping future generations differently, in providing them with a set of planetary moral intuitions better fitting their (technological) status as planetary people. For this purpose, intellectuals can be of help.

3. Intellectuals

The existence of intellectuals is an economical and relatively safe way to maximize those cultural mutations that might prove useful to society. Intellectuals build theories, with the declared aim of finding the truth. On the basis of these theories, of which they have a vast array, they make all kinds of suggestions concerning what practical moves could (or should) be made. Most of the suggestions are worthless, and many of the not so worthless ones are not pursued anyway; but some are, and they eventuate in large or small transformations of the current system of practices, transformations that sometimes have the effect of making life easier. Usually, the theories on the basis of which successful (new) practices were originally proposed are later discarded, but the practices themselves are not, not at least unless more successful ones are found—which, incidentally, shows how delusive the ideal of approximating truth is.

Return to morals. Ordinary people—or better, people insofar as they are involved in ordinary activities—are best advised to follow their existing moral intuitions. If they tried suddenly to make decisions and act on the basis of some new proposal, the chances are that they would mess up. There was much good sense in Descartes's retiring to a private, secluded life (and giving himself a "provisional," very conservative behavioral code) before going on to challenge the whole system of his previous beliefs, as there is in the current psychoanalytic practice of not letting patients change anything important in their lives while they are undergoing treatment.

On the other hand, intellectual activities and intellectuals are (and should be[9]) largely disconnected from everyday concerns, hence largely harmless: they are luxuries that individuals or societies allow themselves to be more effective in the long run. So it is best left to intellectuals and their activities to speculate on what future men and women will have to look *and feel* like. In fact, it may be better for intellectuals to speculate on that than to carry out additional articulations of existing and by now obsolete moral practices, for at least two reasons: (1) given the current rate of technological advances and the consequent high level of environmental instability, the former task is probably (now, though it may not have been in earlier times) more urgent than the latter, and (2) for reasons already indicated no one else is likely (or is advised) to pick it up.

Of course, it will be more satisfying for intellectuals to play their old games instead. I certainly find it more satisfying to discuss Kant's ethical views than to talk about planetary people or the bomb. There is a good reason for this, and for the modest amount of sophistication shown by most discussions of such "contemporary" issues (not excluding the present one): the old games have acquired by now a set of problematics, a repertory of interpretive and argumentative tools, and a system of standards for what counts as an acceptable move, that give the players a clear sense of knowing what they are doing. And it may be profitable to use these old games as a training camp, to make the players practice there so that they become stronger and faster before the season starts, provided they do not forget what *else* they are after. *At some point*, we need to force them away from what they are used to, have them leave safe, conventional moves and explore unknown options, especially when—as is the case with the problems discussed here—we really do not have much of an alternative to exploring options *in thought*. We cannot fight a nuclear war and learn from the experience, so the most effective way of shaping people's intuitions (moral and otherwise) is precluded here. In the absence of this possibility, some concentrated thinking through the issue might help—just might. Many stupid, superficial things will be thought and said in the process, but those who refrain from silliness and prefer to barricade themselves behind their scholarly sophistication and dignity will pay the price of their cowardice by being condemned to irrelevancy.

4. Worries

To further articulate my position, it will be useful to consider some objections to it. The first one is as follows. Am I not confusing 'is' with 'ought' when I infer from claims of the theory of evolution—that is, from *descriptive* claims—statements like "The point of moral commandments is to be found in their adaptive value"? The answer is: no, I am not, because I read the latter statements as descriptive, too. That is, I read them as saying that the *actual functions* fulfilled by a moral code, hence—given my acceptance of the evolutionary mode of explanation—what causes us to have a moral code in the first place, must be found in how it contributes to inhibit aggressiveness, promote cooperation, and in general make it possible for the species to better cope with environmental pressure. So at this level questions concerning whether it is *morally good* to have any moral code, or a specific one, do not arise *yet*.

But the worry will not go away. For I do not limit myself to pointing out what the (actual) functions of morality are: I also say that people (intellectuals) *should* do this and that. And isn't this (an attempt at) inferring value judgments from descriptive statements?

Initially, the way I would tend to defuse this criticism is by pointing out that my statements can be taken as conditionals. That is, I am not necessarily saying that people should (categorically) do this or that. What I could be saying instead is that *if* people want their morality to fulfill its function—more explicitly, *if* they want their species to survive—they should be doing what I suggest. And this is no more questionable an inference from 'is' to 'ought' than, say, a statement to the effect that *if* people want their legs to fulfill their function they should prevent them from atrophying, hence exercise.

But now suppose that I am asked a direct question: "Don't you want the species to survive?" That is, am I not, in fact, ready to separate the consequent of the conditional above, and assert categorically that people should proceed as I suggest, *because* (not simply *if*) the species should survive? Then my answer would be: yes. But this does not mean that I think it *should* be yes, in any absolute (moral) sense. It is just that, like most ordinary human beings, I have an immediate (intuitive) concern for the survival of humankind, and an immediate (intuitive) repulsion by the prospect that my species will be wiped out. So because of the way I am (a descriptive statement), I will tend to express views of this kind, and try to convince people to operate in various ways. I don't know that I *should* be doing this, I don't know that it even makes sense to raise the issue.

The last point deserves additional elaboration. Though most of what I say here is at the descriptive level, if it works at all it will work by mobilizing people's values—values that people *already* have. My views will be accepted, and will be effective, only if they succeed in allying themselves with existing (and possibly dormant) intuitive reactions. People will convince themselves to help the starving populations of Africa—hence eventually convince themselves to educate their children accordingly – only if television or other media coverage succeeds in awakening in them the same natural compassion that they would normally have for their neighbors, and that a few generations ago they could hardly have had for the starving populations of Africa because they had no perceptual access to those populations. A moral revolution of the kind I would like to see will not come about on the basis of factual considerations only: it must manipulate moral intuitions, bring some to the fore and use them to make others recede into the background. But I can *describe* all of this, and *sub*scribe to it, and even work for it, without knowing that it *should* happen.

Suppose now that the above is enough of an answer to the first (kind of) worry. Some might then criticize me from the opposite point of view. Am I, that is, in a position to make (sense of making) any recommendation at all? When you invite people to do something, you ordinarily assume that they *can* do it, but doesn't my "biologism" exclude any such possibility? Nature will work itself out in individual human beings and in the human species according to its own laws, whatever I say, so how is my statement here going to matter? And if it doesn't matter, why is it made? Am I not involved in a pragmatic paradox when I make a proposal while believing that one of the basic presuppositions of the activity of making proposals is not satisfied?

But there is no paradox in my position. There would be if I thought that people will or might be rationally convinced of the correctness of my proposal, and then proceed to make a (rational) choice about what to do next. But I don't think any of that. What I think is that my proposal is one more item in the pandemonium of dissonant voices that surround us. It is to overestimate the decisional capacity of human beings to think that they can freely pick out the "right" message in this pandemonium, but it is to *under*estimate the causal impact of the voices to think that they will make no difference at all. Some will, just like any other (kind of) event, though probably for what a philosopher would consider the wrong reasons: characters like being better able to strike people's imagination, or call upon their biases, or satisfy their sense of beauty and balance. And it is even possible that *my* voice will be effective, as one of the ways in which nature works itself out.

Critics might insist. My tone through most of this chapter is not compatible – they might say – with such a modest construe of the significance of my proposal as I am now trying to sell. Indeed, my tone is often moralistic: I don't just utter words to be added to the general confusion, *I tell people what to do*. So again I seem committed to a pragmatic paradox.

And again, there is no paradox. If I don't have a choice about other things, I don't have a choice about what tone to adopt, either. I don't have a choice about feeling strongly that the species should survive, and if I talk about it I don't have a choice about expressing strong views on the matter. And if this thing is going to convince anyone, it is probably because they don't have a choice about what tone proves convincing to them.

5. Education

A simple way to summarize the position formulated here is the following: moral philosophy must turn from the examination of (the consequences of) current moral intuitions to the formulation of desirable policies of moral *education*.[10] This kind of conclusion is not new. To give only one significant example, when Jean-Jacques Rousseau realized that civilization can only produce unhappiness but the way back to the state of nature is blocked for us civilized people, he inferred that the only hope for a better future was based on the possibility of educating the young differently, and bringing them back to a situation in which the state of nature would really be *natural* for them. However, the centrality that positions such as this one assign to education is not at all shared by the value-system that dominates this country's intellectual (especially academic) life.

There are two complementary aspects to the underrating of education within academia. First, there is the low dignity of the *subject-matter* of education. Departments of education are not considered intellectually high powered: viewed as primarily "practical" in nature, they come to share in the general disregard for all applied disciplines. Within the high-powered discipline of philosophy, education is considered a "soft" subject and is usually relegated to minor figures in minor departments, publishing in minor journals.

Second, there is the low dignity of the *practice* of education, not surprising in a culture that has gone on record saying "Those who cannot do, teach." When one is hired as a junior faculty member in a major philosophy department, one is pompously told that teaching is an area where one is expected to excel, on a par or almost on a par with research. But one quickly realizes that, from a career point of view, time spent teaching is wasted, and that one is never going to be promoted (or, for that matter, not promoted) because of one's good (or bad) teaching. The whole academic hierarchy conveys this message. At the top, it displays the very best research professors, who are paid the most and teach the least: it is a sign of distinction, in fact, to have a "reduced teaching load." At the bottom, comes the crowd of those who work in minor (teaching-oriented) institutions: all they (are expected to) do is teach, and, consequently, they are paid (and valued) the least. As for *what* all of these people would rather teach, the ranking is clear: seminars (especially on "one's own work") are in great demand, whereas "sexy" courses like the one in "Contemporary Moral Problems" that originated my reflections are usually regarded as a burden.

Still, the burden must be sustained, for anyone can use high enrollments. Which is a consolation, because it proves that (luckily!) "nature works itself out" in such a manner that the most urgent problems inevitably (and irritatingly, and embarrassingly) keep on being thrown in our way.

Notes

1. But see the introduction and Chapters 3 and 4 above.
2. A good recent formulation of this distinction can be found in Kekes (1986). Note also that

the context of reference for the qualifications 'old' and 'new' here is analytic philosophy; if we take a wider standpoint we may come to see these two conceptions as the (permanent) extremes of an oscillation which is as old as philosophy itself.

3. When we move away from the (mystifying) ideological level, we may see less of an opposition between this activity and the alternative one described below, since asking for the legitimation of a practice (which is what gets the first activity going) is already challenging it, and often has the effect of weakening its hold on us *even when the legitimation is found*. (I touch on this point in the introduction above.) Thus, in the end, the "logical articulation" of existing moral intuitions and the bold search for new ones may be going in the same direction. The problem with the first method is whether it goes fast enough.

4. For remember: safety devices may miscarry. See the point made in the next paragraph.

5. Lorenz seems to believe that the point of morality is only to inhibit aggressiveness, but his position can be generalized (and my first example below will suggest how).

6. In Section 4 below I consider natural worries that one might have with statements such as this one.

7. One might agree that we now *can* help the Africans, and ask why we *should*. My answer would be based on the high level of global interdependence realized by contemporary technology, and on the resulting difficulties we experience to keep problems (and solutions) at a local level—a point that will be brought into sharper focus by the next example.

8. It is indeed possible—it seems—to (partially) reshape a person's basic intuitions (or basic reactions), for example by a "reparenting" of the psychoanalytic variety (see Chapter 4 above). But, as reassuring as this possibility may sound to many, the time and effort required to turn it into an actuality make it as impractical as if it did not exist at all.

9. That they are is a fact; that they should be is a consequence of my rationalization of the facts. (Further discussion of this theme can be found in the introduction above.) Note also that the qualification 'largely' does not exclude occasional (even devastating) exceptions.

10. Of course, for this summary not to be a caricature of my position it is necessary to understand education as something more than the simple passing on of intuitions from one generation to the next. But this qualification is redundant for those who think that education should proceed in the interest of those who are being educated.

Bibliography

Bibliography

In this book, some references are given by title, and some by original date of publication (by and large, the first category is constituted by classical works). When a translation, a new edition, or a new printing is cited below, it is to this source that references are made in the book, not to the original.

Addison, Joseph. *Works*, edited by G. Greene (New York: Putnam, 1854).

Aristotle. *Complete Works*, edited by J. Barnes (Princeton: Princeton University Press, 1984).

Austin, John. *How to Do Things with Words* (Cambridge, Mass.: Harvard University Press, 1962).

Barcan Marcus, Ruth. "Rationality and Believing the Impossible," *Journal of Philosophy* 80 (1983), 321–38.

Bencivenga, Ermanno. "Alcuni sviluppi nella teoria dell'uso referenziale delle descrizioni," *Lingua e Stile* 9 (1974), 147–58.

———. "Per una logica e un'ontologia delle espressioni descrittive," *Rivista di Filosofia* 69 (1978), 258–69.

———. "Osservazioni sul carattere 'genetico' delle espressioni referenziali," *Atti del Convegno Nazionale di Logica di Montecatini Terme* (Naples: Bibliopolis, 1979), 325–33.

———. "Again on Existence as a Predicate," *Philosophical Studies* 37 (1980), 125–38.

———. "On Secondary Semantics for Logical Modalities," *Pacific Philosophical Quarterly* 62 (1981), 88–94.

———. "Knowledge as a Relation and Knowledge as an Experience in the *Critique of Pure Reason*," *Canadian Journal of Philosophy* 15 (1985), 593–615.

———. "Free Logics," in *Handbook of Philosophical Logic*, vol. III, edited by D. Gabbay and F. Guenthner (Dordrecht: Reidel, 1986), 373–426.

———. *Kant's Copernican Revolution* (New York: Oxford University Press, 1987).

———. *Tre dialoghi* (Torino: Bollati Boringhieri, 1988).

Bennett, Jonathan. *Kant's Dialectic* (Cambridge: Cambridge University Press, 1974).

Brittan, Gordon G., Jr. *Kant's Theory of Science* (Princeton: Princeton University Press, 1978).

Chang, C. C., and Keisler, H. J. *Model Theory* (Amsterdam: North-Holland, 1973).

Chisholm, Roderick. "Intentionality," in *The Encyclopedia of Philosophy*, edited by P. Edwards (New York: Macmillan and Free Press, 1967), 201–4.

Cocchiarella, Nino B. "On the Primary and Secondary Semantics of Logical Necessity," *Journal of Philosophical Logic* 4 (1975), 13–27.

Curley, E. M. *Descartes Against the Skeptics* (Cambridge, Mass.: Harvard University Press, 1978).

Derrida, Jacques. "La mythologie blanche (la métaphore dans le texte philosohique," *Poétique* 5 (1971), 1–52.

———. *Positions* (Paris: Les Editions de Minuit, 1972). Translated by A. Bass (Chicago: University of Chicago Press, 1981).

Dewey, John. *Art as Experience* (New York: Capricorn Books, 1958).

Donnellan, Keith. "Reference and Definite Descriptions," *Philosophical Review* 75 (1966), 281–304.

Dummett, Michael. *Frege: Philosophy of Language* (Cambridge, Mass.: Harvard University Press, 1981).

Feyerabend, Paul. *Against Method: Outline of an Anarchistic Theory of Knowledge* (London: Verso, 1978).

Findlay, John. *Meinong's Theory of Objects and Values* (New York: Oxford University Press, 1963).

Fine, Kit. "Model Theory for Modal Logic," *Journal of Philosophical Logic* 7 (1978), 125–56 and 277–306.

Frege, Gottlob. "Über Sinn und Bedeutung," *Zeitschrift für Philosophie und philosophische Kritik* 100 (1892), 25–50. Translated by M. Black in Frege (1984), 157–77.

———. *Grundgesetze der Arithmetik, begriffsschriftlich abgeleitet*, vol. I (Jena: Hermann Pohle, 1893). Partially translated by M. Furth (Berkeley: University of California Press, 1964).

———. "Logische Untersuchungen. Erster Teil: Der Gedanke," *Beiträge zur Philosophie des deutschen Idealismus* 1 (1918), 58–77. Translated by P. Geach and R. Stoothoff in Frege (1984), 351–72.

———. *Philosophical and Mathematical Correspondence*, edited by G. Gabriel et al. (Oxford: Basil Blackwell, 1980).

———. *Collected Papers on Mathematics, Logic, and Philosophy*, edited by B. McGuinness (Oxford: Basil Blackwell, 1984).

Freud, Sigmund. *Complete Psychological Works*, edited by J. Strachey (London: Hogarth Press, 1953–74).

Friedman, Michael. "Kant's Theory of Geometry," *Philosophical Review* 94 (1985), 455–506.

Galilei, Galileo. *Dialogue on the Great World Systems*, Salusbury edition revised by G. de Santillana (Chicago: University of Chicago Press, 1953).

Getto, Giovanni. *Letture manzoniane* (Florence: Sansoni, 1964).

Gibson, J. J. *The Senses Considered as Perceptual Systems* (Boston: Houghton Mifflin, 1966).

Gombrich, Ernst. *Art and Illusion* (Princeton: Princeton University Press, 1960). Second paperback printing, 1972.

Grice, Paul. "Meaning," *Philosophical Review* 66 (1957), 377–88.

———. "Utterer's Meaning and Intentions," *Philosophical Review* 78 (1969), 147–77.

Grünbaum, Adolf. *The Foundations of Psychoanalysis: A Philosophical Critique* (Berkeley: University of California Press, 1984).

Hacking, Ian. *Why Does Language Matter to Philosophy?* (Cambridge: Cambridge University Press, 1975).

Hintikka, Jaakko. "Existential Presuppositions and Existential Commitments," *Journal of Philosophy* 56 (1959), 125–37.

———. *Knowledge and Belief* (Ithaca: Cornell University Press, 1962).

Hirsch, Eric D., Jr. *Validity in Interpretation* (New Haven: Yale University Press, 1967).

Horwich, Paul. "On Refutations of Skepticism," *Noûs* 16 (1982), 56–61.

Hoy, David. *The Critical Circle* (Berkeley: University of California Press, 1978).

Iser, Wolfgang. *The Act of Reading* (Baltimore: The Johns Hopkins University Press, 1978).

Kant, Immanuel. *Critique of Pure Reason*, translated by N. Kemp Smith (New York: St. Martin's Press, 1965).

———. *Prolegomena to Any Future Metaphysics*, translated by L. Beck (Indianapolis: Bobbs-Merrill, 1950).

———. *Groundwork of the Metaphysic of Morals*, translated by H. Paton (New York: Harper and Row, 1964).

———. *The Critique of Judgement*, translated by J. Meredith (Oxford: Clarendon Press, 1952).

———. *The Conflict of Faculties*, translated by M. Gregor (New York: Abaris Books, 1979).

———. *Anthropology from a Pragmatic Point of View*, translated by M. Gregor (The Hague: M. Nijhoff, 1974).

Kaplan, David. "Quantifying In," in *Words and Objections*, edited by D. Davidson and J. Hintikka (Dordrecht: Reidel, 1969), 178–214.

——. "How to Russell a Frege-Church," *Journal of Philosophy* 72 (1975), 716–29.

Kekes, John. "Moral Intuition," *American Philosophical Quarterly* 23 (1986), 83–93.

Kemp Smith, Norman. *A Commentary to Kant's "Critique of Pure Reason"* (New York: Macmillan, 1923).

Kripke, Saul. "Semantical Considerations on Modal Logic," *Acta Philosophica Fennica* 16 (1963), 83–94. Reprinted in *Reference and Modality*, edited by L. Linsky (Oxford: Oxford University Press, 1971), 63–72.

——. "Naming and Necessity," in *Semantics of Natural Language*, edited by D. Davidson and G. Harman (Dordrecht: Reidel, 1972), 253–355. Revised edition (as a book) Cambridge, Mass.: Harvard University Press, 1980.

——. "A Puzzle about Belief," in *Meaning and Use*, edited by A. Margalit (Dordrecht: Reidel, 1979), 239–83.

Kuhn, Thomas. *The Copernican Revolution* (Cambridge, Mass.: Harvard University Press, 1957).

——. *The Structure of Scientific Revolutions* (Chicago: University of Chicago Press, 1962).

——. "Second Thoughts on Paradigms," in Suppe (1974), 459–82.

Lambert, Karel. "Definitions of E!(xistence) in Free Logic," First Congress of Logic, Methodology, and Philosophy of Science, Stanford 1960.

——. "Existential Import Revisited," *Notre Dame Journal of Formal Logic* 4 (1963), 288–92.

——. "On the Philosophical Foundations of Free Logic," *Inquiry* 24 (1981), 147–203.

——. *Meinong and the Principle of Independence* (Cambridge: Cambridge University Press, 1983).

Lambert, Karel, and Ermanno Bencivenga. "A Free Logic with Simple and Complex Predicates," *Notre Dame Journal of Formal Logic* 27 (1986), 247–56.

Leblanc, Hugues, and Theodore Hailperin. "Nondesignating Singular Terms," *Philosophical Review* 68 (1959), 239–43.

Lehrer, Keith. *Knowledge* (Oxford: Clarendon Press, 1974).

Leonard, Henry. "The Logic of Existence," *Philosophical Studies* 7 (1956), 49–64.

Lewis, David. "Counterpart Theory and Quantified Modal Logic," *Journal of Philosophy* 65 (1968), 113–26.

——. "What Puzzling Pierre Does Not Believe," *Australasian Journal of Philosophy* 59 (1981), 283–89.

Liebert, Robert. *Michelangelo: A Psychoanalytic Study of His Life and Images* (New Haven: Yale University Press, 1983).

Lorenz, Konrad. *Das sogennante Böse* (Vienna: G. Borotha-Schoeler, 1963). Translated by M. Wilson (New York: Harcourt, Brace, and Jovanovich, 1974).

——. *Studies in Animal and Human Behavior*, translated by R. Martin (Cambridge, Mass.: Harvard University Press, 1970).

——. *Die Rückseite des Spiegels: Versuch einer Naturgeschichte menschlichen Erkennens* (Munich: Piper, 1973). Translated by R. Taylor (London: Methuen, 1977).

——. "Analogy as a Source of Knowledge," Nobel Lecture 1973 (Stockholm: The Nobel Foundation, 1974).

Manzoni, Alessandro. *The Betrothed*, translated by B. Penman (Harmondsworth: Penguin Books, 1972).

Marr, David. *Vision: A Computational Investigation into the Human Representation and Processing of Visual Information* (San Francisco: Freeman, 1982).

Meinong, Alexius. "Uber Gegenstandstheorie," in *Untersuchungen zur Gegenstandstheorie und Psychologie*, edited by A. Meinong (Leipzig: Barth, 1904), 1–50. Translated by I. Levi et al. in *Realism and the Background of Phenomenology*, edited by R. Chisholm (New York: Free Press, 1960), 76–117.

Nagel, Thomas. "Moral Luck," *Proceedings of the Aristotelian Society: Supplementary Volumes* 50 (1976), 137–51. Reprinted in *Mortal Questions* (Cambridge: Cambridge University Press, 1979), 24–38.

Nozick, Robert. *Philosophical Explanations* (Cambridge, Mass.: Belknap Press, 1981).

Paratore, Ettore. *Studi sui "Promessi sposi"* (Florence: Olschki, 1972).

Parsons, Terence. *Nonexistent Objects* (New Haven: Yale University Press, 1980).

Popkin, Richard. *A History of Scepticism from Erasmus to Descartes* (Assen: Van Gorcum, 1960).

Pribram, Karl, and Merton Gill. *Freud's "Project" Re-Assessed: Preface to Contemporary Cognitive Theory and Neuropsychology* (New York: Basic Books, 1976).

Ptolemy. *The Almagest*, in *Great Books of the Western World*, vol. XVI (Chicago: Encyclopedia Britannica, 1952), 5–465.

Putnam, Hilary. *Meaning and the Moral Sciences* (Boston: Routledge and Kegan Paul, 1978).

———. Comments on Kripke (1979), in *Meaning and Use*, edited by A. Margalit (Dordrecht: Reidel, 1979), 284–88.

Quine, Willard Van Orman. "Quantifiers and Propositional Attitudes," *Journal of Philosophy* 53 (1956), 177–87.

———. *Word and Object* (Cambridge, Mass.: MIT Press, 1960).

Rapaport, William. "To Be and Not To Be," *Noûs* 19 (1985), 255–71.

Rorty, Richard. *Philosophy and the Mirror of Nature* (Princeton: Princeton University Press, 1979).

———. *Consequences of Pragmatism* (Minneapolis: University of Minnesota Press, 1982).

Russell, Bertrand. "On Denoting," *Mind* 14 (1905), 479–93.

———. *Introduction to Mathematical Philosophy* (London: Allen and Unwin, 1919): 1919a.

———. "The Philosophy of Logical Atomism," *The Monist* 29 (1919), 206–22: 1919b.

Sartre, Jean-Paul. *What Is Literature?*, translated by B. Frechtman (London: Methuen, 1950).

Searle, John. *Speech Acts* (Cambridge: Cambridge University Press, 1969).

———. *Intentionality* (Cambridge: Cambridge University Press, 1983).

Smith, David Woodruff. "The Realism in Perception," *Noûs* 16 (1982), 42–55.

Smith, David Woodruff, and Ronald McIntyre. *Husserl and Intentionality: A Study of Mind, Meaning, and Language* (Dordrecht: Reidel, 1982).

Strawson, P. F. "On Referring," *Mind* 59 (1950), 320–44.

———. *Individuals* (London: Methuen, 1959).

———. *The Bounds of Sense* (London: Methuen, 1966).

Suppe, Frederick (ed.). *The Structure of Scientific Theories* (Urbana: University of Illinois Press, 1974). Second edition 1977.

Thomason, Richmond H. *Formal Philosophy: Selected Papers of Richard Montague* (New Haven: Yale University Press, 1974).

van Fraassen, Bas C. *The Scientific Image* (Oxford: Clarendon Press, 1980).

von Einem, Herbert. *Michelangelo*, translated by R. Taylor (London: Methuen, 1973).

Walker, Ralph. *Kant* (London: Routledge and Kegan Paul, 1978).

Winnicott, D. W. *Playing and Reality* (London: Tavistock, 1971).

Wittgenstein, Ludwig. *Tractatus Logico-Philosophicus*, translated by B. Pears and B. McGuinness (London: Routledge and Kegan Paul, 1961).

———. *Philosophical Investigations*, translated by G. Anscombe (New York: Macmillan, 1953).

———. *On Certainty*, translated by G. Anscombe and G. von Wright (New York: Harper and Row, 1969).

Index

Index

157

Ermanno Bencivenga is professor of philosophy at the University of California, Irvine. Born and raised in Italy, he received his B.A. and Specialist degrees in philosophy from the University of Milano and his Ph.D. in philosophy from the University of Toronto. Bencivenga has served as a visiting professor at the Universities of Pittsburgh, Milano, Bologna, and Salzburg, and at Rice University. He is the author of several books in Italian and German, and two in English: *Logic, Bivalence, and Denotation* (co-authored with Karel Lambert and Bas van Fraassen, 1986) and *Kant's Copernican Revolution* (1987). His articles have appeared in *Noûs*, the *Journal of Philosophy, The Monist, Synthese*, and *Philosophy and Phenomenological Research.*